NEW DIRECTIONS IN REAL ESTATE FINANCE AND INVESTMENT

Maastricht-Cambridge Symposium 2000

A Special Issue of The Journal of Real Estate Finance and Economics

edited by

Piet Eichholtz
Limburg Institute of Financial Economics
Maastricht University, The Netherlands

Kanak Patel
University of Cambridge
United Kingdom

Reprinted from
The Journal of Real Estate Finance and Economics
Volume 24.1/24.2

KLUWER ACADEMIC PUBLISHERS
Boston/Dordrecht/London

The Journal of Real Estate Finance and Economics

Special issue on New Directions in Real Estate Finance and Investment: Maastricht-Cambridge Symposium 2000
Guest Editors: Piet Eichholtz and Kanak Patel

Distributors for North, Central and South America:
Kluwer Academic Publishers
101 Philip Drive
Assinippi Park
Norwell, Massachusetts 02061 USA
Telephone (781) 871-6600
Fax (781) 681-9045
E-Mail ⟨kluwer@wkap.com⟩

Distributors for all other countries:
Kluwer Academic Publishers Group
Distribution Centre
Post Office Box 322
3300 AH Dordrecht, THE NETHERLANDS
Telephone 31 78 6392 392
Fax 31 78 6546 474
E-Mail ⟨services@wkap.nl⟩

Electronic Services ⟨http://www.wkap.nl⟩

Library of Congress Cataloging-in-Publication Data

A C.I.P. Catalogue record for this book is available
from the Library of Congress.

Printed on acid-free paper.

Printed in the United States of America

Journal of Real Estate Finance and Economics, 24:1/2, 5–8, 2002

RICS FOUNDATION

Guest Editorial

PIET EICHHOLTZ
Maastricht University

KANAK PATEL
University of Cambridge

Introduction

Research in real estate finance and economics has developed in an exciting way in the past twenty-five years or so. The resulting theoretical and empirical findings are shining a new light on some of the classic mysteries of the real estate markets. It is good to see that a growing proportion of this research output is concerned with contemporary problems and issues regarding the European and Far Eastern property markets.

To stimulate a creative exchange of new ideas and a debate of the latest research findings regarding the global property markets, we have established the Maastricht-Cambridge Real Estate Finance and Investment Symposium. This initiative aims at bringing together a number of leading researchers in the field for a short, intensive conference. The 2000 Symposium, which was hosted by Maastricht University in the Netherlands in June of that year, is the first in an annual series of such conferences, which will alternate between Maastricht University and Cambridge University.

To decide which themes to include in the first meeting of the Symposium, we began by consulting the members of the advisory board and a number of experts in the field. Although tastes varied with respect to the ordering of important topics, the professional consensus erred in favor of breadth of topics rather than a single unifying theme. This resulted in a first Symposium meeting, which was attended by 42 participants, and which included presentation of twelve papers on a broad range of topics including property companies' capital structure and securitization, real options, rents and mortgage contracts, housing risk and portfolio issues.

The value of the Symposium is greatly increased by the parallel initiative taken by the *Journal of Real Estate Finance and Economics* for a Special Issue of symposium proceedings. This Special Issue, named ''New Directions'', stimulates international discussion of economic and financial issues regarding the global real estate markets.

The twelve articles that were selected for presentation at the Symposium subsequently went through the Journal's normal refereeing process, which resulted in the collection of eight papers published in this issue. These eight articles represent a well-balanced mix of contemporary topics. It does not seek to be a comprehensive guide of the contemporary literature, but rather reflects the selection of major issues that participants at the first Maastricht-Cambridge Symposium meeting considered to be challenging. In choosing individual contributions we used a number of guiding principles, of which importance of the problem at hand, contribution to knowledge and originality were most important. We slightly favored contributions concerning inferences about investors' behavior from observed data. Finally, we did not restrict our attention solely to articles originating from any specific region or country, even though all contributions surviving the screening process are from the United States and Europe. Granted the breadth of the topics, the sketch of the articles provided below may prove to be helpful to the reader.

Calhoun and Deng analyze the prepayment and default experience of fixed-rate mortgages (FRM) and adjustable-rate mortgages (ARM) in the United States. The empirical analysis of the conditional probabilities of prepayment and default, based on a multinomial logit specification, is set in the context of option-theoretic variables, mortgage age effect, and other exogenous factors. The key option-theoretic predictors are the mortgage premium values and the equity position of the borrower. Mortgage age captures the ''structural'' duration-dependence in prepayment rates and the ''residual'' impact of unobserved heterogeneity amongst borrowers. The main other exogenous variables included are dummy variables for origination years, the original loan-to-value ratio, and current seasonal variables that account for whether, school schedules, seasonal employment patterns, and occupancy status. The multinomial logit estimates show that the expected rates of prepayment by age are very similar for FRM and ARM, suggesting that most systematic differences between these two sets of loans are explained by the other explanatory variables. The option-related variables for FRMs and ARMs indicate that borrower behavior is consistent with the option theory of prepayments and default.

Jones and David Nickerson develop a game-theoretic model for both the analysis and valuation of mortgage contracts. Their model emphasizes two aspects of multiperiod loans in a strategic setting: The mortgagor can receive flows of housing services from the property as long as he makes his loan payments, and the option to default is an element of the strategy set of the borrower. The authors derive the value of the mortgage contract to both lender and borrower, and evaluate whether certain features of mortgage contracts and variations in access to mortgage credit can be explained solely in terms of the options each party holds as elements of the strategy sets in lending negotiations, without recourse to asymmetric information. Their results show that both increasing flows of housing services accruing to the mortgagor and an increase in the price volatility of property serving as collateral reduce the willingness to lend. Faster amortization and shorter terms to maturity for fixed mortgages are found to increase the volume of credit offered by the lender. They also show that the mortgage credit offered by a rational lender may be a small fraction of the fair current market value of the collateral, and will decrease as bankruptcy costs or housing service flows increase. Indeed, when bankruptcy costs are sufficiently high, the supply of mortgage funds, as a function of the difference of the yield charged over the riskless rate, becomes negatively sloped.

Hendershott, McGregor and White use a reduced-form error-correction model to explain the ''long-run'' levels and the ''short-run'' movements of commercial property rents. They look at office, retail, and industrial property in eleven market regions in the United Kingdom. In the long run model, supply of occupied space is equal to demand with demand expressed as a function of rent and economic activity. The short run model is the first difference of the long run equation with the addition of an error-correction term. In the retail sector, the error-correction coefficient shows that rents adjust to about 30 percent of the imbalance in the previous period. In the office sector, the error-correction coefficient for London is significant when the lag of rental change is added, and ''for all regions except London'' it is highly significant but has a small magnitude, suggesting a long adjustment process. The implied long run price elasticity and the income elasticity are lower in absolute value in London than in the ''all regions except London'' panel. This study reveals that, while the economic drivers may vary, there is no evidence of differences in the operation of the regional property markets outside London.

Ben-Shahar, Feldman, and Greenberg analyze rent control using an option approach. The rent-control rental contract is modeled as a series of compounded European call options as a complement to the no-arbitrage condition that the tenant's costs of renting in the free market are equal to his or her costs under controlled rent. The solution, the value of the key money for a tenant occupying a controlled rent dwelling unit, is a function of the expected remaining tenure horizon. In the rational expectations equilibrium, the representative agent's expected tenure duration is determined endogenously by accounting for both the nodes on the binomial tree where the tenant selects to vacate the real estate unit and the probabilities of reaching those nodes. An interesting result derived from the simulation of the model is that, for a sufficiently long ''conditional life expectancy,'' the equilibrium levels of both the key money and the expected tenure duration are hardly affected by the distribution of the key money between the departing tenant and the landlord.

Brounen and Eichholtz investigate Initial Public Offering (IPO) underpricing, and the subsequent log-run performance of a sample of 86 European companies that went public during between 1984 and 1999. The average IPO is found to outperform a within-country common stock benchmark by 1.74 percent on the issue date and to underperform its common stock benchmark over the three-year period subsequent to the initial offering. The cross-national differences in market structure and maturity, however, give rise to substantial variation in initial day returns across different countries. The results of a multivariate regression analysis show that factors such as issue size, debt ratio, standard deviation, and sector specialization of the property portfolio affect IPO underpricing. Issues of lesser size, with smaller debt ratios and higher aftermarket standard deviations are associated with more underpricing.

Ling and Naranjo analyze the performance of listed property companies using a database of approximately 600 companies in 28 countries for the period 1984 through 1999. Using a one-factor model with a global stock index as the proxy for the world wealth portfolio, they find a strong global factor in property share returns. They subsequently extend this model with an orthogonal country-specific factor to capture systematic risk factors independent of world-wide systematic risk for each country. This model shows that significant country-specific effects exist, suggesting international diversification opportunities for property share investors.

Cauley and Pavlov use an option approach to explain the fall in liquidity following negative shocks in demand for residential real estate. They base their analysis on a dataset of residential real estate in Los Angeles. They regard the levered purchase of a home as an American option, with the exercise price being the mortgage loan balance. After a negative demand shock, when an owner has little or negative home equity, the exercise price and the value of the option owned by a potential buyer. This would prevent otherwise mutually advantageous transactions, and result in a fall in liquidity. After a positive demand shock, buyer's and seller's option values are likely to be more in line, which implies that mutually advantageous transactions will not be precluded, and that market liquidity will not be affected as much.

Englund, Hwang and Quigley investigate the risk faced by homeowners on the basis of a dataset of Swedish housing transactions between 1981 and 1993. They construct a transaction-based house price index to which they add an imputed rental value to get a total return index of residential property. They use this index to look at the investment performance of housing relative to other assets. Their main contribution is in an investigation of the effect of different holding periods on risk, return and correlations of residential property and other asset classes, and on the efficient portfolios consisting of all these assets. They find that the optimal allocation to home equity increases with longer holding periods, suggesting that the large exposure to home equity that is often observed in homeowners' portfolios may not be sub-optimal, but due to a relatively long investment horizon.

Indebtedness for this Special Issue and for the Maastricht-Cambridge 2000 Symposium meeting runs wide and deep, and we therefore make no attempt to enumerate individually all those whom we owe our thanks. However, in addition to all the authors, discussants and referees who made this Issue possible, some special notes of appreciation are in order.

The Maastricht-Cambridge Symposium owes its existence to C. F. Sirmans, who has provided the stimulus for its inception and facilitated its proceedings to be published in this Journal. We should like to express our gratitude to him and the four other members of the advisory board, Patric Hendershott, Dean Paxson, James Shilling and Charles Ward, who assisted us in the selection process described above. We should also like to thank the RICS Foundation and Maastricht University for generously sponsoring the Special Issue and hosting the Symposium meeting. Stephen Brown, Research Officer, the RICS Foundation, has played a large role in making this a successful venture.

Journal of Real Estate Finance and Economics, 24:1/2, 9–33, 2002

A Dynamic Analysis of Fixed- and Adjustable-Rate Mortgage Terminations*

CHARLES A. CALHOUN
Calhoun Consulting, Annadale, VA 22003-4043
E-mail: calhoun@ix.netcom.com

YONGHENG DENG
University of Southern California, Los Angeles, CA 90089-0626
E-mail: ydeng@usc.edu

Abstract

This paper provides a side-by-side comparison of loan-level statistical models for fixed- and adjustable-rate mortgages. Multinomial logit models for quarterly conditional probabilities of default and prepayment are estimated. We find that the estimated impacts of embedded option values for prepayment and default are generally quite similar across both FRM and ARM loans, providing additional empirical support for the basic predictions of the options theory. We also find that differences in estimates of conditional probabilities of prepayment and default associated with mortgage age, origination period, original LTV, and relative loan size, indicate the continued significance of these other economic and demographic factors for empirical models of mortgage terminations.

Key Words: default, prepayment, option values, event history models, conditional probability, time-varying logit

Introduction

This paper adds to the growing body of empirical research into the causes and correlates of single-family residential mortgage terminations based on the options theory of prepayment and default by presenting a side-by-side comparison of statistical models for fixed- and adjustable-rate mortgages. The empirical analysis is based on a discrete-time/discrete-choice framework that utilizes data on the event histories of individual mortgage loans. A multinomial logit specification is used to account for the discrete-choice nature of default and prepayment decisions and to account for the competing-risks of default and prepayment.[1]

We report estimates of multinomial logit models for quarterly conditional probabilities of prepayment and default for conventional, conforming, 30-year, single-family mortgages. The statistical estimates were obtained using data on nearly 1.3 million

*A previous version of this paper was presented at the American Real Estate and Urban Economics Association Annual Meetings, New Orleans, Louisiana, January 1997, while the authors were employed at the Office of Federal Housing Enterprise Oversight. Any opinions expressed or implied are those of the authors.

mortgages originated over the period 1979–1993.[2] Contemporaneous measures of mortgage premium values and borrower equity distributions were used to reconstruct individual mortgage event histories for analysis in a dynamic discrete-time logit model. We were also able to augment the basic loan-level data with detailed information on the contractual terms that determined the periodic changes in the coupon rates on adjustable-rate mortgages, and to directly compare the performance of fixed-rate and adjustable-rate loans within the same econometric model.

Options theory and mortgage prepayment and default

Options theory has been the dominant paradigm for research on residential mortgage prepayment and default in recent years and holds that mortgage borrowers will exercise embedded call (prepayment) or put (default) options when either of these alternatives becomes financially attractive—that is, when they are "in the money."[3] Many empirical studies have applied financial options theory to the analysis of prepayment and default probabilities for single-family fixed-rate mortgages (FRM).[4] Options-based empirical models of adjustable-rate mortgage (ARM) performance are less prevalent, owing to the greater complexity of the underlying index and coupon dynamics, and the relative paucity of publicly available loan-level data. This has complicated the application of options-based empirical models to ARM loans, and limited direct statistical comparisons of FRM and ARM performance within a common empirical framework.[5] A primary objective of the present paper was to compare FRM and ARM performance when the options values of prepayment and default are computed in a consistent manner by accounting for the unique features of ARM contracts. Evidence that FRM and ARM borrowers respond in similar ways to comparable measures of the options values of prepayment and default would provide additional empirical support for the options theory.[6]

For the research reported in this paper, we used loan-level data on conventional, conforming, single-family residential mortgages to study FRM and ARM prepayment and default behavior in an options-based empirical model. The availability of loan-level data allowed us to account for the dynamics of mortgage coupon rates to reflect the specific characteristics of ARM contracts (e.g., interest rate index, periodic and lifetime adjustment caps, interest rate margins, rate adjustment look-back periods, frequency of interest rate adjustments) and to approximate current coupon rates and monthly payment amounts on ARM mortgages at each period over the lives of the loans. Loan-level data on approximately 630,000 ARM loans originated between 1982 and 1993, and 650,000 FRM loans originated between 1979 and 1993, were used in the empirical analysis.[7] Mortgage performance was measured through the end of 1995.[8]

Statistical methods

Mortgage prepayment and default are highly duration-dependent, exhibiting characteristic age-profiles that increase during the first few years following origination, peak sometime between the fourth and seventh years, and decline over the remaining years. Like other duration- or age-dependent processes, mortgage terminations are highly amenable to analysis using a variety of statistical survival-time models, including parametric hazard models, semi-parametric or proportional hazard models, and discrete-time models.[9] A discrete-time/discrete-choice model is applied in the present paper. In what follows we briefly summarize the different approaches and explain why a discrete-time/discrete-choice approach is appropriate for analyzing mortgage prepayment and default risks.

Parametric models

Parametric models provide a complete parameterization of the probability distribution of survival times. Examples include the exponential, Weibull, gamma, log-logistic, log-normal, and various mixtures of these and other parametric distributions. A key advantage of parametric models is parsimony, since relatively few parameters are needed to completely describe the distribution of survival times. Once one has estimates of these parameters, the distribution of survival times is completely determined, thereby facilitating hypothesis testing, forecasting, or simulation. However, parametric models also impose greater restrictions on the specification and therefore are less likely to provide a good fit to empirical data for processes for which there is no theoretical justification for a given functional form. While one may specify the survival distribution in terms of an arbitrary mixture of different parametric models until the desired goodness-of-fit is attained, it is not clear that this conveys any particular advantage over more flexible specifications that are also easier to implement, such as proportional hazards or discrete-time models.

Proportional hazards models

One popular statistical survival-time model that has been applied to analyzing mortgage prepayment and default is the proportional hazard model.[10] The proportional hazard model is an appropriate method when one is willing to assume that the conditional termination rate or hazard function (defined as the ratio of the density to the survivorship proportion, $\lambda(t) = f(t)/S(t)$) can be written as the product of an exponential function of covariates and a baseline hazard that captures the underlying pattern of the hazard function over time which is identical across all subjects in the sample, $\lambda(t) = \lambda_0(t) \cdot e^{-x\beta}$. The reference to "proportionality" derives from the constant proportional impact of the covariates in the exponential component on the overall hazard rate.[11]

Estimation of the covariate parameter vector β can be achieved using a variety of canned routines for computing Cox (1975) partial-likelihood estimates that do not require specification and estimation of the baseline hazard component given by $\lambda_0(t)$. The Cox proportional hazard specification is particularly convenient when one wishes to test various hypotheses about the possible impact of a covariate on overall survivorship without having to specify a complete distribution of survival times. The proportional hazard model is often referred to as a ''semi-parametric'' model, due to the combination of the partial-likelihood approach with non-parametric estimation of the baseline hazard.[12]

Discrete-time models

Discrete-time models are usually specified in terms of the conditional probabilities of termination within specified time intervals. As such, discrete-time models often conform more closely to the way events are actually measured in empirical data, even when the underlying decision-making process may be defined in continuous time. This is almost always the case in terms of mortgage performance data.[13] Even if borrowers are assumed to decide to exercise embedded default (put) options in continuous time, this exercise may not be revealed until the next payment date when the lender fails to receive the scheduled payment from the borrower.

Whereas the hazard function in continuous time is defined as the instantaneous rate of failure conditional on survival to a given point in time, the discrete-time hazard is the probability that an event occurs at time t, or more precisely, in the interval from t to $t+1$, given that an event has not already occurred prior to t. Specification and estimation of a discrete-time model may be fully consistent with specification of parametric or semi-parametric models in continuous-time, from which it possible to derive the corresponding conditional probabilities of failure within discrete intervals of time by integrating the hazard function.[14] However, in cases where the events are observed only at discrete time points, as is almost always the case with mortgage performance data, a discrete-time model is appropriate. A grouped-duration model can be specified to estimate the discrete time behavior of mortgage prepayment and default. However, the Cox partial likelihood estimation approach, which is designed for estimating a continuous proportional hazard model, is inappropriate for estimating a grouped-duration model if there exist more than one failure observations in each discrete time interval.[15] Though unbiased estimates for a grouped-duration model may be obtained by using a maximum likelihood approach,[16] the approach typically requires significant amount of computational resources, particularly when the grouped-duration model is specified with competing risks and time-varying covariates.

Discrete choice theory and competing risks

The period-by-period decisions by borrowers to prepay, default, or continue payment on a loan conform to a situation of discrete choice for which the multinomial logit model is widely recognized as an appropriate methodology.[17] Given the inherent discreteness of the historical loan-level mortgage performance data, a discrete-time model is a more natural choice than a continuous-time specification. Mortgage prepayment and default may also be viewed as competing risks, since they are mutually exclusive and the occurrence of one event precludes or ''censors'' the chance of ever observing the waiting time until the other event.[18]

The multinomial logit specification provides a joint model for the probabilities of prepayment and default and accounts for the competing risks nature of these events. A joint model for the conditional probabilities of prepayment and default is also implied by the fact that both types of decisions are likely to depend on common unobserved factors so that there is some inherent simultaneity in the decisions of borrowers. Options theory predicts, for example, that borrowers may delay exercising either one of their embedded options if doing so increases the value of future exercise, making an assumption of independent competing risks questionable.

The empirical model

We have estimated the competing risks of mortgage prepayment and default using a discrete-time multinomial logit model that accounts for the event histories of individual mortgage loans.[19] The data used in the present analysis allowed us to reconstruct individual loan event histories for quarterly transitions by combining mortgage origination information with contemporaneous values of time-dependent factors. In the process of creating quarterly event histories, each loan contributes an additional observed "transition" for every quarter from origination up to and including the period of mortgage termination.[20] All of the explanatory variables except mortgage age (measured in quarters) were recoded to categorical values.[21] The use of categorical outcomes for the explanatory variables is an inherently flexible approach to model specification, allowing the data to reveal any underlying non-linearities. The use of categorical explanatory variables also allowed us to "reduce" the data to a smaller number of physical loan records, each representing a unique combination of the categorical variables, to which a frequency count was assigned and applied as a sampling weight in subsequent statistical analyses.[22] Given sufficient computer resources, this approach avoids the need to undertake choice-based sampling in order to assure that sufficient numbers of rare events like mortgage defaults are obtained.[23]

The empirical model is specified in terms of the age-specific conditional probabilities of prepayment and default given by:

$$\pi_P(t) = f_P(t, MP(t), EQ(t), X(t)) \tag{1}$$

$$\pi_D(t) = f_D(t, MP(t), EQ(t), X(t)) \tag{2}$$

where t is mortgage age. The two key options-theoretic predictors of mortgage prepayment and default are the mortgage premium value at age t, given by $MP(t)$; and the equity position of the borrower at age t, given by $EQ(t)$. The remaining explanatory variables are represented by $X(t)$, comprising a collection of exogenous fixed-effects and time-varying factors related to the conditional probabilities of prepayment and default. The direct dependence of the conditional probabilities on mortgage age recognizes the existence of other borrower processes and unobserved heterogeneity that induce duration dependence in the conditional rates of termination and help to explain the typical age patterns of default and prepayment.[24]

3.1. Mortgage premium value

The options theory views mortgages as long-term bonds issued by borrowers who retain embedded call (prepayment) and put (default) options. The call option value of the mortgage is a function of the difference between the present value of the "anticipated" future stream of mortgage payments discounted at the current market rate of interest, $R(t)$, and the present value of the mortgage evaluated at the current note rate, $C(t)$.[25] Following Deng et al. (1996), we have elected to approximate the call option value using the relative mortgage premium given by:

$$MP(t) = \frac{\sum_{\tau=1}^{T-t} PAY(t) \cdot \left\{\frac{1}{1+R(t)}\right\}^{\tau} - \sum_{\tau=1}^{T-t} PAY(t) \cdot \left\{\frac{1}{1+C(t)}\right\}^{\tau}}{\sum_{\tau=1}^{T-t} PAY(t) \cdot \left\{\frac{1}{1+R(t)}\right\}^{\tau}} \tag{3}$$

where T is the original term to maturity for a mortgage originated at $t=0$ (first payment due at $t=1$), and $PAY(t)$ is the current monthly payment that will fully amortize the outstanding mortgage balance over remaining term $T-t$ at the current coupon rate $C(t)$. This expression can be rewritten as:

$$MP(t) = \frac{\left\{\left[1 - \left(\frac{1}{1+R(t)}\right)^{T-t}\right] \Big/ R(t)\right\} - \left\{\left[1 - \left(\frac{1}{1+C(t)}\right)^{T-t}\right] \Big/ C(t)\right\}}{1 - \left(\frac{1}{1+R(t)}\right)^{T-t} \Big/ R(t)}. \tag{4}$$

For moderately large values of the remaining term, $T-t$, the terms in powers of $T-t$ are close to zero, so that mortgage premium can be approximated by the following expression for the relative spread between the current coupon rate on the mortgage and the market rate of interest:

$$MP(t) = \left\{\frac{C(t) - R(t)}{C(t)}\right\}. \tag{5}$$

The relative mortgage premium values for ARMs and FRMs were derived in exactly the same manner, except that the current coupon is always equals to the coupon at origination for FRMs.[26]

Borrower equity

The equity position of the borrow is determined by the difference between the market value of the property securing the loan, $P(t)$, and the unpaid mortgage balance, $UPB(t)$:

$$EQ(t) = P(t) - UPB(t). \tag{6}$$

Consistent with the assumptions of the financial options theory, which emphasizes the total value of the financial instrument, the definition of borrower equity is often expanded to include the current mortgage value, $MV(t)$, given by:

$$MV(t) = \sum_{\tau=1}^{T-t} PAY(t) \cdot \left\{\frac{1}{1+C(t)}\right\}^{\tau} - \sum_{\tau=1}^{T-t} PAY(t) \cdot \left\{\frac{1}{1+R(t)}\right\}^{\tau} \tag{7}$$

when this value is positive. Thus, an expanded definition of borrower equity is given by:

$$EQ(t) = P(t) + \max[0, MV(t)] - UPB(t). \tag{8}$$

The expression for borrower equity in (8) assumes that when borrowers assess the current value of the default option, they consider the financial benefit of having a below market rate of interest on their current loan, under the assumption that once they have defaulted they will immediately take out another loan to purchase another property.[27]

Ideally, periodic observations on the values of individual properties would be used to update individual house values and borrower equity at the same frequency (monthly) at which the decision to prepay or default can be exercised. In fact, the lack of continuous updating of individual housing values introduces significant asymmetries in the information sets of borrowers and lenders, and complicates the implementation and testing of the options theory of prepayment and default. In light of the measurement difficulties associated with borrower equity at the loan level, researchers have resorted to various means of simulating the distribution of borrower equity.[28]

We have characterized the equity positions of individual borrowers using ex ante probabilities of negative equity. The probability of negative equity is a function of the current loan balance and the probability of individual house price outcomes that lie below this value. Distributions of individual housing values relative to the value at mortgage origination were determined by applying estimates of house price drift and volatility obtained from independent estimates based on the OFHEO House Price Index (Calhoun, 1996). The House Price Index (HPI) is based on a modified version of the weighted-repeat-sales (WRS) methodology (Case and Shiller, 1987, 1989), and is consistent with the assumption that housing values are generated by a log-normal diffusion process.[29]

Individual house prices are assumed to obey a non-stationary log-normal diffusion process in which individual house price appreciation since mortgage origination is normally distributed with variance $\sigma^2(t)$ around the expected rate of appreciation from the HPI given by $\beta(t)$.[30] For the individual borrower with original house price $P(0)$, the probability of negative equity is given by:

$$PNEQ(t) = Pr\{EQ(t) < 0\} = \Phi\left\{\frac{\ln(UPB(t)) - \ln(P(0)e^{\beta(t)} + \max[0, MV(t)])}{\sigma(t)}\right\} \tag{9}$$

where $\Phi(x)$ is the standard normal cumulative distribution function evaluated at x, and where we have included the mortgage value as a component of borrower equity when this value is positive. The final expression for the probability of negative equity shows that the equity position of the borrower depends on the drift and volatility of house price appreciation rates, the expected current LTV, and loan amortization. Rather than representing a point estimate for the expectation of the borrower regarding his current equity status, this variable characterizes the entire distribution of equity values underlying these expectations.

ARM coupon rate dynamics

To represent the current financial value of the prepayment option, we needed to trace the path of the coupon rate over the active life of individual ARM loans. The coupon rate resets periodically to a new level that depends on the underlying index, plus a fixed margin, subject to periodic and lifetime caps and floors that specify the maximum and minimum amounts by which the coupon can change on any one adjustment and over the life of the loan.[31] Accordingly, the current ARM coupon rate $C(t)$ can be specified as follows:

$$\begin{aligned} C(t) = \max\{&\min[Index(t-S) + \text{Margin}, \\ &C(t-1) + A(t) \cdot Period\_UpCap,\ C(0) + A(t) \cdot Life\_UpCap], \\ &C(t-1) - A(t) \cdot Period\_DownCap(t),\ C(0) - A(t) \cdot Life\_DownCap\} \end{aligned} \tag{10}$$

where $Index(t)$ is the underlying index value at time t, S is the "lookback" period, and *Margin* is the amount added to $Index(t-S)$ to obtain the "fully-indexed" coupon rate. The periodic adjustment caps are given by *Period_UpCap* and *Period_DownCap*, and are multiplied by dummy variable $A(t)$ which equals 0 except during scheduled adjustment periods when it equals 1. The maximum lifetime adjustments are determined by *Life_UpCap* and *Life_DownCap*.

Additional interest rate variables

Recent studies of mortgage terminations have emphasized the importance of path dependence in interest rates for distinguishing among borrowers more or less likely to exercise the prepayment option when the opportunity arises.[32] The tendency for the most responsive borrowers to prepay first, so that the remaining sample of borrowers are those with lower conditional probabilities of prepayment, contributes to the observed seasoning or ''burnout'' of mortgage pools. We have included a dummy variable (BURNOUT) that indicates whether the borrower has missed a previous refinance opportunity.[33]

Expectations about future interest rates and differences in short-term and long-term borrowing rates associated with the slope of the Treasury yield curve influence the choice between FRM and ARM loans and the timing of refinancing. We have used the ratio of the 10-year Constant Maturity Treasury yield (CMT10) to the 1-year Constant Maturity Treasury yield (CMT1) to define the slope of yield curve. A high value for the slope of the yield curve indicates relatively favorable short-term rates, increasing the likelihood that a borrower refinances to an ARM to take advantage of the lower initial coupons.

Mortgage age

Conditional probabilities of mortgage default and prepayment exhibit characteristic age-profiles that increase during the first years following origination, peak sometime between the fourth and seventh years, and decline thereafter. Under a pure options model, the typical age patterns of conditional default and prepayment rates might be attributed entirely to the diffusion of housing values and the introduction of unobserved differences (heterogeneity) in the equity positions of individual borrowers, resulting in differences in the rates of default and prepayment among particular subsets of individual borrowers. As these differences emerge following mortgage origination, the observed average conditional default and prepayment rates will initially increase. Eventually, as ''high risk'' borrowers depart the sample or mortgage pool, the average conditional rates of default and prepayment will decline. The existence of other demographic and economic processes that may ''trigger'' mortgage default, and the inability to measure the diffusion of house prices and the distribution of borrower equity precisely, imply the need to account directly for age-specific differences in conditional rates of default and prepayment. For this reason, mortgage age is included as an additional explanatory variable in the empirical model.

Other variables

Dummy variables for origination years were included to account for differences in the performance of specific mortgage origination cohorts due to excluded factors such as regional income growth and unemployment, or changes in mortgage underwriting standards.[34] Dummy variables for the original loan-to-value (LTV) ratio were also included. The LTV ratio serves as an indicator of the income and net worth of the borrowers at mortgage origination, and directly determines the initial equity position of the borrower. Higher values of LTV at origination increase the probability of default and lower the probability of prepayment because there is a greater likelihood that the borrower will be in a negative equity position early in the life of the loan. High LTV borrowers are also more likely to have fewer economic resources to finance the transactions costs of prepayment or endure spells of unemployment or other trigger events that might otherwise cause them to exercise the default option in a sub-optimal manner. Finally, high LTV borrowers have demonstrated a willingness to ''leverage'' the financing of the home purchase, which may portend a greater sophistication or ''ruthlessness'' in the exercise of the default option.

Dummy variables were also included to account for the current season (quarter) of the calendar year, in recognition of the potential impact of weather, school schedules, and seasonal employment patterns on residential mobility. A dummy variable for the occupancy status of the property was included to distinguish mortgages on owner-occupied units from investor loans. Owner occupants should be less likely than investors to exercise the default option given the direct benefits they receive from the consumption of housing services. Owner occupants should be more likely to prepay than investors for non-financial reasons such as residential mobility.

The ability to bear the transactions costs of refinancing, and the ability to weather economic stress and avoid default will be correlated with the income level of the household. Given the lack of data on household income at origination, we elected to use a measure of relative loan size as a proxy for the relative income level of the household. Relative loan size was defined as the ratio of the original loan amount relative to the average-sized loan originated in the same state during the same origination year.[35] Loan size and borrower income may be assumed to be highly correlated given the existence of loan qualification requirements that limit monthly payments, and therefore loan size, to a multiple of borrower income, and the fact that housing services (and therefore demand for mortgage debt) are a normal good for most mortgage borrowers.

For the estimation results reported in this paper, all the explanatory variables were entered into both the default and prepayment functions. While our stated justifications for including particular variables have emphasized their specific relevance to either prepayment or default, the estimated models represent a ''reduced-form'' specification in which all of the explanatory variables are included in the logit ''regression'' functions for both prepayment and default. In the vernacular of survival analysis, mortgage prepayment and default are ''competing risks,'' each having direct actuarial impacts on the probability of occurrence of the other event. In addition, the underlying hazards for prepayment and default may be causally related, although we lack sufficient information to identify such a model.[36]

Empirical results

Table 1 reports multinomial logit coefficient estimates for quarterly conditional probabilities of mortgage prepayment and default. Separate estimates are reported based

Table 1. Comparison of multinomial logit parameter estimates for quarterly conditional prepayment and default probabilities.

	30-Year FRM		ARM	
Explanatory Variables	Prepayment	Default	Prepayment	Default
Constant	– 4.795	– 6.873	– 4.932	5.916
	(0.00)	(0.00)	(0.00)	(0.00)
Age	0.094	0.113	0.090	0.065
	(0.00)	(0.00)	(0.00)	(0.00)
Age squared	– 0.002	– 0.002	– 0.002	– 0.002
	(0.00)	(0.00)	(0.00)	(0.00)
1979	– 0.201	0.273		
	(0.00)	(0.00)		
1980	– 0.161	0.402		
	(0.00)	(0.00)		
1981	0.238	0.970		
	(0.00)	(0.00)		
1982	0.347	0.853	0.531	1.393
	(0.00)	(0.00)	(0.00)	(0.00)
1983	0.030	0.394	0.079	1.213
	(0.02)	(0.00)	(0.00)	(0.00)
1984	0.134	0.202	– 0.412	0.705
	(0.00)	(0.00)	(0.00)	(0.00)
1985	0.026	– 0.103	– 0.130	0.390
	(0.00)	(0.03)	(0.00)	(0.00)
1986	– 0.221	– 0.496	– 0.908	– 0.995
	(0.00)	(0.00)	(0.00)	(0.00)
1987	– 0.245	– 0.559	– 0.044	– 0.285
	(0.00)	(0.00)	(0.00)	(0.00)
1988	– 0.067	– 0.437	– 0.036	– 0.114
	(0.00)	(0.00)	(0.00)	(0.00)
1989	0.033	0.148	– 0.114	– 0.170
	(0.00)	(0.00)	(0.00)	(0.00)
1990	0.089	0.250	0.340	0.369
	(0.00)	(0.00)	(0.00)	(0.00)
1991	0.225	– 0.051*	0.472	0.062*
	(0.00)	(0.27)	(0.00)	(0.13)
1992	0.025	– 0.584	0.241	– 0.707
	(0.00)	(0.00)	(0.00)	(0.00)
1993	– 0.251	– 1.263	– 0.009	– 1.977
$LTV \leq 60$	0.134	– 1.348	0.094	– 1.310
	(0.00)	(0.00)	(0.00)	(0.00)
$60 < LTV \leq 70$	0.024	– 0.090	– 0.017	– 0.260
	(0.00)	(0.03)	(0.00)	(0.00)
$70 < LTV \leq 75$	– 0.077	0.416	– 0.100	0.257
	(0.00)	(0.00)	(0.00)	(0.00)
$75 < LTV \leq 80$	– 0.000*	0.197	– 0.059	0.209
	(0.90)	(0.00)	(0.00)	(0.00)
$80 < LTV \leq 90$	– 0.017	0.309	0.082	0.448
	(0.00)	(0.00)	(0.00)	(0.00)
$90 < LTV \leq 100$	– 0.063	0.516	0.000	0.656

Table 1. (*continued*)

Explanatory Variables	30-Year FRM Prepayment	30-Year FRM Default	ARM Prepayment	ARM Default
PNEQ ≤ 0.05	0.412	− 1.147	0.700	− 1.052
	(0.00)	(0.00)	(0.00)	(0.00)
0.05 < PNEQ ≤ 0.10	0.200	− 0.222	0.264	− 0.317
	(0.00)	(0.00)	(0.00)	(0.00)
0.10 < PNEQ ≤ 0.15	0.149	− 0.056*	0.060	− 0.182
	(0.00)	(0.11)	(0.00)	(0.00)
0.15 < PNEQ ≤ 0.20	0.086	− 0.031*	0.046	− 0.036*
	(0.00)	(0.47)	(0.00)	(0.21)
0.20 < PNEQ ≤ 0.25	− 0.078	0.191	− 0.010*	0.165
	(0.00)	(0.00)	(0.53)	(0.00)
0.25 < PNEQ ≤ 0.30	− 0.143	0.414	− 0.158	0.314
	(0.00)	(0.00)	(0.00)	(0.00)
0.30 < PNEQ ≤ 0.35	− 0.150	0.376	− 0.289	0.451
	(0.00)	(0.00)	(0.00)	(0.00)
0.35 < PNEQ	− 0.475	0.475	− 0.613	0.658
MP ≤ − 0.20	− 1.101	− 0.326	− 1.335	− 0.233
	(0.00)	(0.00)	(0.00)	(0.00)
− 0.20 < MP ≤ − 0.10	− 0.704	− 0.147	− 0.506	0.028*
	(0.00)	(0.00)	(0.00)	(0.18)
− 0.10 < MP ≤ 0.0	− 0.605	− 0.377	− 0.279	− 0.029*
	(0.00)	(0.00)	(0.00)	(0.11)
0.0 < MP ≤ 0.10	− 0.432	− 0.283	− 0.031	− 0.169
	(0.00)	(0.00)	(0.00)	(0.00)
0.10 < MP ≤ 0.20	0.585	0.077	0.362	− 0.051
	(0.00)	(0.00)	(0.00)	(0.00)
0.20 < MP ≤ 0.30	1.093	0.451	0.837	0.150
	(0.00)	(0.00)	(0.00)	(0.00)
0.30 < MP	1.163	0.605	0.901	0.304
CMT 10/CMT1 < 1.0	− 0.224	0.239	0.134	0.001*
	(0.00)	(0.00)	(0.00)	(0.98)
1.0 ≤ CMT10/CMT1 < 1.2	− 0.261	0.261	− 0.182	0.083
	(0.00)	(0.00)	(0.00)	(0.00)
1.2 ≤ CMT10/CMT1 < 1.5	0.038	− 0.083	− 0.068	− 0.002*
	(0.00)	(0.00)	(0.00)	(0.90)
1.5 ≤ CMT10/CMT1	0.447	− 0.517	0.116	− 0.082
Burnout	0.143	− 0.272	0.071	− 0.026*
(no chance to Refinance)	(0.00)	(0.00)	(0.00)	(0.05)
Burnout	− 0.143	0.272	− 0.071	0.026
(missed chance to Refinance)				
Winter	− 0.152	− 0.128	− 0.104	− 0.056
	(0.00)	(0.00)	(0.00)	(0.00)
Spring	0.148	0.023*	0.044	0.035
	(0.00)	(0.26)	(0.00)	(0.01)
Summer	− 0.008	− 0.044	− 0.009	0.023*
	(0.01)	(0.03)	(0.01)	(0.08)
Fall	0.012	0.145	0.069	− 0.001

Table 1. (*continued*)

	30-Year FRM		ARM	
Explanatory Variables	Prepayment	Default	Prepayment	Default
Investor	−0.126	0.272	−0.121	0.647
	(0.00)	(0.00)	(0.00)	(0.00)
Owner-occupant	0.126	−0.272	0.121	−0.647
Loan size ≤ 0.40	−0.616	0.017*	−0.389	−0.134*
	(0.00)	(0.76)	(0.00)	(0.10)
$0.40 <$ loan size ≤ 0.60	−0.339	−0.035*	−0.290	0.074
	(0.00)	(0.28)	(0.00)	(0.01)
$0.60 <$ loan size ≤ 0.75	−0.119	−0.078	−0.139	0.051
	(0.00)	(0.01)	(0.00)	(0.03)
$0.75 <$ loan size ≤ 1.00	0.066	−0.079	0.005*	0.007*
	(0.00)	(0.00)	(0.29)	(0.73)
$1.00 <$ loan size ≤ 1.25	0.221	−0.40*	0.171	0.027*
	(0.00)	(0.10)	(0.00)	(0.17)
$1.25 <$ loan size ≤ 1.50	0.334	0.078	0.279	0.021*
	(0.00)	(0.01)	(0.00)	(0.35)
$1.50 <$ loan size	0.452	0.137	0.363	−0.046

Notes. All models were estimated by the method of maximum likelihood using the SAS® CATMOD procedure. Empirical *p*-values are shown in parentheses. An asterisk (*) indicates that the coefficient is not statistically significant from zero at the 5-percent level for an asymptotic-normal test. CATMOD treats the last category for each variable grouping as the omitted category and computes the coefficient estimate for this category as the negative sum of the other coefficients for that variable group, and no standard error estimate is reported for this category.

on separate applications of the model to FRM and ARM loan data. In what follows we briefly review the estimates for the mortgage age effects before moving on to discuss the other variables.

Selected sets of coefficient estimates (all except seasonality) are also shown graphically in Exhibits 1 and 2. Some explanation of the exhibits may be helpful in interpreting the results. For all variables except mortgage age, the vertical axis represents the contribution of the explanatzory variable to the logit ''regression'' function, $X_k \cdot \beta_k$, for explanatory variable k, where the value of X_k is equal to 1 when the loan falls into a particular category and 0 otherwise, and the values of the β_k coefficients are the same as those reported in Table 1 for the logit prepayment and default functions, respectively. Because all of the explanatory variables (except mortgage age) are 0 or 1 dummies, the same scale applies to every panel in Exhibits 1 and 2. For the panels in Exhibits 1 and 2 showing the results for mortgage age, the vertical axis reports the sum of the corresponding logit intercept coefficient and the quadratic age function. Thus, the intercepts reported in the first panel of each of the exhibits correspond to the overall intercept of the respective logit regression functions. Although these panels are drawn to different scales than the others, the units are the same as for the other panels and correspond directly to the coefficient values reported in Table 1.

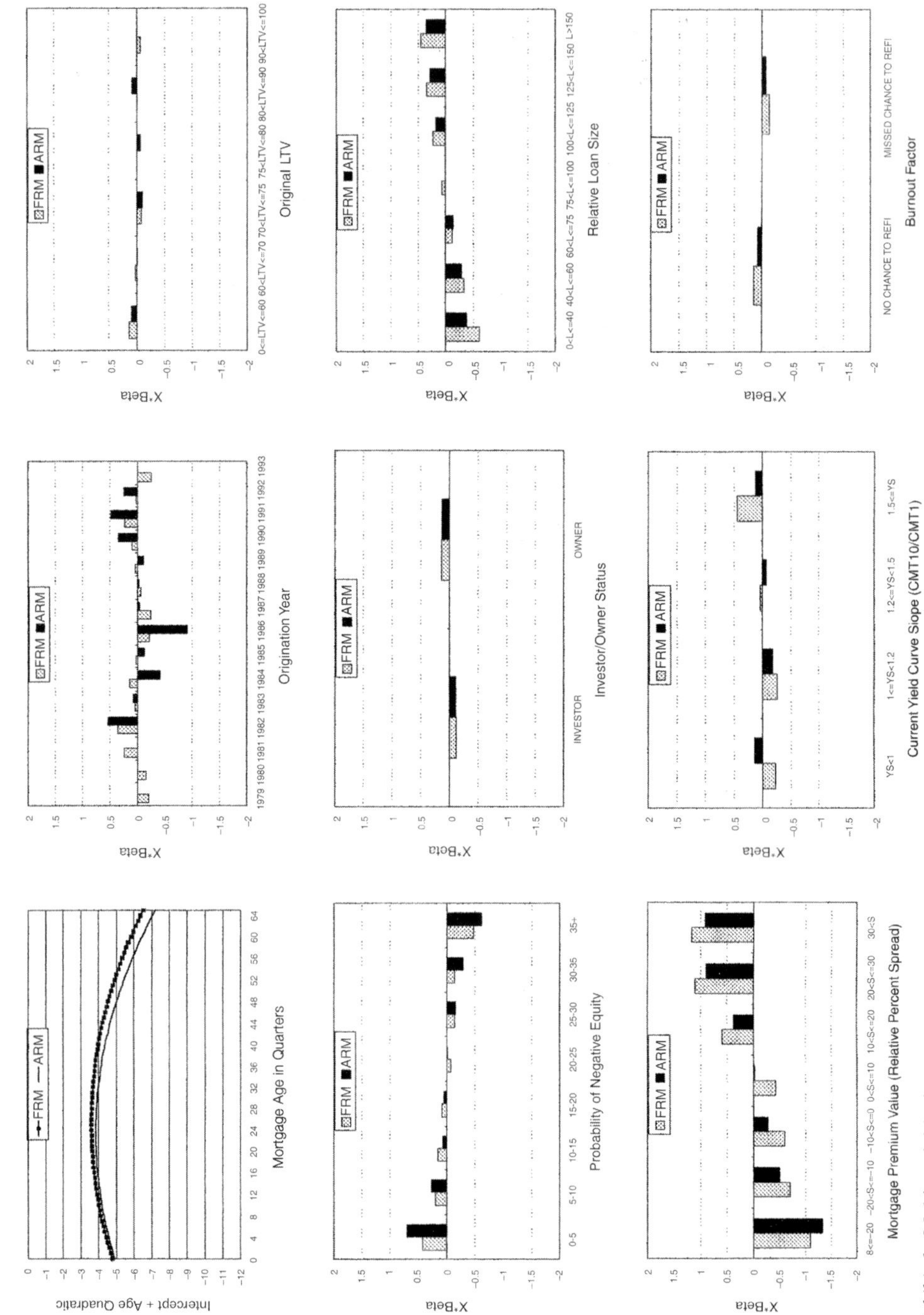

Exhibit 1. Multinomial logit prepayment parameter estimates.

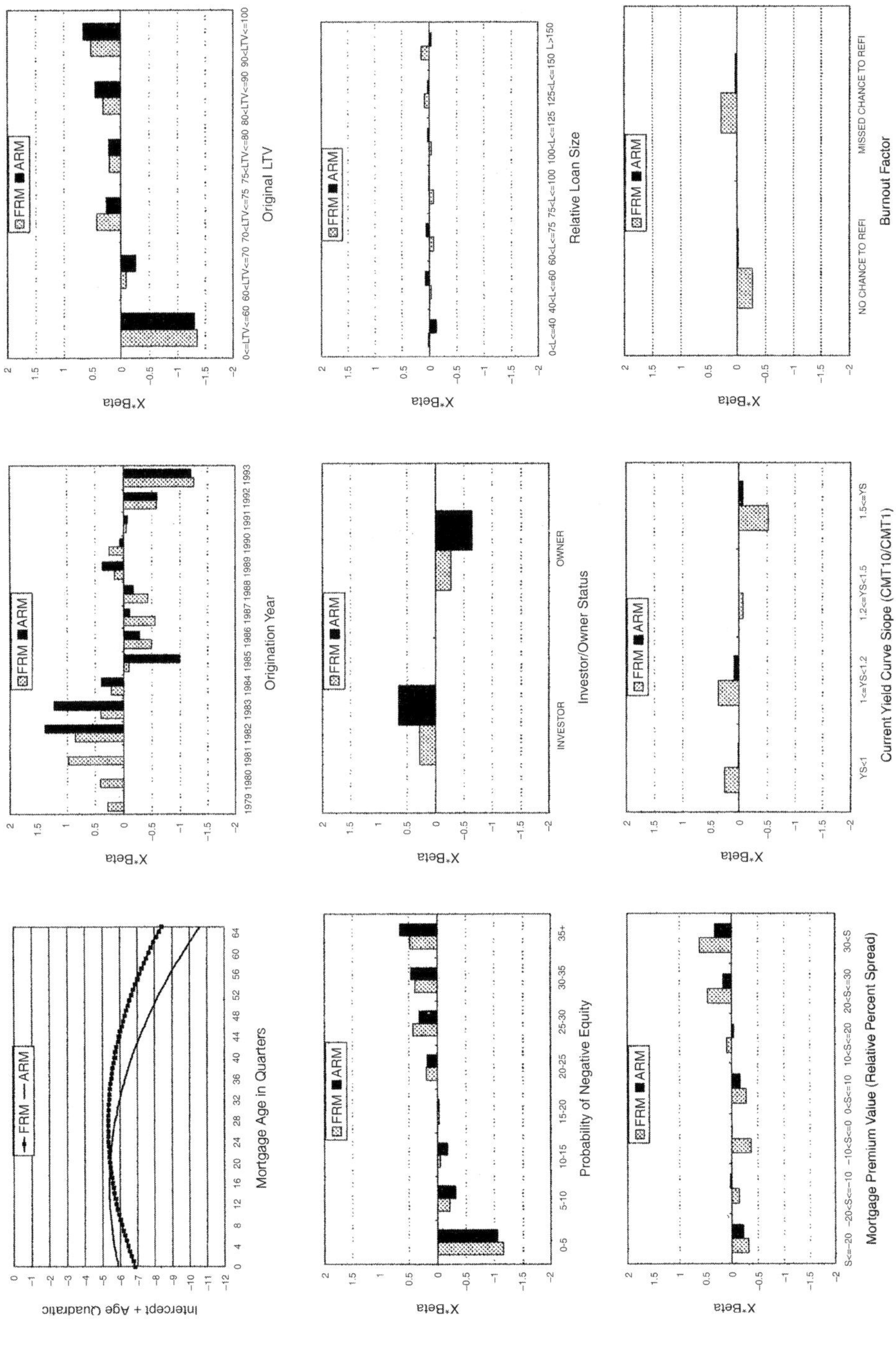

Exhibit 2. Multinomial logit default parameter estimates.

Mortgage age effects

Exhibit 1 shows that the underlying expected rates of prepayment by age are very similar for FRM and ARM loans. This has particular significance for assessing the validity of the options-based empirical model. As discussed above, mortgage age plays a dual role in capturing both "structural" duration-dependence in prepayment rates, as well as the "residual" impact of unobserved heterogeneity among borrowers that contributes to "spurious" duration dependence in prepayment rates.[37] The fact that the underlying age patterns for FRM and ARM loans are so similar suggests that most systematic differences have been explained by the other explanatory variables. The fact that the most influential variable is the mortgage premium representing the call option value of prepayment represents strong empirical support for the options model, and confirms the basic consistency of FRM and ARM borrower behavior. We will return to the discussion of the impact of the mortgage premium variables below.

Exhibit 2 shows that the underlying average rates of default are initially higher for ARMs, but they subsequent rise less rapidly with age and eventually decline more rapidly than the corresponding estimates for FRMs. The more rapid decline in the underlying age-specific conditional probabilities of default for ARM borrowers may indicate a greater level of unobserved heterogeneity in the determinants of mortgage default than exists for FRM borrowers, or additional differences related to the mortgage selection process.

The selection of an ARM contract over a FRM loan may signal a number of differences among borrowers not fully measured by the included explanatory variables. For example, ARM borrowers may have more limited time horizons for residential mobility, so they are less risk averse regarding future changes in interest rates. Alternatively, the lower initial coupons and monthly payments on ARM loans make it easier for lower income borrowers to qualify, and they may be more likely to default earlier in the life of the mortgage. The resulting age patterns of mortgage default indicate higher early defaults, and more rapid improvement in the underlying risk profile of the sample of ARM borrowers than occurs among FRM borrowers.

The impact of option values

The estimates for the option-related variables for FRMs and ARMs indicate that borrower behavior on these loans is consistent with the predictions of the options theory of prepayment and default. Conditional probabilities of prepayment are negatively related to the mortgage premium value (positively related to relative spreads), and conditional probabilities of default are positively related to the probability of negative equity. Conditional default rates are also negatively related to the mortgage premium values. Although the mortgage value was included as a component of borrower equity, we find that the mortgage premium value also has a direct impact on conditional default rates.[38] In addition, conditional prepayment rates are negatively related to the probability of negative equity, which is consistent with the expectation that borrowers will be less likely to refinance or sell their properties in declining markets.

The overall consistency of the independent estimates for FRM and ARM termination models provides strong empirical support for the options-based model. While the patterns of estimates across product types are quite similar, the multinomial logit estimates do indicate some differences in the responsiveness of FRM and ARM borrowers to comparable option value outcomes. For example, ARM prepayment and default probabilities appear to be more responsive to the likelihood of extreme outcomes for borrower equity than those of FRM borrowers, given the larger difference in the range of borrower equity coefficient estimates for ARM borrowers shown Table 1 and Exhibits 1 and 2. ARM prepayment and default probabilities are generally somewhat less sensitive to differences in the mortgage premium value, with the exception of the coefficient estimate for the probability of prepayment for loans in the most negative spread category (i.e., largest mortgage premium category). Again, this finding seems consistent with the hypothesis that borrowers with more limited time horizons for remaining in the home are more like to choose ARM contracts and will be less responsive to the value of the mortgage premium.

Other interest rate variable effects

There are some interesting differences in the impact of the yield curve slope and burnout variables on FRM and ARM prepayment and default probabilities. These variables have relatively smaller impacts on conditional probabilities of prepayment and default for ARM borrowers. This is also consistent with what one would expect from an options-theoretic viewpoint. For example, when confronted with an upward sloping yield curve, an FRM borrower has a financial incentive to switch to an ARM mortgage to take advantage of lower short-term rates offered by lenders. ARM borrowers, many of whom have coupon rates indexed to relatively short-term Treasury yields or other cost-of-funds indexes, already enjoy this advantage, and would be less likely to refinance. In addition, if borrowers select ARM mortgages because they have shorter time horizons for residential mobility, they have no incentive to incur the transactions costs associated with refinancing that would be required to take advantage of a steeply sloped yield curve.[39]

There appears to be no impact of path dependence in interest rates on ARM prepayment and default probabilities. The burnout variable is used primarily to distinguish borrowers who have failed to prepay when the prepayment option was previously in-the-money. ARM borrowers should be in this situation less frequently than FRM borrowers, due to the periodic adjustment of ARM coupons. In addition, as discussed above, even when market rates decline enough to produce significant spreads on ARM mortgages, the original selection of an ARM contract may indicate a limited time horizon, reducing the potential benefits of exercising the prepayment option on lifetime wealth, and making it less likely that ARM borrowers respond to prepayment opportunities.

Origination year effects

Both the FRM and ARM models produced a wide range of default coefficient estimates for the origination year dummies. This indicates that there are important factors associated with specific mortgage cohorts that are not completely captured by the two key options related variables. The range of origination year coefficient estimates for conditional default probabilities is greatest for ARMs, but mainly in the early years when this product was a relatively new innovation, and prior to standardization of ARM underwriting guidelines after 1985.

Origination year effects are generally smaller for prepayment, but still indicate that there is a great deal of variation in prepayment probabilities that is not explained by the options value of prepayment. One source of difference in the pattern of ARM prepayment origination year effects could be the timing of the introduction of different types of ARM contracts into the historical sample. Although information on different ARM products was used to provide accurate updating of ARM coupon rates, no attempt was made to account for the changing composition of the sample as different ARM product types were introduced to the market and began to appear in the sample.[40]

Original loan-to-value ratios

The impact of LTV at origination is quite similar for the FRM and ARM models, showing a strong positive relationship between LTV and default, and very little impact on prepayment. This is consistent will numerous other studies and confirms the continued significant of this key underwriting factor on subsequent mortgage performance. The default coefficient estimates for LTV indicate a slight deterioration in performance in the 70–75 LTV category, which is consistent with less stringent screening of loans for which borrowers have 25–30 percent equity at origination.[41]

Other variables

Conditional probabilities of default vary significantly for loans secured by owner-occupied properties versus those for investor loans. The impact on ARM default rates is substantially larger than that estimated for FRMs. The impact of occupancy status on both FRM and ARM prepayments is quite small, but does indicate a tendency for owner-occupants to prepay at higher rates than investors.

Relative loan size appears to be much more important for explaining differences in prepayment rates than it is for default. Smaller loans are less likely to prepay regardless of product type, although the range of coefficient estimates is slightly greater for FRM loans. Surprisingly, relative loan size has only negligible impact on the probability of default for both FRM and ARM loans. Combined with the results for prepayment, this seems to suggest that, to the extent that loan size is a proxy for borrower income, it is more likely to be associated with differences in non-financial prepayments, such as those due to residential mobility, rather than an indicator of the ability of the household to avoid default.[42]

Both FRM and ARM loans exhibit seasonal variation in conditional probabilities of prepayment and default, although the range of coefficient estimates is greater for fixed-rate loans. If ARM borrowers were generally more likely to relocate, that being one reason for selecting an ARM rather than a FRM, then one would expect seasonal factors to be less important. If an ARM were selected in part because a move was anticipated, then this would be consistent with the attenuation of seasonal effects for ARM borrowers.

Summary and conclusions

The empirical analysis used individual mortgage event histories to estimate a discrete-time hazards model for FRM and ARM performance based on a multinomial-logit specification for quarterly conditional probabilities of default and prepayment. The explanatory variables for both ARMs and FRMs comprised a variety of fixed-effects and time-varying covariates, including contemporaneous indicators of the current values of the embedded default and prepayment options. Information on individual ARM contract terms was used to reconstruct the dynamics of ARM coupons. Using this increased level of detail, the empirical analysis explored the relationship between FRM and ARM termination rates and the dynamics of the underlying options-related determinants of prepayment and default.

The estimated impacts of the options values on conditional probabilities of prepayment and default are generally quite similar across both FRM and ARM borrowers. We believe that this provides additional support for the basic predictions of the options theory, as it implies similar behavior by FRM and ARM borrowers when faced with the same financial incentives. When FRM and ARM behavior differs, it is mainly with respect to other fixed-effects. In many cases, these differences can be related to the alternative motivations of FRM and ARM borrowers in the mortgage selection process.

What are the potential implications of these findings for the pricing of FRM and ARM securities? One implication of the similarities between the FRM and ARM estimates is that in the absence of historical data on ARM loan performance one could apply a model of FRM performance combined with realistic modeling of changes in ARM coupons under different interest rate scenarios. Our estimates confirm that the underlying options-related incentives to default and prepay are very similar, so that one would expect very little difference in valuations based on either set of model estimates. This does not imply that ARM and FRM securities would receive similar prices under the same assumptions about future changes in housing values and interest rates, only that the underlying propensities to default or prepay will be similar when individual borrowers are faced with the same financial incentives.

We have attempted to assess the significance of options-related determinants of prepayment and default outcomes in the context of an empirical model that must accommodate the existence of other economic and demographic events and observed and unobserved heterogeneity among individual borrowers (i.e., violations of the assumptions of a pure options model). While the results support the basic predictions of the options theory, differences in estimates of conditional probabilities of prepayment and default associated with mortgage age, year of origination, original LTV, and relative loan size, indicate the continued significance of these other processes for empirical models of mortgage terminations.

This paper has attempted to advance the state of empirical research on mortgage terminations by modeling FRM and ARM loans with comparable levels of precision. We report empirical estimates based on a large, temporally and geographically diverse sample of historical mortgage experience, supplemented by detailed characteristics on the dynamics of ARM coupons rates. Like many other empirical studies of mortgage terminations, the analysis was subject to limitations in our ability to measure the option values of prepayment and default. These limitations notwithstanding, the results support the application of similar options-based empirical models to the analysis of FRM and ARM loan performance.

Notes

1. A number of recent studies analyze mortgage prepayment and default in a competing risks hazard-modeling framework. See, for example, Deng et al. (1996, 2000), and Deng (1997). Further discussion of the relationship of the statistical method to alternative approaches such as proportional hazards models is provided later in the paper.
2. Conventional loans are not government insured. Conforming loans meet underwriting and maximum loan amount requirements for eligibility for purchase by U.S. government-sponsored housing enterprises Fannie Mae and Freddie Mac. The data used in the empirical analysis were from a historical mortgage database compiled by OFHEO to support a broad range of research and analysis activities.
3. See Dunn and McConnell (1981), Foster and Van Order (1984, 1985), Buser and Hendershott (1984), Brennan and Schwartz (1985), Kau et al. (1985, 1990), and Hendershott and Van Order (1987).
4. See, for example, Green and Shoven (1986), Schwartz and Torous (1989), Quigley and Van Order (1990, 1995), Archer et al. (1996), Deng et al. (1996, 2000), and Deng (1997).
5. Previous empirical studies have tended to either: (1) model ARM prepayment and default rates as functions of variables observed at mortgage origination; (2) study ARM prepayment and default at the aggregate level; or (3) use prepayment and default rates on FRMs as a benchmark to estimate the relative termination rates of ARMs using empirical multiples. For example, Sa-Aadu (1988) used only variables observed at the time of origination to analyze ARM defaults but did not address prepayment. Lea and Zorn (1986) analyzed ARM termination experience in response to changes in macro-level variables. Cunningham and Capone (1990) studied relative termination experience of ARM to FRM in a small sample of loans from Houston, Texas.
6. This does not imply that FRM and ARM loans will have similar observed rates of prepayment and default over the same economic cycle, as changes in ARM coupons will result in different realized values for the prepayment and default options.
7. Data on FRM loans were limited to conventional, conforming, 30-year (greater than 240 months original term to maturity) mortgages on single-family, single-unit properties. The FRM sample is a 10 percent random sample from a much larger database of historical mortgage originations.
8. Default and prepayment events correspond to the occurrence of last-paid-installments that are subsequently identified as defaults or prepayments. In the case of default events, there may exist delays of a few months to as long as two years following a borrower's decision to cease payment on a loan and the culmination of foreclosure proceedings that result in a loan being classified as a default. Thus, it is necessary to limit the sample to cohorts with at least two years actual experience.
9. Standard references in statistics and economics include Kalbfleish and Prentice (1980), and Lancaster (1990).
10. See, for example, Deng et al. (1996, 2000), and Deng (1997).
11. Covariate vector X may be functions of time, in which case they are referred to as ''time-varying'' covariates.
12. Han and Hausman (1990) have proposed a method by which a flexible baseline function can be estimated

non-parametrically together with the proportional hazard parameters given by β. A preliminary effort to apply the Han and Hausman (1990) approach to default and prepayment hazards is described in Calhoun (1998).

13. Allison (1995), in introducing discrete-time methods, specifically mentions mortgage payment behavior as a case where ''a discrete-time model is the natural way to go.''
14. As discussed in Allison (1982), in some cases the parameters estimates obtained from a discrete time model will be identical to those in the continuous time specification, such as when the hazards can be specified in terms of a log-linear model and all the explanatory variables are categorical.
15. See Kalbfleish and Prentice (1980) for a discussion.
16. See, for example, Deng et al. (2000).
17. See, for example, McFadden (1978).
18. In the case of parametric and semi-parametric models, the assumption of independent competing risks can simplify the estimation of model parameters. For example, a standard approach is to view different types of terminations as arising from the existence of latent or potential failure times for each termination type. If these random failure times are independently distributed then we have an independent competing risks model, and the derivation of marginal distributions and accounting for censoring is greatly simplified. Whether or not the form of the dependence can be identified in the case where the underlying competing risks are not independent depends on whether we have information in addition to the proportions surviving and the type of failure. In the absence of additional information any dependent competing risks model will be observationally equivalent to an independent competing risks model. These points follow the discussion of competing risks and identification issues in Lancaster (1990), pp. 154–155.
19. Several empirical studies have applied static from of the logit or other qualitative response models to analyze mortgage prepayment and default behavior. Examples of previous applications of the multinomial logit model are Campbell and Dietrich (1983), Zorn and Lea (1989), and Cunningham and Capone (1990).
20. The term ''transition'' is used here to refer to periods in which loans remain active, or in which default or prepayment is observed to occur.
21. The categorical outcomes were subsequently treated as dummy variables in the logit estimation. This has the additional benefit of avoiding over-parameterization of the model through the use of specific functional forms (i.e., linear, quadratic, logarithmic). The only variable entered directly using a specific functional form was the age variable, which was entered as a quadratic. The implications of this specification for the empirical result are discussed in greater detail below in summarizing the model estimates.
22. The original ARM sample of approximately 630,000 mortgage originations produced a weighted event-history sample of 3.8 million records representing nearly 10.6 million quarterly transitions. The FRM sample of approximately 650,000 mortgage originations produced a weighted event-history sample of 1.64 million records representing 9.9 million quarterly transitions. The smaller number of weighted event-history records for FRMs is consistent with the fact that each loan contributes fewer unique combinations of the explanatory variables because the coupon rates on these loans are fixed at origination and do not change over the life of the loan.
23. It has been demonstrated for static logit models that choice-based sampling results in biased estimates of the coefficients of the logit constant terms, for which relatively simple corrections are available, based on the sample versus population distributions of the explanatory variables across groups defined by dependent variable outcomes (Costlett, 1981).
24. Other borrower processes include residential mobility, employment mobility, involuntary unemployment, and demographic events related to household formation and dissolution, mortality, and fertility. Ideally, given suitable household-level data, these other processes would be modeled jointly with mortgage terminations. See Lancaster (1990) for a discussion of the impact of unobserved heterogeneity on estimates of duration dependence in econometric models of transition probabilities.
25. The precise value of the mortgage premium is unknown, and depends on the uncertain future time path of mortgage payments and the associated future probabilities of prepayment and default. In this paper, we have elected to approximate the mortgage premium using empirical values known, or at least knowable, by both borrowers and observers of borrower behavior. To facilitate the comparison of FRM and ARM performance,

we have also imposed the additional simplification of using the current payment amount to represent current and future payment amounts, although for ARM loans these payments will vary along with the levels of future interest rates. The dependence of current premium values on the uncertain exercise of financial options has been one motivation for the development of ''option-adjusted spreads'' in valuing the payment streams associated with financial assets (for example, see Fabozzi and Richard, 1995). For a discussion of the implications of stochastic term structure for the construction of mortgage premium values in default models, see Deng (1997).

26. Note that negative spreads between the current coupon and the market rate of interest are associated with positive values of the mortgage premium and vice versa.
27. See Foster and Van Order (1984). This ignores the potential implications for a borrower's credit standing and their subsequent ability to qualify for another mortgage.
28. The most familiar example is Foster and Van Order (1984, 1985). They used a Monte Carlo simulation of a synthetic mortgage pool in conjunction with a house price diffusion process and actual default and prepayment rates to reconstruct a time-series for the number of borrowers in a negative equity position. Under additional restrictions on the model (i.e., that only borrowers with negative equity default, and only borrowers with positive equity prepay), the time-series for the number of borrowers in a negative equity position. Under additional restrictions on the model (i.e., that only borrowers with negative equity (various levels) was used in regressions for conditional default and prepayment probabilities.
29. Estimates of the parameters of the log-normal diffusion process are produced as by-products of the application of the WRS methodology. Deng et al. (1996) applied a similar approach using WRS indexes for 26 metropolitan areas estimated using Freddie Mac data.
30. Estimates of expected appreciation or drift in house prices are obtained directly form the estimated values of the HPI for each of the nine U.S. Census divisions. Estimates of diffusion volatility $\sigma^2(t)$ are computed using the estimated parameters for the error variance of individual log-differences in housing prices that are obtained from the second-stage of the WRS method for each Census division. See Calhoun (1996) for additional details.
31. Detail on specific ARM contracts was obtained in some cases from loan-level information, and in other cases was obtained using plan-level detail for loans in certain product categories.
32. For example, see the discussions of borrower heterogeneity and path dependence in Bartholomew et al. (1988), and the discussion of burnout in Richard and Roll (1989).
33. The dummy variable equals one if the spread between the note rate on the mortgage and the average market rate of interest has been 200 basis points or greater during any two of the past 8 quarters. We experimented with a number of alternative burnout specifications such as the sum of all past negative spreads. One practical problem with utilizing cumulative measures like the sum of all past negative spreads arises when one intends to apply the model to project mortgage cash flows under the extreme interest rate assumptions of a stress test. For example, the risk-based capital stress test being develop by OFHEO for Fannie Mae and Freddie Mac assumes that interest rates increase by up to 600 basis points and then remain at historically high levels for up to 10 years. In this case the burnout variable specified in terms of the sum of past negative spreads takes on unrealistically high values and drives prepayment rates to unrealistically low levels. As an alternative we experimented with specifications that would be much more limited in terms of the range of outcomes they may describe, but which are also more constrained in terms of the values they can take on under extreme interest rate scenarios. The particular specification reported here was selected from among several alternatives that used different numbers of quarters and different threshold levels for interest rates changes. The estimation results were generally quite similar across the different combinations and we selected the combination of looking back 8 quarters for at least 2 quarters of interest rate spreads of at least 200 basis points as a reasonable compromise, and one that corresponds to conventional wisdom about the magnitude of changes that have been required historically to motivate borrowers to prepay. We found that the hurdle of 200 basis points worked well in comparison with the tested alternatives, including 100 and 300 basis point hurdles.
34. The sample includes ARM loans for origination years 1982–93 and FRM loans for origination years 1979–1993. As noted by Vandell (1993), significant changes in underwriting guidelines for Fannie Mae and Freddie Mac occurred in 1985 and 1988, respectively.

35. Price Waterhouse (1990) reported significant differences in claim rates for FHA mortgages stratified by loan size. Smaller loans were observed to fail at significantly higher rates than other loans.
36. For an example of simultaneous equations hazards models, see Lillard (1993).
37. The use of a quadratic function for age conveniently reduces the number of discrete parameters that must be estimated. We also experimented with estimating models that included separate categorical variables for each age, so that the age function was essentially unrestricted. The results of this analysis confirm that a quadratic age function fits almost perfectly for default, and somewhat less so for prepayment. In the case of prepayment, the unrestricted age function showed that prepayment probabilities would initially be closer to zero in the first year, then rise more rapidly over years 1 to 3, peak slightly sooner and higher around year 4, and then decline more or less linearly after year 5. Due to the small number of loans surviving to years 9 to 12, the coefficient estimates become highly variable at these outer years. The quadratic is generally consistent with the overall pattern of prepayment intensities and does not allow for erratic estimates at the higher ages, so that it smoothes the data in the way one would like. In future research we plan to experiment with alternatives such as combinations of cubic and linear splines that will allow more flexibility in the earlier ages and still smooth the estimates at the later ages.
38. The finding of a direct effect of the mortgage premium on conditional default rates may be explained in part by the fact that we cannot measure borrower equity directly at the loan level.
39. ARM borrowers have already revealed themselves as unwilling to pay higher fixed coupon rates to acquire the full benefit of the embedded prepayment option on a fixed-rate mortgage.
40. Although the FRM and ARM samples cover different time periods, we do not believe this presents any problems given the inclusion of separate origination year dummies and additional contemporaneous explanatory variables specific to time periods in which loans are at risk of prepayment or default (e.g., equity, mortgage premium, burnout, seasonality, yield curve slope). We experimented with more flexible functional forms, such as estimating separate models for each origination cohort and interacting origination years with other explanatory variables. We found that these specifications tended to produce more erratic coefficient patterns and to highlight historical anomalies rather than identifying consistent patterns.
41. A similar finding is reported in a recent analysis by MacDonald and Holloway (1996) comparing the relative early payment performance of balloon and FRM loans. The authors suggest that this result may be due to the presense of low-documentation loan products in the 71–75 percent LTV category.
42. This view is supported by recent research on securitization of low-income loans meeting the requirements of the Community Reinvestment Act (CRA). The relatively more stable prepayment speeds of CRA-eligible loans is cited as a feature increasing their value as a collateral for securitization. See Brown and Westhoff (1998).

References

Allison, P. D. (1992). "Discrete-Time Methods for the Analysis of Event Histories." In S. Leinhardt (ed.), *Sociological Methodology 1982* (pp. 61–98). San Francisco: Jossey-Bass.

Allison, P. D. (1995). *Survival Analysis Using the SAS® System: A Practical Guide*. Cary, N.C.: SAS Institute.

Archer, W. R., D. C. Ling, and G. A. McGill. (1986). "The Effect of Income and Collateral Constraints on Residential Mortgage Terminations," *Journal of Regional Science and Urban Economics* 26(3–4), 235–261.

Bartholomew, L., J. Berk, and R. Roll. (1988). "Adjustable Rate Mortgages: Prepayment Behavior," *Housing Finance Review* 7, 31–46.

Brennan, M. J., and E. S. Schwartz. (1985). "Determinants of GNMA Mortgage Prices," *AREUEA Journal* 13, 209–228.

Brown, N., and D. Westhoff. (1998). "Packaging CRA Loans into Securities," *Mortgage Banking*, May 1998, 32–41.

Buser, S. A., and P. H. Hendershott. (1984). "Pricing Default Free Mortgages," *Housing Finance Review* 3, 405–429.

Calhoun, C. A. (1996). "OFHEO House Price Indexes: Technical Description," Washington, D.C., Office of Federal Housing Enterprise Oversight, April 1996.

Calhoun, C. A. (1998). ''Bivariate Ordered-Probit Estimates of Simultaneous Competing-Risk Hazards Models for Residential Mortgage Default and Prepayment.'' *Proceedings of the American Statistical Association 1997*, Epidemiology Section, 92–97.

Campbell, T. S., and J. K. Dietrich (1983). ''The Determinants of Default on Insured Conventional Residential Mortgage Loans,'' *Journal of Finance* 38, 1569–1581.

Case, K. E., and Shiller, R. J. (1987). ''Prices of Single Family Real Estate Prices,'' *New England Economic Review*, Sept./Oct., 45–56.

Case, K. E., and Shiller, R. J. (1989). ''The Efficiency of the Market for Single-Family Homes,'' *The American Economic Review* 79, 125–137.

Costlett, S. (1981). ''Efficient Estimation of Discrete-Choice Models.'' In C. F. Manski and D. McFadden (eds.), *Structural Analysis of Discrete Data with Econometric Applications* (pp. 51–111). Cambridge, Massachusetts: MIT Press.

Cox, D. R. (1975). ''Partial Likelihood,'' *Biometrika* 62, 269–276.

Cunningham, D., and C. Capone. (1990). ''The Relative Termination Experience of Adjustable to Fixed-Rate Mortgages,'' *The Journal of Finance* 45(5), 1687–1703.

Deng, Y. (1997). ''Mortgage Termination: An Empirical Hazard Model With Stochastic Term Structure,'' *The Journal of Real Estate Finance and Economics* 14(3), 309–331.

Deng, Y., J. M. Quigley, and R. Van Order. (1996). ''Mortgage Default and Low Downpayment Loans: The Costs of Public Subsidy,'' *Journal of Regional Science and Urban Economics* 26(3–4), 263–285.

Deng, Y., J. M. Quigley, and R. Van Order. (2000). ''Mortgage Termination, Heterogeneity, and the Exercise of Mortgage Options,'' *Econometrica* 68(2), 275–307.

Dunn, K. B., and J. J. McConnell. (1981). ''Valuation of Mortgage-Backed Securities,'' *The Journal of Finance* 36, 599–617.

Fabozzi, F. J., and S. F. Richard. (1995). ''Introduction to the Option-Adjusted Spread Method.'' In F. J. Fabozzi (ed.), *The Handbook of Mortgage Backed Securities*, 4th Edition, (pp. 611–624). New York: McGraw-Hill, 1995.

Foster, C., and R. Van Order. (1984). ''An Option-Based Model of Mortgage Default,'' *Housing Finance Review* 3(4), 351–372.

Foster, C., and R. Van Order. (1985). ''FHA Terminations: A Prelude to Rational Mortgage Pricing,'' *AREUEA Journal* 13(3), 273–291.

Green, J., and J. B. Shoven. (1986). ''The Effect of Interest Rates on Mortgage Prepayment,'' *Journal of Money, Credit and Banking* 18, 41–50.

Han, A., and Hausman, J. A. (1990). ''Flexible Parametric Estimation of Duration and Competing Risk Models,'' *Journal of Applied Econometrics* 5, 1–29.

Hendershott, P. H., and R. Van Order. (1987). ''Pricing Mortgages: An Interpretation of the Models and Results,'' *Journal of Financial Services Research* 1, 77–111.

Kalbfleisch, J. D., and R. L. Prentice. (1980). *The Statistical Analysis of Failure Time Data*. New York: John Wiley & Sons.

Kaplan, E. L., and P. Meier. (1958). ''Nonparametric Estimation from Incomplete Observations,'' *Journal of the American Statistical Association* 53, 457–481.

Kau, J. B., D. C. Keenan, W. J. Muller, and J. F. Epperson. (1985). ''Rational Pricing of Adjustable Rate Mortgages,'' *AREUEA Journal* 13(2), 117–128.

Kau, J. B., D. C. Keenam, W. J. Muller, and J. F. Epperson. (1990). ''The Valuation and Analysis of Adjustable Rate Mortagages,'' *Management Science* 36(12), 1417–1431.

Lancaster, T. (1990). *The Econometric Analysis of Transition Data*. New York: Cambridge University Press.

Lillard, L. A. (1993). ''Simultaneous Equations for Hazards: Marriage Duration and Fertility Timing,'' *Journal of Econometrics* 56, 189–217.

MacDonald, G. D., and T. H. Holloway (1996). ''Early Evidence on Balloon Performance,'' *Journal of Real Estate Finance and Economics* 12, 279–293.

McFadden, D. (1978). ''Modelling the Choice of Residential Location.'' In A. Karquist et al. (eds.), *Spatial Interaction Theory and Planning Models*. Amsterdam: North-Holland Publishing Company.

McFadden, D. (1981). "Econometric Models of Probabilistic Choice." In C. F. Manski and D. McFadden (eds.), *Structural Analysis of Discrete Data with Econometric Applications* (pp. 198–272). Cambridge, Mass.: MT Press.

Price Waterhouse (1990). *An Actuarial Review of the Federal Housing Administration's Mutual Mortgage Insurance Fund.* Washington, DC: Price Waterhouse, 1990.

Quigley, J., and R. Van Order. (1995). "Efficiency in the Mortgage Market: The Borrower's Perspective," *AREUEA Journal* 18(3), 237–252.

Quigley, J. M., and R. Van Order. (1995). "Explicit Tests of Contingent Claims Models of Mortgage Default," *The Journal of Real Estate Finance and Economics* 11(2), 99–117.

Richard, S. F., and R. Roll (1989). "Prepayments on Fixed Rate Mortgage Backed Securities," *Journal of Portfolio Management* 15(3), 73–82.

Roll, R. (1987). "Collateralized Mortgage Obligations: Characteristics, History, Analysis." In F. J. Fabozzi (ed.), *The Handbook of Mortgage-Backed Securities* (pp. 7–44). Chicago: Probus.

Sa-Aadu, J. (1988). "Legal Restriction, Credit Allocation and Default Risk Under Fixed and Adjustable Rate Mortgage," *Housing Finance Review* 7, 225–247.

Schwartz, E. S., and W. N. Torous (1989). "Prepayment and the Valuation of Mortgage-Backed Securities," *The Journal of Finance* 44(2), 375–392.

Stanton, R., and N. Wallace (1995). "ARM Wrestling: Valuing Adjustable Rate Mortgages Indexed to the Eleventh District Cost of Funds," *AREUEA Journal* 23, 311–345.

Vandell, K. D. (1993). "Handing Over the Keys: A Perspective on Mortgage Default Research," *AREUEA Journal* 21(3), 211–246.

Zorn, P., and M. Lea. (1986). "Adjustable Rate Mortgage, Fluctuations in the Economic Environment and Lender Portfolio Change," *AREUEA Journal* 14, 432–447.

Journal of Real Estate Finance and Economics, 24:1/2, 35–58, 2002

Mortgage Contracts, Strategic Options and Stochastic Collateral

ROBERT A. JONES
Simon Fraser University

DAVID NICKERSON
Colorado State University and FreddieMac
Email: david.nickerson@colostate.edu

Abstract

This paper offers a game-theoretic model for both the analysis and valuation of mortgage contracts in the context of an economy with complete information and complete contingent claims markets. We analyze the equilibrium strategy of the lender, who holds an option over the magnitude of mortgage credit extended per dollar of collateral offered, and the mortgagor, who holds options to default or prepay, in a class of intertemporal mortgage contracts collateralized by property evolving according to a random process which is common knowledge to both parties to the mortgage contract. Using continuous–time arbitrage valuation principles, we derive the value of the mortgage contract to both parties and show, through both analytical solutions and numerical simulations, that Markov perfect equilibria exist in which, among other properties, a lower flow of housing services accruing to the borrower, per dollar of initial house value, and a correspondingly lower rate of effective depreciation, will elicit a larger volume of funds offered by a lender; the amount of credit offered, the values of the contract to both lender and mortgagor, and the expected losses to both parties from costly bankruptcy are highly sensitive to the perceived volatility of the value of the property collateralizing the mortgage, even in an economy with complete markets or risk neutrality on the parts of lender and borrower; the upper limit on mortgage credit offered by a rational lender may be a small fraction of the current fair market value of the property, regardless of the contractual yield offered by the borrower, and will decrease, at each such yield, as bankruptcy costs or housing service flows increase; and under significant but plausible values for bankruptcy and costs of liquidating property under foreclosure, the flow of mortgage credit can become negatively related to the spread of the mortgage yield over the riskless rate, with the lender preferring a lower contractual yield to a higher one.

Key Words: regulated Brownian motion, real options, differential games

1. Introduction

The nature of mortgage lending and the efficiency of residential mortgage markets are important topics in financial economics and in public policy. A prerequisite for assessing the state of the mortgage market is the ability to model the strategic behavior of both the lender and borrower and to value the claims of each party in the mortgage contract which emerges in the resulting equilibrium.

Author for correspondence: Professor David Nickerson, Department of Economics, Colorado State University, Clark Hall C310, Fort Collins, Colorado 80523-1771, USA.

This paper offers a game-theoretic model for both the analysis and valuation of mortgage contracts in the context of an economy with complete information and complete contingent claims markets. We analyze the equilibrium strategy of the lender, who holds an option over the magnitude of mortgage credit extended per dollar of collateral offered, and the mortgagor, who holds options to default or prepay, in a class of intertemporal mortgage contracts collateralized by property evolving according to a known random process, and in which the lender and borrower have identical information at the time the mortgage is negotiated, and it is common knowledge that the borrower has no discretion over the subsequent riskiness of his activities. The object is to provide a benchmark analysis of mortgage contract design and the effects on mortgage credit availability of various terms in the mortgage contract, based only on the strategic exercise of the options inherent in secured debt.[1]

The type of contract we consider is the multi-period, specified collateral, non-recourse mortgage loan, exemplified by standard mortgage contracts in many jurisdictions within the United States and elsewhere. The lender advances a sum to the borrower or mortgagor, who promises to make a scheduled stream of payments. If the mortgagor fails to make a payment as agreed, the lender seizes the property collateralizing the contract and sells it, refunding any excess over the outstanding loan balance to the borrower.[2] The initial market value of the collateral for the mortgage, such as a house or other property, is known to both agents but, owing to fluctuations in its market value, the future worth of the collateral is uncertain. We seek to determine the maximum proportion of initial market value a rational lender will advance against given collateral, with particular interest in situations where variations in the non-price terms of the mortgage contract cause that fraction to become noticeably less than one, regardless of the yield the borrower offers to pay, and where this fraction may become completely inelastic or even negatively related to the offered yield.

Our model of the mortgage contract emphasizes two aspects of multi-period loans in a strategic setting. The first is that the mortgagor can receive flows of housing services from owning the property serving as collateral as long as he makes his loan payments.[3] The value of past flows of housing services is not retrievable by the lender in the event of default; to the extent that the prospect of these flows contributed to the initial market value of the collateral, that value is effectively absent as security to the lender should default subsequently occur. The relevant value from the lender's perspective is, approximately, the expected market value of the collateral at the (unknown) time of default, discounted to the present. This will, for a given initial value, be lower the higher the intervening housing service flows are.[4]

The second aspect we consider is that the option to default is an element of the strategy set of the borrower. He controls the timing of its exercise, and will do so in his own best interest. A lender would prefer the borrower to follow a policy of defaulting at the last moment the loan could be fully repaid by the liquidated property serving as collateral. If, however, there is some chance the property might rise in value, the borrower will generally prefer to postpone the irreversible exercise of his option to default, especially if the mortgage loan payments are less than the value of the housing service flows from the collateral.[5] Any promise by the mortgagor to do otherwise would not be credible, and the lender will, in equilibrium, take this incentive of the mortgagor into account when deciding upon the volume of mortgage credit to be offered.[6] These two considerations—the irretrievability of past housing service flows and the control of default timing by the borrower—provide a focus for our analysis of mortgage credit availability under symmetric information in an economy with complete markets.[7]

The model is set in continuous time, using arbitrage-free valuation principles familiar from modern asset pricing theory and the properties of optimal stopping rules for continuous-time stochastic games as analyzed in Dutta and Rustichini (1993) and Grenadier (1995, 1996).[8] The riskless interest rate is assumed constant. Fluctuations in the market value of the collateral are exogenous to the agents but can be hedged, if they so choose, at the prevailing market terms. Both parties are assumed to rationally exercise the options available to them and to select strategies which are a best reply to the other.[9]

The advantages of using a complete market, symmetric information environment are compelling in attaining our objective of providing a benchmark measure of the efficiency of standard mortgage contracts. It permits one to obtain equilibrium option exercise strategies that are independent of risk attitudes, endowments and expectations about future collateral values. It enforces consistency between collateral characteristics such as cash flows and rate of change in value. Finally, it offers the promise of an operational means of valuing the mortgage contract to both lender and mortgagor, and evaluating the magnitude and effects of inefficiencies, such as bankruptcy costs.[10]

Our analysis can be placed within the context of several earlier strands of literature relevant to mortgage lending, contract design and credit access. A traditional approach to explaining certain features of bank lending, most notably an inelastic or backward-bending supply of credit with respect to offered yields, was originally made by Hodgman (1960) and Freimer and Gordon (1963), among others, directly in terms of the effects of default on the funds advanced by a lender to meet an exogenous demand for credit. Jaffee and Modigliani (1969), Baltensperger (1976), Barro (1976) and others, while rejecting the rationale offered by these earlier authors, re-focused the question of credit access by positing an exogenous inability of lenders to perfectly discriminate across individual borrowers in the pricing of default risk.[11] Stiglitz and Weiss (1981, 1986) endogenized this inability to assess the actuarial risks of default through adverse selection and/or moral hazard, leading to recognition of the screening role of yields in loan contracts and to credit rationing in pure debt markets in equilibrium. More recently, Parigi (1992), Bester (1994), Hart (1995), Choe (1998), Hart and Moore (1998) and Gorton and Kahn (2000), among others, have examined various aspects of asymmetric information, monitoring costs and renegotiation on the design of loan contracts, while Plaut (1986), Buckley et al. (1993), Buckley (1994), and others have examined the specific effects of asymmetric information and capital market imperfections on mortgage contracts in the context of both developed and developing economies.

Our paper differs from these latter papers, which base explanations of the features of observed loan contracts and differential access to credit on an inability to price discriminate, on the basis of default risk, across borrowers because of asymmetric information, in that we adopt the antipodal assumptions of complete capital markets and common knowledge of the actuarial risk of default in an explicit continuous-time game framework. This allows us to both apply the familiar replication techniques of contingent claims analysis, which requires capital market completeness, in order to explicitly value the mortgage contract to both lender and borrower, and, as well, to evaluate whether certain features of mortgage contracts and variations in access to mortgage credit can be explained solely in terms of the options each party holds as elements of their strategy sets in lending negotiations, without recourse to asymmetric information. While more closely related to the earlier literature on default risk, our paper also differs from those earlier studies by explicitly endogenizing the demand for mortgage credit, as well as the supply of such credit, in an explicit game-theoretic context.[12]

Extant non-strategic explanations of the incidence of termination in residential mortgage lending are also based on the default and prepayment options possessed by the mortgageholder. Foster and van Order (1984), Dokko and Edelstein (1991), Archer and Ling (1993), Kau et al. (1993), Kau et al. (1992, 1995), Archer et al. (1996), Kau and Keenan (1999), Crawford and Rosenblatt (1995), Phillips et al. (1996), and Deng et al. (2000), among others, have used contingent claims methods to value both fixed-rate and adjustable rate-mortgage contracts. These option-based models generate predictions for default based on the current value of housing relative to the discounted value of future mortgage payments.[13]

Our paper differs from these in analysing the option to default, possessed by the borrower, in a *strategic* setting, in which borrower and lender play a well-defined game. By explicitly analyzing the lender's best response to the borrower's default option, as well as analyzing the optimal timing of borrower default as a best-response to the contract offered by the lender, our model enlarges the option-based literature on mortgage termination to include the endogenous response of the supply of mortgage credit to both the strategic timing of default or prepayment by the borrower, and simultaneously to the characteristics of the collateral offered by the borrower, in a perfect equilibrium.

This paper is organized as follows. Section 2 describes the features of the negotiation between lender and borrower that determine the features of the mortgage contract and the principles determining its value to both lender and borrower. Section 3 provides analytical results on the incentives for mortgagors to delay the irreversible decision to default, as well as explict analytical solutions for the value of mortgage contracts, to both lender and borrower, in the two alternative situations in which the mortgage can only default at maturity and in which the mortgage has an unbounded term to maturity. We also derive an analytical value of the inefficiencies generated by bankruptcy costs and borne by both parties to the loan. Section 4 uses numerical solutions to examine the equilibrium properties of mortgage contracts in a variety of circumstances in which parameters of the loan contract are calibrated to ranges of empirically realistic values. We focus here on the best-response strategy of the lender, examining how variations in loan terms affect the flow of available mortgage credit. Concluding remarks appear in the final section.

2. A Model of mortages

2.1. The class of mortgage contracts

We consider strategic behavior by lender and borrower within a broad class of standard mortgage contracts. In return for an advance of one unit of wealth by the lender at date 0, contracts in this class obligate the borrower or mortgagor to make continuous coupon payments, at a rate of c, and a terminal payment C at maturity date T. If the contractual loan rate is y per year, continuously compounded, the mortgage balance $m(t)$ outstanding at date t, $0 \leq t \leq T$, satisfies:[14]

$$1 = C\int_0^t \mathrm{e}^{-y\tau} + m(t)\mathrm{e}^{-yt}, \quad \text{for } 0 \leq t \leq T, \tag{1}$$

where $C = m(T)$.

We assume the market value $h(t)$ of the house collateralizing the mortgage evolves according to the diffusion,

$$\mathrm{d}h(t) = \alpha(h,t)\mathrm{d}t + \sigma h(t)\mathrm{d}z(t), \tag{2}$$

where $z(t)$ is a standard Brownian motion, σ is a constant volatility parameter and $\alpha(h,t)$ is the instantaneous expected drift in the state variable $h(t)$.[15] Possession of the collateral entitles the holder to a flow of housing services accruing at the rate $\eta(h,t)$, unless the mortgagor defaults by withholding the coupon payment c. If the mortgagor defaults, the lender seizes the collateral and sells it for $h(t) - b(h,t)$, where $b(h,t)$ is the bankruptcy cost incurred by the lender in the liquidation procedure, with any funds from this procedure in excess of the outstanding mortgage balance $m(t)$ refunded to the mortgagor.[16]

Finally, we assume that both lender and mortgagor may trade costlessly and continuously in markets that are complete with respect to h-risk, the randomness imposed by variation in the value of the house collateralizing the mortgage.[17] Additionally, both parties may trade in riskless bonds at constant and continuously compounded yield r.[18]

2.2. Strategy spaces of borrower and lender

We consider, within this general class of mortgage contracts, a simple environment in which failure on the part of the mortgagor to make scheduled coupon payments results in termination of the contract and liquidation of the property collateralizing the contract.[19] The principal element of the strategy space of the mortgagor, in this context, is his option to default. He may, at any time, cease making the contractual payments c, or at maturity fail to make the terminal payment C, and forfeit the property serving to collateralize his mortgage. Upon this occurring, the lender liquidates the collateral immediately, with the lender receiving max $\{0, m(t) - b(h,t)\}$ if default occurs at time t and the mortgagor receiving any excess of the liquidated value of his house over the outstanding balance $m(t)$ on the mortgage.[20] Since housing prices may rise without bound, the strategy space of the mortgagor also includes the option to terminate the mortgage prior to maturity by making a payment equal to the outstanding balance $m(t)$. If he does so, he incurs refinancing costs $f(m(t))$ of negotiating a new loan to refinance the old, in addition to incurring a new obligation whose market value equals the amount of the new mortgage.[21]

The principal element of the strategy space of the lender is the magnitude of funds he offers to the borrower, contingent on the qualities of the property offered as collateral by the mortgagor, and in full knowledge of both the options possessed by the mortgagor and the distribution (2) of the collateral.[22]

2.3. Equilibrium contract values

The observed features of the mortgage contract reflect the equilibrium achieved in the noncooperative game played between lender and mortgagor, in which each individual selects a best-reply strategy for exercising the options available to him over the course of the loan. Based on the distribution of the random house value $h(t)$, we analyze the Markov perfect equilibria of a continuous time game of perfect information, in which both the process (2) describing the evolution of the value of the house collateralizing the mortgage and the realization of the sample path of this evolution are common knowledge, at each date t, to both players, and in which the current value of the state variable, $(h(t), t)$ embodies all relevant information upon which the current actions of the individuals are based.[23] The mortgagor selects the value, c, or 0, of coupon payments at each moment to maximize the value of the mortgage contract to him, conditional on the current state variable, while the lender's observed response, in terms of the magnitude of mortgage funds proferred per dollar of collateral value, maximizes the value of his respective claims, as embodied in the mortgage contract.

Denoting by $\mathscr{H} \equiv [0, \infty]$ the range of housing values h, and by $\mathscr{T} \equiv [0, T]$ the continuum of decision dates during the life of the mortgage, the Markov nature of the game implies that $\mathscr{H} \times \mathscr{T}$ is the support of all potential states relevant to the contingent actions constituting the strategies selected by each player. Since the mortgage is assumed to terminate when either default occurs, prepayment occurs, or T is reached, the strategy for the mortgagor is represented by the union $\mathscr{D} \cup \mathscr{P}$ of two closed subsets of $\mathscr{H} \times \mathscr{T}$. A realization of $(h, t) \in \mathscr{D}$ induces default through a zero coupon payment by the mortgagor while a realization of $(h, t) \in \mathscr{P}$ induces termination of the extant mortgage through prepayment.[24] Since the lender is assumed to foreclose immediately upon default by the mortgagor, the strategy selected by the lender consists only of amount of funds to extend to the mortgagor, per dollar of collateral, at the onset of the mortgage contract, and so his strategy space, $\mathscr{L}$, is the set $\mathscr{H} \times \{0\} \subset \mathscr{H} \times \mathscr{T}$. The open subset $\mathscr{S} \subset \mathscr{H} \times \mathscr{T}$, the complement of $\mathscr{D} \cup \mathscr{P}$, consists of all values of the state variable in which the mortgage contract remains active.

Each player's choice of an optimal strategy maximizes the value of his claims embodied in the mortgage contract, and, in our Markovian context, consists of the solution to an optimal stopping problem.[25] Denote by $L(h,t)$ the value to the lender of the cash flows from the contract if the value at time t is h and $(h,t) \in \mathscr{S}$ and denote by $M(h,t)$ the value of the mortgagor's position in the contract, inclusive of his default and prepayment options. Note that $L(h,0) \in \mathscr{L}$, the value of the promised cash flows at the time of origination of the loan, is also the value of mortgage funds advanced by the lender.

Appealing to the standard arbitrage valuation procedures of contingent claims analysis, the value functions $L(h,t)$ and $M(h,t)$ must satisfy the following Bellman equations in the open set $\mathscr{S}$:

$$L(h,t) = c\ \mathrm{d}t + E_t L^*(h,t), \tag{3}$$

$$M(h,t) = (\eta - c)\mathrm{d}t + E_t M^*(h,t), \tag{4}$$

where $\eta = \eta(h,t)$ is the instantaneous flow of housing services obtained by the mortgagor from his property, $E_t(\cdot)$ is the expectations operator under the unique equivalent martingale measure induced by our assumption of complete markets, and $L^*(h,t) = (\exp(\tau,\ \mathrm{d}t))L(h + \mathrm{d}h, t + \mathrm{d}t)$ and $M^* = ((\exp r, \mathrm{d}t))M(h + \mathrm{d}h, t + \mathrm{d}t)$ are the respective risk-adjusted values of future claims of the lender and mortgagor, discounted at the riskless interest rate.[26] These conditions, in turn, must satisfy the respective partial differential equations over $\mathscr{S}$,

$$\frac{1}{2}\sigma^2 h^2 L_{hh} + (rh - \eta)L_h + c + L_t = rL, \tag{5}$$

$$\frac{1}{2}\sigma^2 h^2 M_{hh} + (rh - \eta)M_h + (\eta - c) + M_t = rM, \tag{6}$$

where $(rh - \eta)$ is the risk-adjusted drift in the value of the house, representing the expected rate of appreciation, for the diffusion (2), under the equivalent martingale measure relevant to our valuation.

These differential equations state that the expected increase in wealth from holding each position (the left hand sides) must be the same as the increase in wealth from holding riskless bonds of the same value. The first terms on the left hand sides reflect a convexity effect arising from the volatility of h. The second terms reflects the (risk adjusted) expected drift in h. The third terms are the net payment or service flows received by lender and mortgagor respectively. The last terms capture the decreasing time to maturity.[27]

Unique solutions for the valuation equations (5) and (6) are determined by the relevant boundary conditions delineating the strategy spaces $\mathscr{D}$ and $\mathscr{P}$. Denoting by $\bar{L}(h,t)$ and $\bar{M}(h,t)$ the respective values of the players' claims if termination occurs at (h,t) and the respective boundaries of the spaces $\mathscr{D}$ and $\mathscr{P}$ by $(\underline{h},t)$, and $(\bar{h},t)$, the boundaries $\underline{h}$ and $\bar{h}$ are determined by the value-matching condition, which requires continuity in the value function of the mortgagor on the boundary of $\mathscr{D}$, $M(\underline{h},t) = \bar{M}(h,t)$, and $\mathscr{P}$, $M(\bar{h},t) = \bar{M}(\bar{h},t)$, and by the smooth-pasting or high contact conditions, which require continuity in the first derivatives of these functions at the same points.[28]

Qualitative properties of the boundaries of the strategy spaces $\mathscr{D}$ and $\mathscr{P}$ can be described by using the value-matching conditions with the Bellman equations in (3) and (4). At maturity T, the mortgagor's optimal default decision is dictated by the value of his claim relative to the value of his house,

$$M(h,t) = \begin{cases} h(T) - C, & \text{if } C < h(T); \\ 0, & \text{if } h(T) \le C; \end{cases} \tag{7}$$

and so, at maturity, $(h, T) \in \mathscr{D}$ if and only if $h(T) \le C$. Claims of the lender at maturity consequently satisfy the residual condition,

$$L(h,T) = \begin{cases} C, & \text{if } C < h(T); \\ \max\{0, h(t) - b(h,t)\} & \text{if } h(T) \le C. \end{cases} \tag{8}$$

Prior to maturity, the mortgagor will cease his coupon payment and lapse into default only if the value of the mortgage contract to him, $M(h,t)$, becomes zero, since at the relevant values of (h,t), default will imply his termination value $\bar{M}(h,t)$, is zero. Using (4) in this value matching condition, the boundary $(\underline{h}, t)$ of $\mathscr{D}$ is defined by

$$\eta(\underline{h}, t) - c + E_t M^*(\underline{h}, t) = 0. \tag{9}$$

Claims of the lender at this boundary satisfy

$$L(\underline{h}, t) = \max\{0, \underline{h} - b(\underline{h}, t)\}. \tag{10}$$

A similar argument can be used to delineate the boundary (h, t) of the prepayment region, $\mathscr{P}$, which must satisfy

$$\eta(\bar{h}, t) - c + E_t M^*(\bar{h}, t) = \bar{h}(t) - m(t) - \min\{b(\bar{h}, t), f(m(t))\}. \tag{11}$$

Here the lender's claim is simply[29]

$$L(\bar{h}, t) = m(t).$$

3. Mortgage credit: Analytical results

We examine, within a set of alternative parametric specifications, properties of the equilibria of our lending game, as reflected in the terms of the mortgage contract and in the equilibrium strategies adopted by lender and mortgagor. We place a particular emphasis on the qualities of the best-response strategy of the lender in these equilibria, with two objectives in mind. First, we wish to use our analytical framework to examine circumstances under which non-price components of the vector of mortgage terms, such as the amortization rate, flow of housing services, bankruptcy costs and the term over which the mortgage yield is fixed, affect the flow of mortgage credit forthcoming, per dollar of house value collateralizing the loan. These effects provide insight into both the positive and normative aspects of mortgage contract design. Second, we are also interested in what insights our model can offer on how the moments of the distribution of house price affect the mortgage contract and the volume of mortgage funds available to borrowers. We are especially interested in how both types of variable affect the elasticity of mortgage credit supplied with respect to the yield spread or risk premium on the mortgage in equilibrium.[30]

The perfect equilibrium of the lending game is described by the linked partial differential equations (5) and (6), combined with the free boundary conditions (9) and (11) characterizing mortgagor strategies. Although these cannot, in general, be solved analytically, an analytical characterization of the equilibrium is possible in two specific circumstances. First, if the two termination options of the mortgagor would only be rationally exercised at loan maturity, then optimal strategies are described by single critical values for $h(T)$ and contract values to both lender and mortgagor can be readily determined. Second, if the mortgage features an unbounded term to maturity, approximating the long terms that some fixed rate mortgages exhibit in the United States and elsewhere, the decision problems faced by borrowers and lenders are stationary and optimal strategies are described, in terms of both the default and prepayment decision of the mortgagor, by constant critical values for $h(t)$.[31]

Prior to considering these two cases, we can use Bellman equations and the free boundary conditions to characterize default behavior in equilibrium, under all parametric specifications. The presence of bankruptcy costs and irrecoverable housing service flows will, in equilibrium, have adverse effects on the value of mortgage funds lent and on the magnitude of allocational inefficiencies in the exchange between lender and mortgagor. These effects result from the incentive of the mortgagor to delay default, should default occur, beyond the state where the net collateral value obtained by the lender would be sufficient to cover the extant balance $m(t)$ of the mortgage. This incentive is characterized by the following proposition:

Proposition 1: The mortgagor will refrain from default for a range of house values less than the extant mortgage balance, net of bankruptcy costs:

$$\forall h \quad h \in \underline{H}(\underline{h}) \rightarrow M(h,t) > 0,$$

where $\underline{H}(\underline{h})$ is a set of strictly positive measure defined by

$$\underline{H}(\underline{h}) = \{h | \underline{h} < h(t) < m(t) + b(\underline{h}, t)\}.$$

Proof of this proposition is immediate from equations (4), (9) and (10). Since the expected discounted future claims of the mortgagor, $E_t M^*(h,t)$, are always non-negative, current claims $M(h,t)$, which are obviously positive whenever the flow of housing services $\eta(h,t)$ exceeds the flow of coupon payments c, will also remain positive even when

$\eta(h,t) < c$, as long as sufficient time to maturity remains so that a positive probability of house price appreciation renders $E_t M^*(h,t) > 0$. Under such circumstances, $M(h,t)$ is positive for an interval $\underline{H}$ of housing values $h(t)$ satisfying $\underline{h} < h(t) < m(t) + b(\underline{h},\ t)$. Lenders would clearly prefer default to occur at housing values at least as great as $m(t) + b(h,t)$, and will, consequently, take the behavior of the mortgagor in these circumstances into account when deciding upon the value of mortgage funds to lend at date 0. The range of such housing values, $\underline{H}$, is increasing in the magnitude of housing services accruing to the mortgagor, $\eta(h,t)$, and losses to the lender in the event of eventual default are increasing in the magnitude of bankruptcy costs, $b(h,t)$.

3.1. Default only at maturity

If circumstances insure that the loan will continue to maturity with certainty, the only relevant action in the mortgagor's strategy set is to default at maturity or, equivalently, to exercise his option to retain his property by paying the terminal value C.[32] Assuming that bankruptcy costs $b(h,t)$ and the flow of housing services $\eta(h,t)$ are both proportional to the house value $h(t)$ at each moment, the value of the mortgage contract to both lender and borrower, in this case, can be derived analytically:

Proposition 2: If default cannot occur prior to maturity T, coupon payments are constant at c, and the proportional bankruptcy cost and housing service flows are constant at rates b and η, then the respective values of the mortgage contract to lender and mortgagor are:

$$L(h,0) = (1-b)[h(0)e^{-\eta T} - \phi_1(h,T,C)] + \left(\frac{c}{r}\right)(1-e^{-rT}) + \phi_2(h,T,0)C \quad (12)$$

$$M(h,0) = h(0)(1-e^{-\eta T}) - \left(\frac{c}{r}\right)(1-e^{-rT}) + \phi_1(h,T,C), \quad (13)$$

where $\phi_1(h,T,C)$ is the value of a European call option on the house collateralizing the mortgage, with expiry date T and exercise price equal to the payment at maturity, C, and ϕ_2 is a call paying b dollars whenever ϕ_1 is exercised, and zero otherwise.[33]

Proof is direct from the differential equations (5) and (6). This proposition states that the value of the contract to the lender is the value of the house, net of bankruptcy costs, plus the discounted value of contractual mortgage loan payments, less the market value of the housing service flows received by the mortgagor and the value of the mortgagor's terminal call option to retrieve his collateral by making the balloon payment C. Similarly, the value of the contract to the mortgagor consists of the current value of the flow of housing services accruing to him over the life of the mortgage, plus the value of the call option to retrieve his collateral or default at maturity, less the discounted flow of coupon payments required to maintain the mortgage. Observe that the value of the contract to the lender (mortgagor) is decreasing (increasing) in the flow of housing services η, the volatility of the value of the house collateralizing the mortgage, and the term to maturity of the mortgage, while the deadweight losses to both parties are increasing in the proportional bankruptcy cost, b. This leads to the following corollaries:

Corollary 2.1: If the proportional cost of bankruptcy is positive, the combined values of the mortgage contract to lender and mortgagor are less than the value of the house collateralizing the mortgage by $B(h,0)$, the expected current value of the costs of bankruptcy, which are given by

$$B(h,0) = b[h(0)e^{-\eta T} - \phi_1(h,T,C)] - \phi_2(h,T,0)C. \tag{14}$$

Corollary 2.2: If the mortgagor receives a constant proportional flow of housing services $\eta(h(t))$, the supply of mortgage credit in circumstances precluding early default is limited to:

$$L(h,0) \leq (1-b)h(0)e^{-\eta T}. \tag{15}$$

These corollaries both follow from the preceding proposition, the non-negativity of the value of the call option C, and the role of positive bankruptcy costs play in lowering the combined values of the mortgage contract to lender and mortgagor. They respectively illustrate that, in an equilibrium specification of a standard mortgage contract, the ratio of mortgage funds offered by the lender, per dollar of collateral value, is diminishing in the flow of housing services η, and the expected present value of the loss to the lender from this flow of services forms an upper bound on the volume of mortgage funds available which is strictly less than the value of the house collateralizing the mortgage.[34]

3.2. Perpetual loans

Consider now a perpetual mortgage loan with constant contractual flow of coupon payments c. If the proportional flow of housing services η is constant and the moments of the Markov process governing h are stationary, then the optimal termination strategy of the mortgagor and the current value functions L and M are also stationary. The mortgagor's strategy, in this case, can be simply described as constant critical values of the house value h at which default or prepayment will, respectively, occur.[35] This perpetual loan may be interpreted as approximating long-term fixed-rate mortgages of the form found in the United States, or, alternatively, mortgages for which there is a high probability of termination before contractual maturity. This case highlights the value of timing options to the mortgagor and the implications of the mortgagor's incentives on the availability of mortgage credit relative to collateral. Owing to its tractability, we focus on the specific case where default is the only action available.[36] In this case, we have:

Proposition 3: An interest-only mortgage with unbounded maturity, constant payments c, constant proportional bankruptcy charges b and a constant proportional flow of housing services η, will be defaulted at time t in equilibrium if and only if

$$h(t) \leq \underline{h} = \left(\frac{\lambda}{\lambda - 1}\right)\left(\frac{c}{r}\right), \tag{16}$$

and have respective values to the lender and mortgagor of

$$L(h) = \frac{c}{r} + \left(\underline{h} - b\underline{h} - \frac{y}{r}\right)\left(\frac{h}{\underline{h}}\right)^{\lambda}, \tag{17}$$

$$M(h) = h + \left(\frac{c}{r} - \underline{h}\right)\left(\frac{h}{\underline{h}}\right)^{\lambda}, \tag{18}$$

where

$$\lambda = \frac{\gamma - \sqrt{\gamma^2 + 8r/\sigma^2}}{2},$$

$$\gamma = 1 - \frac{2(r - \eta)}{\sigma^2}.$$

Proof of this proposition relies on the properties of parabolic differential equations, as first discussed in this context by Merton (1973), and is available from the authors on request. Note that $\lambda < 0$ in the above expressions and, consequently, $h < (c/r)$.

This proposition provides both insight into the valuation of risky long-term fixed-term mortgages and offers implications for mortgage contract design. First, note that the default value $\underline{h}$ is proportional to the coupon payment c. Since the principal is never repaid, it is only the level of coupon payments relative to the value of the house collateralizing the mortgage that concerns the borrower. Whether it was a large mortgage loan at a low yield or a small loan at a high yield that resulted in the specified c is irrelevant, as is any expected rate of appreciation in the house value $h(t)$. Second, the value of the house at optimal default is strictly less than c/r, which is the current value of the remaining mortgage loan payments, capitalized at the riskless interest rate. As a consequence, a mortgagor will rationally default only if the value of his house relative to his mortgage payments is exceptionally low: the simple but standard comparison of current house value to total mortgage payment obligations is *not* a valid indicator of impending default.[37]

4. Mortgage credit: numerical results

Analytical solutions for the valuation equations (5) and (6), and the attendant boundaries of the termination regions in which the options held by the mortgagor are optimally exercised, cannot be obtained when these boundaries vary with the term remaining on the loan, such as with loans with finite term to maturity. Numerical solutions can be applied in these cases, permitting us to consider the nature of the lending equilibrium in realistic parametric cases and providing additional insight into factors affecting the flow of mortgage credit. We focus our reported results on the value of the mortgage contract to the lender, $L(h, 0)$, which coincides with the volume of mortgage funds loaned in equilibrium, as other variables in the mortgage contract change their values in equilibrium.[38]

We use a finite difference procedure to solve the problem for representative parametric cases. The set $\mathscr{H} \times \mathscr{T}$ is represented by a discrete rectangular grid of h and t values. A solution is a set of L and M values for these gridpoints, together with an indication whether each point is or is not in $\mathscr{D}$, $\mathscr{P}$ or $\mathscr{S}$. Working backwards from time T, the valuation equations are "solved" for each time step using the Crank-Nicholson discrete approximation for the partial derivatives.[39] After each step, one checks, for each individual and each value of h, whether either could do better by exercising the options available to him. If so, the value functions of both individuals are appropriately adjusted to reflect this. One continues moving recursively in this fashion until the origination date of the loan is attained.

The parametric cases examined below assume that bankruptcy costs $b(h, t)$, flows of housing services $\eta(h, t)$ and refinancing costs $f(m(t))$ are independent of time and are homogeneous in their other arguments.[40] The optimal strategy of the lender, for each case, can consequently be reported independently of the absolute size of the mortgage.

A benchmark set of values for the terms of the mortgage contract is used to evaluate the effects on the volume of mortgage funds $L(h, 0)$, lent per dollar of the market value $h(0)$ of the house collateralizing the mortgage. This benchmark set is calibrated as follows: the riskless interest rate is $r = 0.05$ per year; annualized proportional volatility of the value of the house collateralizing the mortgage is $\sigma = 0.2$; the term to maturity of the mortgage is $T = 5$ years; no payments are due before maturity, so that $c = 0$; the contractual loan rate spread over the riskless rate, $y - r$, is 0.02 per year; there are no flows of housing services from the collateral and no bankruptcy or refinancing costs. The amount due at maturity is 1.419 per unit of currency initially lent.[41]

Tables 1–4 show how the value of the mortgage contract to the lender, and his

Table 1. Effects of coupon rate c and the term to maturity T on the offer of mortgage funds, for a constant value of the yield spread $y - r$.

Coupon		Loan Term	
c	$L(1,0)$	T	$L(1,0)$
0.00	0.717	1	0.810
0.02	0.781	2	0.771
0.04	0.840	3	0.747
0.06	0.890	4	0.731
0.08	0.928	5	0.717
0.10	0.952	8	0.690
0.20	0.992	10	0.676
0.30	0.999	12	0.660

corresponding offer of mortgage funds to loan per dollar of collateral, changes as we alter various terms of the mortgage contract, while keeping other terms fixed at their benchmark levels. In each table, the columns $L(1,0)$ give the proportion of the initial market value of the house or collateral a competitive mortgage lender would be willing to advance to a prospective mortgagor.

Table 1 demonstrates the respective effects of two contractual terms, the coupon rate c and the term to maturity T, on the offer of mortgage funds, for a constant value of the yield spread $y-r$. The first case demonstrates how faster loan amortization through larger payment flows significantly increases the willingness to lend, with an elasticity of funds advanced, per dollar of collateral, for a unit increase in the proportional coupon rate of approximately 7–10 percent as the coupon rate increases from 2 percent to 10 percent. The second case shows the negative and convex impact on available credit of lengthening the term to maturity. An initial doubling of the term to maturity lowers the proportion of funds offered by approximately 4 percentage points, while an increase in the term from four to five years lowers the funds offered by approximately 1.5 percentage points, with a smooth convex decline throughout the range of contract durations.

Table 2 demonstrates the respective effects of two aspects of the property serving as collateral, the proportional flow of housing services and the volatility of the value of the property, on the offer of mortgage funds. The first case demonstrates how increased flows of housing services accruing to the mortgagor reduces the willingness to lend, with each 2 percentage point increase in the proportional flow of housing services reducing the funds offered in a convex fashion, from an initial decline of 0.068 of the current value of collateral to a decline of 0.05 for a change in η from 0.06 to 0.08, for example. The second case illustrates a negative, and initially strictly concave, relation between volatility in the price of the property serving as collateral and the proportion of funds offered, with an increase in the standard deviation of the property price from 0.00 to 0.05 reducing the funds offered by 0.016 percentage points, with an increase in the magnitude of the decline from 0.066 to between 0.100 and 0.105 percentage points as the standard deviation increases, in increments of 0.05, from 0.05 to 0.35, with a convergence of the difference in

Table 2. Effects of proportional flow of housing services and volatility of the value of property on the offer of mortgage funds.

Services		Volatility	
η	$L(1,0)$	σ	$L(1,0)$
0.00	0.717	0.00	0.999
0.02	0.649	0.05	0.983
0.04	0.587	0.10	0.917
0.06	0.531	0.15	0.822
0.08	0.481	0.20	0.717
0.10	0.435	0.25	0.612
0.12	0.394	0.30	0.512
0.14	0.356	0.35	0.409

Table 3. Effects of increased housing service flows on the positive relation between mortgage funds offered and the spread $y - r$.

Spread $y-r$	Case One ($\eta = 0.00$) $L(1,0)$	Case Two ($\eta = 0.10$) $L(1,0)$	Case Three ($\eta = 0.20$) $L(1,0)$
0.00	0.000	0.000	0.000
0.02	0.717	0.435	0.264
0.04	0.827	0.502	0.304
0.06	0.890	0.540	0.327
0.08	0.930	0.564	0.342
0.10	0.955	0.579	0.351
0.12	0.972	0.590	0.358
0.14	0.983	0.596	0.362
0.16	0.990	0.600	0.364
0.18	0.994	0.603	0.366
0.20	0.997	0.605	0.367

the successive rates of change for volatility values above 0.15. These values encompass the range of average housing price volatilities across neighborhoods in most U.S. cities. Such a result suggests, for example, the existence of a relation between differential mortgage credit conditions across different neighborhoods, for identical yields and other terms of mortgage loans, if those neighborhoods exhibit a significant difference in the volatility of property prices.[42]

Table 3 illustrates the effects of increased housing service flows on the positive relation between mortgage funds offered and the spread between the fixed mortgage yield and the riskless interest rate. When the proportional flow η of housing services is zero, in Case One, each 2 percentage point increase in the spread $y - r$ elicits a positive but declining increase in the percentage of mortgage funds offered per dollar of initial collateral value, with an initial 2 percentage point increase in the spread, from 2 to 4 percent, increasing $L(1,0)$ from 71.7 percent of collateral value to 82.7 percent, while an increase in the spread from 10 to 12 percent, for example, increasing $L(1,0)$ from 95.5 to 97.2 percent. Case Two illustrates that a 10 percentage point increase in the proportional flow of housing services, from $\eta = 0$ to $\eta = 10$ percent, serves to reduce both the level and change in the proportion of funds offered, $L(1,0)$, to approximately 60 percent of the corresponding value in Case One, for each 2 percentage point increase in the spread: for example, an increase in $y - r$ from 4 to 6 percent increases $L(1,0)$ in Case Two (where $\eta = 10$ percent) from 50.2 to 54.0 percent, which are each respectively 0.607 of their corresponding values in Case One. A further 10 percentage point increase in the flow of housing services to $\eta = 20$ percent, as illustrated in Case Three, has an analogous relationship with the corresponding values and rates of change in Case Two, with each value of $L(1,0)$ and change in that value, per 2 percentage point increase in $y - r$, being approximately 60 percent of the corresponding values in Case Two.

Finally, Table 4 illustrates the effects of changes in proportional bankruptcy costs on the same positive concave relation between mortgage funds offered and the spread between

Table 4. Effects of changes in proportional bankruptcy costs on the positive concave relation between mortgage funds offered and the spread $y-r$.

Spread $y-r$	Case One ($b=0.00$) $L(1,0)$	Case Two ($b=0.15$) $L(1,0)$	Case Three ($b=0.30$) $L(1,0)$
0.00	0.000	0.000	0.000
0.02	0.717	0.632	0.576
0.04	0.827	0.723	0.650
0.06	0.890	0.772	0.686
0.08	0.930	0.804	0.707
0.10	0.955	0.823	0.718
0.12	0.972	0.835	0.721
0.14	0.983	0.842	0.721
0.16	0.990	0.846	0.719
0.18	0.994	0.848	0.716
0.20	0.997	0.849	0.712

the fixed mortgage yield and the riskless interest rate. In this situation, two features stand out. First, an increase in proportional bankruptcy costs from 0 to 15 percent, as in Case Two, reduces the percentage of funds offered per dollar of collateral, for each value of the spread $y-r$, but at a rate decreasing in the value of the spread: for example, at $y-r=0.02$, the proportional value $L(0,1)$ of funds offered with 15 percent bankruptcy costs is approximately 88 percent of the proportion of funds offered with zero bankruptcy costs, but at a spread of $y-r=0.08$, the value $L(0,1)$ of funds offered with 15 percent bankruptcy costs is now only approximately 86 percent of funds offered with zero bankruptcy costs. A similar pattern is repeated when bankruptcy costs are increased again, from $b=15$ percent in Case Two to $b=30$ percent in Case Three, but with commensurately higher percentages: for the same two respective yield spreads, the value $L(0,1)$ of funds offered with 30 percent bankruptcy costs is now 91 percent and 87 percent of funds offered with 15 percent bankruptcy costs. Second, as a result of the respective magnitudes of the shifts induced in the concave relation between the yield spread $y-r$ and the funds offered $L(1,0)$ by the successive increases in proportional bankruptcy costs, the increasingly inelastic offer of mortgage funds with respect to the yield spread actually *reverses* sign when bankruptcy costs are sufficiently high: for $b=30$ percent in Case Three, the proportion of funds offered per dollar of collateral, $L(1,0)$, attains a maximum of approximately 72 percent for yields over the riskless rate between 0.12 and 0.14, decreasing for additional increases in the spread. The supply of mortgage funds, as a function of the difference of the yield y charged over the riskless rate r, becomes negatively sloped in these circumstances, implying that potential mortgagors may be unable to procure sufficient credit to finance a house purchase, regardless of the yield they offer to the lender. This occurs because the lender rationally anticipates the higher default probability induced by the higher yield spread, which, in the presence of deadweight losses from bankruptcy proceedings, restricts the flow of mortgage credit to borrowers.

These results have a variety of empirical implications for mortgage contracts. They suggest, for example, both a potential rationale for cyclical fluctuations in the availability of mortgage credit and for observations of neighborhood "redlining." Cyclical patterns in housing and other types of credit could depend on the nature of volatility in the assets used to collateralize loans. This would be consistent with recent empirical evidence that a "mortgage credit crunch," especially for low-income applicants or potential mortgagors in non-recourse states, might indeed occur during business downturns, when uncertainty about collateral values tends to increase.[43] Similarly, since the volatility of properties used to collateralize mortgages can be assumed to be highly correlated by neighborhood or region, lenders may be seen to be engaging in redlining a particular neighborhood when the high volatility of property values in that neighborhood imply that lenders have a rational incentive to offer a relatively inelastic supply of mortgage credit, regardless of the demographic characteristics of the affected borrowers.

5. Concluding remarks

By taking into account the strategic interactions between lender and mortgagor in a standard class of multi-period mortgage contracts with symmetric information, our model illustrates the nature of equilibrium lending and the influences of various features of the mortgage on both the respective values of the mortgage to both lender and borrower, and on the amount of mortgage funds available per dollar of property serving as collateral for the mortgage. We have examined, to summarize, rational behavior by both lender and borrower in a mortgage market featuring explicit consideration of the best-replies of borrower and lender to each other's strategies, as embodied in the mortgage contract, in an environment that is complete with respect to financial risk. Principal qualitative results include: (1) Faster amortization and shorter terms to maturity for fixed-rate mortgages increase the volume of credit offered, at any fixed yield; (2) a lower flow of housing services enjoyed by the borrower, per dollar of initial house value, and a correspondingly lower rate of effective depreciation, will elicit a larger volume of funds offered by a lender than will a higher flow of housing services; (3) the amount of credit offered and the values of the contract to both lender and mortgagor are highly sensitive to the perceived volatility of the value of the property collateralizing the mortgage, even in an economy with complete markets or risk neutrality on the parts of lender and borrower; (4) the upper limit on mortgage credit offered by a rational lender may be a small fraction of the current fair market value of the collateral, regardless of the contractual yield offered by the borrower, and will decrease, at each such yield, as bankruptcy costs or housing service flows increase; and (5) under significant but plausible values for bankruptcy and costs of liquidating property under foreclosure, the supply of mortgage credit can bend backward, with the lender preferring a lower contractual yield over a higher one.

Our model and its results, while preliminary and valid only for a simple, though realistic, lending environment, have both positive implications and normative applications. Our results offer, within the class of Markov perfect equilibria, a precise delineation of the relationship between all the alternative features of the class of standard mortgage contracts found in the United States and elsewhere, and an endogenous explanation of the effects of changes in contract terms or in various qualities of the property collateralizing the mortgage on the volume of mortgage credit available and the relation between the supply of such credit and the yield offered by mortgagors. Our model offers the possibility of extending the contingent claims approach to the valuation of mortgages to a strategic environment, in which the options of both lender and mortgagor are reflected in the strategies adopted by each party in equilibrium. This ability to incorporate the strategic aspects of lender and borrower behavior, within a complete markets environment, also offers the possibility of engineering the features of mortgage contracts to increase the availability of mortgage credit to different classes of borrowers.

Acknowledgment

We would like to offer thanks to Lanny Arvan, John Benjamin, Zvi Bodie, Rick Boebel, Amy Bogdon, Bob Buckley, Gabriele Camera, Marsha Courchane, James Follain, Ed Golding, Fred Graham, Hans Haller, Greg Hildebrandt, Art Hogan, Tom Husted, David Ling, Robert Mackay, Michael Marrese, James Moser, Frank Nothaft, Doug Pearce, David Persellin, Ron Phillips, Leigh Riddick, John Seater, Bob Van Order, Neil Wallace, Jim Wilcox, Elaine Worzala, Zhong Yi Tong, seminar participants at American University, Colorado State University, the Fannie Mae Foundation, University of British Columbia, University of Maryland, University of Miami, University of Otago, Virginia Tech, the 1999 North American Summer Meetings of the Econometric Society at University of Wisconsin, the First Annual Cambridge-Maastricht Conference on Real Estate Finance, our referees and especially to Wayne Archer and editors Piet Eicholtz and Kanak Patel for their comments on various earlier versions of this paper. The usual disclaimer applies and, in particular, opinions expressed are those of the authors and not necessarily those of Freddie Mac.

Notes

1. Such options are possessed by both lenders and borrowers and are present in all mortgages, whether or not informational asymmetries are also plausible features of relations between participants in mortgage markets. Our premiss is that some observations about mortgage credit, including the possibility of an interest inelastic supply of mortgage credit, adverse effects of bankruptcy costs and differential access to credit among different groups of mortgagors can be explained in terms of strategic option exercise alone, without recourse to the additional complications posed by asymmetric information.
2. Our results can also be applied to mortgage loans made in jurisdictions with recourse to assets of the mortgagor beyond the property being financed, if the collateral for the loan is interpreted as including these other assets as well as the property.
3. These services can either be measured in terms of their direct consumption value or in terms of the rental value of property. We assume that the depreciation of the property, as a result of this flow of services, is exogenous and common knowledge to both lender and mortgagor, or that the observed evolution of the value of the property includes all investment in the property by the mortgagor.
4. Such a situation for the creditor is analogous to the holder of a call option on a dividend-paying stock.

5. While this response is analogous to the option value of irreversible investments in the literature on real options, as surveyed in Pindyck (1991), we analyze these options in a strategic setting, as discussed in Kulatilaka (1999).
6. Ironically, the adverse incentive in such a case is that the borrower will not default soon enough, from the lender's perspective.
7. We focus our analysis on standard mortgage contracts, which, in the spirit of Williamson (1986) and Lacker (2000), are motivated by implicit considerations of the costs to state verification. Although our model could apply to more elaborate debt contracts, which in theory could be indexed or made contingent, at each moment, on the random value of collateral, we presume in this paper that such alternative arrangements are infeasible because of regulation, uncertain legal enforceability, or simply the difficulties in negotiating fully-contingent debt contracts.
8. Our model differs from that of Grenadier (1996), however, in incorporating arbitrage-free valuation conditions into our calculation of the Nash equilibria of our game, rather than directly considering excess demand.
9. Options for the borrower to renegotiate his coupon payments, and an option for the lender to call for immediate full payment if monitoring reveals a ''technical default'' has occurred, can be easily introduced into this framework, as in Jones (1999). These additional elements of the players' strategy spaces do not alter the qualitative nature of the value of the mortgage contract to the parties nor the flow of mortgage credit, although they will change the quantitative predictions of the basic model.
10. It provides, consequently, the natural benchmark from which to see if, or where, additional features, such as adverse selection or moral hazard, are needed for the understanding of actual mortgage markets.
11. See Baltensperger (1978), Koskela (1979) and Jaffee and Stiglitz (1990) for surveys of these two literatures.
12. More notably, our approach to the design and valuation of mortgage contracts parallels that of Anderson and Sundaresan (1996), who introduce endogenous renegotiation and bankruptcy costs into a standard Merton (1973) model of corporate debt. Our model differs from theirs, however, in its modelling of collateral and its focus on the best-response strategy of the lender in his offer of credit as a function of housing service (dividend) flows and the stochastic nature of the property collateralizing the mortage loan.
13. Equity and the value of the home relative to the current value of mortgage debt outstanding is, following the general case of risky debt first described by Merton (1974), the determinant of optimal default when mortgage repayment is viewed in terms of the default and prepayment options implicit in the mortgage contract, capital markets are perfect in the sense of exhibiting a spanning condition such as that described by Duffie (1992), and homeowners possess well-diversified financial portfolios. Exercise of the default option may also, in this non-strategic environment, depend on the value of the option to prepay the mortgage. Keenan and Kau (1995) offer a comprehensive survey of option-based models of mortgage valuation while Hendershott and van Order (1996) assess the empirical relevance of such models.
14. We abstract from the stochastic nature of interest rates, such as is found in standard models of *non-strategic* mortgage default (Kau et al. (1992), Kau and Keenan (1999), as well as from contingent adjustments of the loan rate, in order to focus on the strategic nature of the default option implicit in the mortgage and the best-reply of lenders to this option in the simplest possible setting. Incorporation of adjustable rate mortgages is, in the current setting, equivalent to adjusting the term to maturity over which the yield is fixed, and incorporating stochastic interest rates and resulting analyzes of prepayment behavior will serve only to monotonically reduce the magnitude of mortgage funds advanced by the lender in the perfect equilibria analyzed here.
15. The expected drift $\alpha(h, t)$ is assumed to satisfy Lipschitz and growth conditions in h, uniformly in t, to assure existence and uniqueness of this diffusion (see Duffie, 1992). The house value $h(t)$ may, consequently, be characterized as mean reverting, growing in mean at a constant proportional rate, being (almost) confined within fixed upper and lower bounds, or conforming to a wide variety of other patterns consistent with observed time series of housing prices in the United States and elsewhere.
16. Note that, in addition to explicit legal, administrative and transaction expenses, bankruptcy costs can include the opportunity cost of receiving neither loan payments nor interest on the value of the collateral during the interval between default and the time the collateral is sold. Estimates by the U.S. Department of Housing and

Urban Development (1996) of the average costs of liquidating residential properties in the United States range between fifteen to thirty percent of the market value of the property at the time of foreclosure.

17. Complete markets requires that any random variable with finite variance can be obtained as the terminal value of some self-financing trading strategy, which is equivalent to assuming that there exist portfolios of assets that are (locally) perfectly correlated with the housing price h, allowing either party to hedge against the random part of the change in h if desired. This assumption precludes the relevance of adverse selection or moral hazard to the design and valuation of the mortgage contract and allows standard no-arbitrage valuation methods to be applied. See Duffie (1992) for a more complete discussion of the implications of this assumption.
18. The simultaneous ability of the mortgagor to borrow at a yield spread $y - r$ to finance a housing purchase while borrowing at the riskless rate in some other transactions is made to simplify the calculation of the optimal stopping rule that forms his strategy in the lending game analyzed here, without qualitative effect on the nature of our results. Such an assumption could be empirically rationalized by collateralization and alternative recourse requirements for different types of loans.
19. Jones (1999) and Jones and Nickerson (2001) consider respective variants of the game analyzed here, in which the contingent action (coupon payment) of the mortgagor at each t can assume any value between c and 0, which, in the presence of significant bankruptcy costs, may trigger renegotation of the loan terms rather than foreclosure, and in which, owing to state law, the borrower retains the "statuatory right of redemption," which requires the addition of second state variable measuring the value, at each date t, of payments foregone over a previous duration. These variants, while realistic, do not change the qualitative nature of the equilibria analyzed here. See Keyles (1995) for information on various aspects of statuatory rights of redemption and foreclosure restrictions in U.S. states germane to the issue of mortgage contract design and Clauretie and Herzog (1989) for an economic analysis of these restrictions.
20. We permit the lender to abandon the collateral if liquidation costs exceed its market value. We are grateful to a referee who also points out the presumption that default by the mortgagor can be regarded as an option only if the evolution of the house value collaterizing the mortgage is exogenous to the maintenance and other investment decisions of the mortgagor. Although this is literally true in the current model, as exemplified by our assumptions about independence of the moments of the diffusion (2) representing the evolution of property value, repair and maintenance investment by the mortgagor could readily be incorporate into the parameters of (2), and, as long as this investment was common knowledge to both parties, our results would be qualitatively unaltered, although the valuation of the default decision would then become a complex option, rather than the simple option examined here.
21. Observe that such prepayment is not a result of fluctuations in interest rates, as in conventional models of mortgage pricing, but instead could result from a situation in which the mortgagor's collateral has appreciated to such an extent that continuing to pay the original premium $y - r$ is no longer commensurate with the default risk posed to the lender by the mortgage. While the mortgagor will exercise this option if the benefit of the lower rate over the remaining term of the loan exceeds the refinancing costs, this prepayment option remains costly to the lender, as in the conventional prepayment literature, and will adversely affect the lender's willingness to proffer mortgage funds per dollar of house value.
22. The strategy space of the lender may also be expanded to include the option to declare a "technical default," as studied by Jones (1995), in which the lender monitors the collateral value according to a Poisson process and in which the mortgagor is legally regarded as being in default, even though he has made all agreed upon payment, if the value of the collateral falls below some fixed fraction δ of the outstanding loan balance, in which case the lender has the option to force liquidation immediately. While the choice of monitoring intensity increases the dimension of the strategy space of the lender, it leads to no significant change in the nature of the results reported here.
23. Markov strategies are strategies in which current actions of the players are contingent only upon the vector of state variables which serve as sufficient statistics for the history of the game, and a Markov perfect equilibrium is a set of Markov strategies yielding a subgame perfect Nash equilibrium which, in our game of complete information, is an equilibrium of each realization of the state vector $(h(t), t)$.
24. Expanding the strategy spaces of the mortgagor or lender to include additional actions or indentures are

reflected in the consequent definition of additional closed subsets of $\mathscr{S} \times \mathscr{T}$, which define, through the entry of (h, t), the timing of the optimal exercise of these options.

25. See Dutta and Rustichini (1993).
26. Observe that we abstract from the influence of divergent expectations between lender and mortgagor, through the assumption that both players value their contractual claims through the expectations operator $E_t(\cdot)$ corresponding to the equivalent martingale measure for this game. The empirical relevance of divergent expectations, however, has been widely acknowledged in the literature, as discussed in Vandell and Thibodeau (1985).
27. An alternative interpretation of these differential equations, termed the Feynman–Kac solution, is that the value of each agent's position equals the expected discounted value of his future receipts, where the equivalent martingale measure used in calculating the expected value is that actuarial measure that would prevail if a followed the process $dh = (rh - \eta)dt + \sigma h dz$. A noteworthy property of these relations is their absence of taste parameters: they apply for any individual, regardless of his level of risk aversion and of his expectations about the drift α in h. This is a consequence of assuming that markets are in equilibrium and are effectively complete with respect to h-risk. All individuals, at the margin, have the same marginal rate of substitution between riskless assets and the positions represented by L, and M. Trading in other securities mediates differences in risk tolerance, just as trading in default-free bonds mediates differences in personal rates of time preference in the standard Fisherian model of consumption and investment.
28. More specifically, value matching conditions and terminal boundary conditions determine unique solutions for L and M in (5) and (6) for arbitary policies $\mathscr{D}$ and $\mathscr{P}$ while the equilibrium strategies must also satisfy ''smooth-pasting'' conditions, when we specify linear bankruptcy costs and ''high contact'' conditions in the case of proportional costs. See van Moerbeke (1976), Dumas (1991), Dixit (1991) and Myneni (1992).
29. When the prepayment option is absent, a borrower never rationally defaults when $h(t) > m(t)$. Owing to notational simplicity, we suppress here explicit inclusion of the return by the lender to the borrower of any excess of liquidated value over the loan balance.
30. Our analysis can, for example, offer both a positive explanation for ''credit crunches'' in the mortgage markets, in terms of both the stochastic properties of the value of the house collateralizing the mortgage and in terms of the bargaining equilibrium between lender and mortgagor, as reflected in both price and non-price features of the mortgage and, as well, normative considerations in the design of mortgage contracts which might enhance the flow of available mortgage credit through changing both lender and mortgagor incentives.
31. See Lea and Diamond (1992) and Courchane and Nickerson (2001) for a survey of mortgage terms in a variety of developed and developing economies. We do not attempt to endogenize the term to maturity of mortgages in this paper.
32. Examples of circumstances in which default will not occur prior to maturity include the case of the coupon payment c being zero or sufficiently small, relative to $\eta(h, t)$.
33. The appearance of $C\phi_2$ in (12) is required to offset the discontinuity in the lender's payoff between the default and no-default states at maturity, caused by the presence of positive bankruptcy costs. The values of ϕ_1 and ϕ_2 can be given by the Black–Scholes formula, modified to allow for the positive flow of housing services, or dividend rate, on the property underlying the mortgage.
34. If, alternatively, the collateral provides a constant absolute flow of services η to the mortgagor while in his possession, the value of the contract to the lender becomes:

$$L(h, 0) = h(0) + (1 - e^{-rT})\frac{c - \eta}{r} - C(h, T, C),$$

and the limit on the supply of credit under these circumstances becomes:

$$L(h, 0) \leq h(0) - (1 - e^{-rT})\frac{\eta}{r}.$$

Of course, for a constant absolute dividend flow to be consistent with h being non-negative, the proportional volatility σ could not be constant, and, as a consequence, the value C of the call option would not be that given by the Black–Scholes formula.

35. Stationarity, implying the independence of L and M from t, allows the partial derivatives, with respect to t, in the valuation equations (5) and (6) to vanish, leaving more tractable ordinary differential equations.
36. The situation with both default and prepayment options is qualitatively similar. The boundary conditions, however, result in a pair of simultaneous quadratic equations in the optimal default and prepayment values, $\underline{h}$ and $\bar{h}$, that would require numerical solution for particular parameter values, and consequently is not presented.
37. Notice also that the size of the loan offered by the lender will be influenced by the (common) knowledge that, were renegotiation possible at subsequent dates, the value of the loan to the lender is decreasing in the payment p in the vicinity of default if there are positive liquidation costs to the lender. There could, consequently, be an incentive for the lender to renegotiate the loan in an environment in which renegotiation was possible, offering *permanently reduced* payments if default is imminent, either by reducing the contractual loan rate or by forgiving a portion of the notional principal, and foreknowledge of this incentive will further reduce the initial value of the loan offered.
38. Each case we analyze, consequently, will focus on the best-response strategy of the lender, taking as given the other features of the mortgage contract. We do not single out, in this section, any specific vector of loan terms as a unique perfect equilibrium in our lending game.
39. See, for example, Press et al. (1986). The procedure approximates partial derivatives by the average of difference expressions in the gridpoint values of M and L at time t, for which one has the last solution, and time $t+k$, for which one does not. Requiring the valuation equations to hold at all gridpoints results in a tridiagonal system of simultaneous linear equations in the unknown values at the current time slice. This is then solved for the values at $t+k$, and so on. The method has the virtue of being numerically stable for all sizes of k, and second order accurate in both the t and h directions.
40. That is, $b(h,t) = bh(t)$, $\eta(h,t) = \eta h(t), f(m(t)) = fm(t)$.
41. The annualized volatility is chosen to approximate the same order of magnitude as that in a sample of urban housing markets in both developed and developing countries over the period 1990–1995, as reported in Courchane and Nickerson (2001).
42. This could, in the presence of both fixed and variable bankruptcy or liquidation costs, suggest an explantion for more adverse credit conditions in transitional neighborhoods within a city, relative to more stable neighborhoods, when all aspects of the mortgage contract itself are held constant.
43. See Gertler (1988).

References

Anderson, R. W., and S. Sundaresan. (1996). ''Design and Valuation of Debt Contracts,'' *Review of Financial Studies* 9(1), 37–68.

Archer, W., and D. Ling. (1993). ''Pricing Mortgage-Backed Securities: Integrating Optimal Call and Empirical Models of Prepayment,'' *American Real Estate and Urban Economics Association Journal* 21(4), Winter, 373–404.

Archer, W., D. Ling, and G. McGill. (1996). ''The Effect of Income and Collateral Constraints on Residential Mortgage Terminations,'' *Regional Science and Urban Economics* 26(3), 235–261.

Baltensperger, E. (1976). ''The Borrower–Lender Relationship, Competitive Equilibrium, and the Theory of Hedonic Prices,'' *American Economic Review* 66 (June), 401–405.

Baltensperger, E. (1978). ''Credit Rationing: Issues and Questions,'' *Journal of Money, Credit and Banking* 10(2), 170–183.

Barro, R. (1976). ''The Loan Market, Collateral and Rates of Interest,'' *Journal of Money, Credit and Banking* 8(1), 439–456.

Bester, H. (1994). ''The Role of Collateral in a Model of Debt Renegotiation,'' *Journal of Money, Credit and Banking* 26(1), 72–86.

Buckley, R. (1994). ''Housing Finance in Developing Countries: The Role of Credible Contracts,'' *Economic Development and Cultural Change* 42(2), 317–332.

Buckley, R., B. Lipman, and T. Persaud. (1993). ''Mortgage Design Under Inflation and Real Wage Uncertainty: The Use of a Dual Index Instrument,'' *World Development* 21(3), 455–464.

Choe, C. (1998). ''A Mechanism Design Approach to an Optimal Contract under Ex Ante and Ex Post Information,'' *Review of Economic Design* 3(3), 237–255.

Clauretie, T., and T. Herzog. (1989). ''How State Laws Affect Foreclosure Costs,'' *Secondary Mortgage Markets* 6(1), 25–28.

Courchane, M., and D. Nickerson. (2001). ''International Mortgage Contracts: A Survey,'' Housing Economics and Financial Research Working Paper, FreddieMac.

Crawford, G., and E. Rosenblatt. (1995). ''Efficient Mortgage Default Option Exercise: Evidence from Loss Severity,'' *Journal of Real Estate Research* 10(5), 543–555.

Deng, Y., J. Quigley, and R. van Order. (2000). ''Mortgage Terminations, Heterogeneity and the Exercise of Mortgage Options,'' *Econometrica* 68(2), 275–307.

Dixit, A. (1991). ''A Simplified Exposition of the Theory of Optimal Regulation of Brownian Motion,'' *Journal of Economic Dynamics and Control* 15(4), 657–673.

Dokko, Y., and R. H. Edelstein. (1991). ''Interest Rate Risk and Optimal Design of Mortgage Instruments,'' *Journal of Real Estate Finance and Economics* 4, 59–68.

Duffie, D. (1992). *Dynamic Asset Pricing*. Princeton: Princeton University Press.

Dumas, B. (1991). ''Super Contact and Related Optimality Conditions,'' *Journal of Economic Dynamics and Control* 15(4), 675–685.

Dutta, P., and A. Rustichini. (1993). ''A Theory of Stopping Time Games with Applications to Product Innovations and Asset Sales,'' *Economic Theory* 3, 743–763.

Foster, C., and R. Van Order. (1984). ''An Option-based Model of Mortgage Default,'' *Housing Finance Review*. 3(4), 351–372.

Freimer, M., and M. Gordon. (1965). ''Why Bankers Ration Credit,'' *Quarterly Journal of Economics* 79, 397–410.

Gertler, M. (1988). ''Financial Structure and Aggregate Economic Activity: An Overview,'' *Journal of Money, Credit and Banking* (August), 559–588.

Gorton, G., and J. Kahn. (2000). ''The Design of Bank Loan Contracts,'' *Review of Financial Studies* 13(2), 331–364.

Grenadier, S. (1995). ''The Persistence of Real Estate Cycles,'' *Journal of Real Estate Finance and Economics* 10, 95–119.

Grenadier, S. (1996). ''The Strategic Exercise of Options: Development Cascades and Overbuilding in Real Estate Markets,'' *Journal of Finance* 51(5), 1653–1679.

Harris, M., and A. Raviv. (1992). ''Financial Contracting Theory.'' In J.-J. Laffont (ed.), *Advances in Economic Theory*, vol. II. (Econometric Society 6th World Congress), Cambridge: Cambridge University Press.

Hart, O. (1995). *Firms, Contracts and Financial Structure*. Oxford: Oxford University Press.

Hart, O., and J. Moore. (1998). ''Default and Renegotiation: A Dynamic Model of Debt,'' *Quarterly Journal of Economics* 113(1), 1–41.

Hendershott, P., and R. Van Order. (1996). ''Pricing Mortgages: An Interpretation of Models and Results,'' *Journal of Financial Services Research* 1, 77–111.

Hodgman, D. (1960). ''Credit Risk and Credit Rationing,'' *Quarterly Journal of Economics* 74(2), 258–278.

Jaffee, D., and F. Modigliani. (1969). ''A Theory and Test of Credit Rationing,'' *American Economic Review* 59(5), 850–872.

Jaffee, D., and J. Stiglitz. (1990). ''Credit Rationing.'' In B. M. Friedman and F. H. Hahn (eds.), *Handbook of Monetary Economics*, vol. II. Elsevier Science Publishers B.V.

Jones, R. (1995). ''Credit Risk, Stochastic Collateral and Credit Rationing,'' Working Paper, Simon Fraser University.

Jones, R. (1999). ''Credit Risk and Credit Access,'' Working Paper, Simon Fraser University.

Jones, R., and D. Nickerson. (2001). ''Mortgage Contracts, Renegotiation and Stochastic Collateral,'' Working Paper, Colorado State University.

Kau, J., and D. Keenan. (1999). ''Patterns of Rational Default,'' Working Paper, University of Georgia.

Kau, J., D. Keenan, and T. Kim. (1993). ''Transactions Costs, Suboptimal Termination and Default Probabilities,'' *Journal of the American Real Estate and Urban Economics Association* 21(3), 247–263.

Kau, J., D. Keenan, and T. Kim. (1994). ''Default Probabilities for Mortgages,'' *Journal of Urban Economics* 35(3) 278–296.

Kau, J., D. Keenan, W. Muller, and J. Epperson. (1995). ''The Valuation at Origination of Fixed-Rate Mortgages with Default and Prepayment,'' *Journal of Real Estate Finance and Economics* 11(1), 5–36.

Kau, J., D. Keenan, W. Muller, and J. Epperson. (1992). ''A Generalized Valuation Model for Fixed-Rate Residential Mortgages,'' *Journal of Money, Credit and Banking* 24(3), 279–299.

Kau, J., and T. Kim. (1994). ''Waiting to Default: The Value of Delay,'' *Journal of the American Real Estate and Urban Economics Association*, 22(3), 539–551.

Keenan, D., and J. Kau. (1995). ''An Overview of the Option-Theoretic Pricing of Mortgages,'' *Journal of Housing Research* 6(2), 217–244.

Keyles, S. (1995). *Foreclosure Law and Related Remedies: A State-by-State Digest*, Chicago, IL: Section of Real Property, Probate and Trust Law, American Bar Association.

Koskela, E. (1979). ''On the Theory of Rationing Equilibria with Special Reference to Credit Markets: A Survey,'' *Zeitschrift fur Nationalokonomie* 39(1), 63–82.

Kulatilaka, N. (1999). *Real Options: Managing Strategic Investments in an Uncertain World.* Cambridge: Harvard University Press.

Lacker, J. (1998). ''Collateralized Debt as the Optimal Contract,'' Federal Reserve Bank of Richmond Working Paper.

Lea, M., and D. Diamond. (1992). ''Housing Finance in Developed Countries: An International Comparison of Efficiency,'' *Journal of Housing Research* 3(1), 1–271.

Merton, R. (1973). ''The Theory of Rational Option Pricing,'' *Bell Journal of Economics and Management Science* 4 (Spring), 141–183.

Moerbeke, P. van. (1974). ''Optimal Stopping and Free Boundary Problems,'' *Rocky Mountain Journal of Mathematics* 4 (Summer), 539–577.

Myneni, R. (1992). ''The Pricing of the American Option,'' *Annals of Applied Probability* 2, 1–23.

Parigi, B. (1992). ''Repeated Lending with Limited Liability Under Imperfect Monitoring,'' *Economic Notes* 21(3), 468–489.

Phillips, R., E. Rosenblatt, and J. VanderHoff. (1996). ''The Probability of Fixed- and Adjustable-Rate Mortgage Termination,'' *Journal of Real Estate Finance and Economics* 13(2), (September), 95–104.

Pindyck, R. (1991). ''Irreversibility, Uncertainty, and Investment,'' *Journal of Economic Literature* 29(3), 1110–1148.

Plaut, S. (1986). ''Mortgage Design in Imperfect Capital Markets,'' *Journal of Urban Economics* 20, 107–119.

Press, W. H., B. P. Flannery, S. A. Teukolsky, and W. T. Vetterling. (1986). *Numerical Recipes: The Art of Scientific Computing.* New York: Cambridge University Press.

Stiglitz, J., and A. Weiss. (1981). ''Credit Rationing in Markets with Imperfect Information,'' *American Economic Review* 71 (March), 393–410.

Stiglitz, J., and A. Weiss. (1986). ''Credit Rationing and Collateral.'' In J. Edwards, J. Franks, C. Mayer and S. Schaefer (eds.), *Recent Developments in Corporate Finance.* Cambridge: University Press.

U.S. Department of Housing and Urban Development. (1996). *Providing Alternatives to Mortgage Foreclosure: A Report to Congress.* Washington, D.C.

Vandell, K. (1993). ''Handing over the Keys: A Perspective on Mortgage Default Research,'' *American Real Estate and Urban Economics Association Journal* 21(3), 211–246.

Vandell, K., and T. Thibodeau. (1985). ''Estimation of Mortgage Defaults Using Disaggregate Loan History Data,'' *American Real Estate and Urban Economics Association Journal* 13(3), 292–316.

Williamson, S. (1986). ''Costly Monitoring, Financial Intermediation, and Equilibrium Credit Rationing,'' *Journal of Monetary Economics* 18 (September), 159–179.

Journal of Real Estate Finance and Economics, 24:1/2, 59–87, 2002

Explaining Real Commercial Rents Using an Error Correction Model with Panel Data

PATRIC HENDERSHOTT

BRYAN MACGREGOR

MICHAEL WHITE

Department of Land Economy, University of Aberdeen, Kings College, Aberdeen

E-mail: m.white@abdn.ac.uk

Abstract

This paper presents rent models for retail and office property in the United Kingdom. Panel data are used covering eleven regions for 29 years, enabling us to overcome the limitations of a relatively short time series. We use an error correction model (ECM) framework to estimate long-run equilibrium relationships and short-term dynamic corrections. The combination of panel data and an ECM is an innovative approach that is still being developed in economics. We construct new supply series that combine infrequent stock data with more frequent construction data. Separate regional models are estimated for retail and office properties. The regions are then combined into a number of panels on the basis of the income and price elasticities in the long-run and short-run models. Unlike previous studies, we find no evidence of a board north–south divide between low growth and high growth regions. Like these studies we do find a London effect: in London, demand elasticities for space with respect to both price (rent) and income are much lower in magnitude. We conclude that, while the economic drivers may vary, there is no evidence of differences in the operation of the regional property markets outside London. Elasticities for retail and office are similar. Our final models are parsimonious with single measures of economic activity and of supply and always support the use of an ECM.

Key Words: panel estimation, error correction, regional rent models

1. Introduction

Forecasts of rent are a fundamental input into both individual property valuations and the construction of optimal portfolio allocations. Until the last decade, the short time series data available for rents tended to limit the scope and reliability of econometric models of rents. More recently, with nearly 30 years of data available in the United States and the United Kingdom, and with developments in time series analysis and econometrics software, there has been a substantial expansion in the modeling of commercial property markers (Ball et al., 1998). In this paper, we apply one of the most recent approaches in econometrics, an error correction model (ECM) with panel data, to explain real retail and office rents in eleven U.K. regions.[1]

The published work on property market modeling is dominated by U.S.- and U.K.-based

Author for correspondence: Dr Michael White, Department of Land Economy, University of Aberdeen, Kings College, Aberdeen AB24 3UF.

researchers and has dealt primarily with the office market. In the main, U.S. models have included equations for the development and user markets and a rental adjustment equation. A characteristic of these models is an embodiment of the theoretical notion of equilibrium. Thus, when vacancy rates diverge form their natural level, rents will also tend to diverge from their equilibrium value and this acts as a signal to developers. In the U.K. and elsewhere in Europe, these models have had limited application, reflecting the lack of vacancy rate data (exceptions are models of the City of London office markets where vacancy data are available) and, perhaps, model preference. Instead, reduced from demand–supply equations have been estimated with real rent as the dependent variable and demand drivers (such as consumer expenditures or service sector employment) and supply (stock or new construction orders, if available) as explanatory variables. Outside the U.K., supply data are not generally available.

This paper considers the different approaches of the U.S. and the U.K. within a single framework that both takes account of the notion of adjustment towards equilibrium prevalent in the American literature and uses a reduces-from model common in the U.K. literature. The basic model is extended into an error correction framework and takes advantage of the availability of U.K. rental data by using a panel approach on regional data for both retail and office properties. We consider the need for more than one panel based upon possible differences in elasticities across regions.

The paper is arranged as follows. Section 2 provides a literature review. Section 3 sets out the basic modeling approach, and Section 4 covers the data. Section 5 presents the estimation strategy and the results, and Section 6 provides a discussion and conclusion.

2. Literature review

The U.S. literature on rental modeling in the office market is dominated by the use of the rental adjustment approach. The basic rental adjustment model makes the percentage change in real rents a linear function of the difference between the actual and natural vacancy rates:

$$(R_t - R_{t-1})/R_{t-1} = \lambda(\nu^* - \nu_{t-1}) \tag{1}$$

where λ is the adjustment factor. The model has its origins in labor economics and was described for rental housing by Black and Winnick (1953). Early support for the rental housing hypothesis was provided by Smith (1969, 1974) and later by Rosen and Smith 1983. The approach was used by Shilling et al. (1987 and 1992) to explain local U.S. office market rents, while Gabriel and Nothaft (1988) employed pooled data to estimate the natural rental housing vacancy rate for U.S. cities. Wheaton and Torto (1988) estimated the model for the aggregate U.S. office market.[2]

The basic rental adjustment equation appears in most multi-equation office models. These tend to have a common structure of three behavioural equations (for space demand, supply and rent) linking exogenous variables to the property market. Rosen (1984) considers the San Francisco office market; Wheaton (1987) models the U.S. national market; Pollakowski et al. (1992) use a panel approach for twenty-one U.S. metropolitan areas and consider the importance of market size; and Wheaton et al. (1997) examine the London market.

Hendershott (1955, 1996) extends the basic model by introducing the impact of deviations from equilibrium rents, thereby allowing both a more plausible and more general adjustment path:

$$(R_t - R_{t-1})/R_{t-1} = \lambda(\nu^* - \nu_{t-1}) + \beta(R_t^* - R_{t-1}) \tag{2}$$

where equilibrium rents depend on real interest through a user–cost relationship. Note the similarity to an ECM: rents adjust to the difference between long-run (equilibrium) and actual values. He provides support for the expanded model using Sydney office data, and Hendershott et al. (1999) obtain similar results with London office data. The latter also estimate space demand and supply (construction) responses.

In Europe, vacancy data are not generally available (London being an obvious exception), and modellers have predominantly estimated a reduced form demand–supply equation. Early works include Hetherington (1988) and Silver and Goode (1990) on retail, Gardiner and Henneberry (1988, 1991) on offices, and Dobson and Goddard (1992) on retail, office and industrial markets. All consider different U.K. regions.

Key et al. (1994) also model rent levels for all three property types using a panel approach for eleven regions and find that offices require two panels: one for London and three southern regions; the other for the remaining regions. The ''north–south'' divide in economic performance and social conditions is a recurrent theme of much U.K. economic geography and regional literature (see Hamelink et al., 2000, for a review of some of the current debates). In general, Key et al. (1994) find lagged rents, the current and lagged demand variables and interest rates to be significant. Floorspace and construction starts are significant only in the southern offices and industrial models, and the authors suggest that these markets are demand driven with little speculative development.

Many of these models employ approaches that would not satisfy current econometric practices. Estimations are often done in levels and stationarity and cointegration are rarely considered. Tsolacos with a variety of co-authors has addressed these issues. Giussani et al. (1993) utilize a cross section model of ten European city office markets, and D'Arcy et al. (1997) extend the study to 22 European cities and adopt a panel approach. Change in rent is estimated as a function of change in GDP and the level of lagged short-term real interest rates. Both are significant. The cities are classified according to size and rate of service sector employment growth.

Thompson and Tsolacos (1999) model real rent change in the U.K. industrial market as a function of lagged changes in GDP, industrial vacancy rates and lagged values of rental change. The multi-equation model found in the U.S. literature is used by Tsolacos et al. (1998) for the U.K. office market. Instead of a rental adjustment model using vacancy rates, their estimated model links rental change to lagged changes in GDP, in employment in the banking, finance and insurance sector and in the volume of new office building output. Finally, a somewhat different approach to those outlined above was adopted by

McGough and Tsolacos (1995) who estimated ARIMA models for one-period-rent forecasts and found that retail rents are linked to their past values while office and industrial rents are more linked to demand and supply shocks.

Estimates of difference relationships have not considered adjustment to an estimated long run equilibrium relationship: to do this requires an ECM approach. Such an approach is not featured much in the property literature, although Hendershott's generalized rental adjustment model is close to it. A formal ECM is used by RICS (1999) to model real property returns in the United Kingdom, by Hoesli and MacGregor (2000) to model U.K. retail property rents, and by Hendershott et al. (1999) to explain London office demand. None of these uses panel data.[3]

Despite the differing approaches, a broad consensus emerges from the U.K. literature on the appropriate demand variables, particularly for the more extensively studied office market. In constant, supply creates problems: some studies do not find it significant, some use construction orders (a flow variable) rather than a stock, some use other proxy variables and some omit it because data are not available.

3. Methodology

3.1. The reduced form long run model

Consider demand for property as a function of rent and economic activity:

$$D = \lambda_0 R^{\lambda_1} EA^{\lambda_2} \tag{3}$$

where D is demand, R is rent, EA is economic activity, $\lambda_1 < 0$ is the "price" elasticity and $\lambda_2 > 0$ the "income" elasticity. By definition, this demand equals the supply of occupied space $(l - \nu)SU$, where SU is supply and ν is the vacancy rate. Equating demand and occupied supply, taking logs and solving for $\ln R$ gives

$$\ln R = -\gamma_2 \ln \lambda_0 + \gamma_t \ln EA + \gamma_2 \ln SU + \gamma_2 \ln(1 - \nu) \tag{4a}$$

where $\gamma_1 = -\lambda_2/\lambda_1 > 0$ and $\gamma_2 = 1/\lambda_1 < 0$.

Vacancy rate data are generally not available for the United Kingdom. To account for the normal vacancies that would exist in equilibrium, we add and subtract $\gamma_2 \ln(1 - \nu^*)$ from the right side of (4a) and treat ν^* as a constant, obtaining

$$\ln R = -\gamma_0 + \gamma_1 \ln EA + \gamma_2 \ln SU + \text{err} \tag{4b}$$

where $\gamma_0 = \gamma_2[\ln(1 - \nu^*) - \ln \lambda_0]$ and $\text{err} = \gamma_2[\ln(1 - \nu) - \ln(1 - \nu^*)]$. Lacking data on v, its impact is embedded in the error term.

3.2. The short run adjustment model

The reduced-form rent equation can be set within an ECM framework and estimated using a panel approach. The residual form the estimated long-run relationship, equation (4b), is

$$u_t = \ln R_t - \hat{\gamma}_0 - \hat{\gamma}_1 \ln EA_t - \hat{\gamma}_2 \ln SU_t, \tag{5}$$

the difference between the observed and estimated long run log rental values. If these variables are co-integrated, this error is stationary and can be used in short run dynamic model as an adjustment process.[4]

The short run model is the first difference of equation (4b) with the addition of the error correction term. To this basic model, we also add the lagged value of real rental change because the rent series are autoregressive:

$$r_t = \alpha_0 + \alpha_1 ea_t + \alpha_2 su_t + \alpha_3 u_{t-1} + \phi r_{t-1} \tag{6}$$

where lower case letters, except u, represent log differences. Thus, real rent adjusts to short run changes in the causal variables and also to lagged market imbalances as measured in equation (5). In the estimations, it is expected that α_0 will be approximately zero, α_1 will be positive, α_2 and α_3 will be negative, and ϕ will be between 0 and 1. $\alpha_3 = 0$ means no adjustment; $0 > \alpha_3 > -1$ means partial adjustment; $\alpha_3 = -1$ means full adjustment; and $\alpha_3 - 1$ means over-adjustment. This basic model is estimated in panels for each of the two property types.

As noted in the literature review, the lagged imbalance between space demand and supply, as reflected in the lagged vacancy rate, is the primary driver in the U.S. rental-adjustment model. Comparing equations (4b) and (5), the residual in (5) is almost certainly dominated by the missing $\gamma_2[\ln(1-\nu) - \ln(l-\nu^*)]$ term in equation (4b). Because $\ln(1-\nu)$ approximates $-\nu$ for small values of ν, the lagged residual in our EC model is, in effect, a proxy for $-\gamma_2(\nu^* - \nu_{-1})$. (Recall that γ_2 is negative.) That is, our EC model can be viewed as an expansion of the traditional U.S. rental-adjustment model.

3.3. Tests for coefficient restrictions

The general model set out in equation (6) embeds more commonly used models. If equation (5) is substituted into equation (6) and we substitute for lnR *ad infinitum*, we get (ignoring the hats):

$$\ln R_t = (\alpha_3\gamma_0 - \alpha_0)/\alpha_3 + \alpha_1 \ln EA_t + \alpha_3(\alpha_1 - \gamma_1)\left[\ln EA_{t-1} + \sum_{i=2}^{\infty}(1+\alpha_3)^{i-1} \ln EA_{t-i}\right]$$
$$+ \alpha_2 \ln SU_t + \alpha_3(\alpha_2 - \gamma_2)\left[\ln SU_{t-1} + \sum_{i-2}^{\infty}(1+\alpha_3)^{i-1} \ln SU_{t-i}\right] \tag{7}$$

If $\gamma_1 = -\alpha_1/\alpha_3$ and $\gamma_2 = -\alpha_2/\alpha_3$, then the model reduces to a Koyck specification (of which the standard partial adjustment and adaptive expectations models are particular cases (Berndt, 1991; Dougherty, 1992).

While the above model allows partial adjustment to a long-run relationship, if $\alpha_0 = 0$, $\alpha_1 = \gamma_1$, $\alpha_2 = \gamma_2$, and $\alpha_3 = -1$, equation (7) reduces to the long run model of equation (4a).

3.4. Unit roots and co-integration in panel data

A preliminary step in this study is an analysis of the time series properties of the variables used. Hence unit root tests were uniformly performed on all variables in this study. The standard regression for this technique is

$$\Delta x_t = \alpha + \beta_1 x_{t-1} + \sum_{i=1}^{\rho-1} \delta_i \Delta x_{t-i} + \mu_t \tag{8}$$

where the chosen value for ρ is such that μ_t will be a white noise error term. The coefficient of interest is β_1. Its t-statistic is compared with the critical values found in Fuller (1976). When only the lagged value of x is present, the test is referred to as a Dickey–Fuller (DF) test. When lagged difference terms are added, the resulting test is an augmented Dickey–Fuller (ADF) test. An alternative approach to adding lagged values of the dependent variable has been suggested by Phillips (1987) and extended by Perron (1988) and Phillips and Perron (1988). They suggest adding a non-parametric correction to the t-test statistic. This accounts for autocorrelation that may be present.

However, Levin and Lin (1993) suggest that DF/PP tests cannot be directly applied to panel data and they develop an alternative procedure. They consider three variants distinguished by the deterministic variables that are included (i.e., a model without a constant, one with a constant and another with a constant and a time trend). The estimated equation is

$$\Delta x_{it} = \delta_i x_{it-1} + \sum_{L-1}^{P_i} \delta_{iL} \Delta x_{it-L} + \delta_{mi} d_{mt} + \mu_t \tag{9}$$

which is similar in structure to (8) but where i represents the region or panel to be examined and d is the deterministic variable. Testing the null hypothesis of non-stationarity requires the residuals from this regression to be normalized in order to control for inter-regional heterogeneity. We normalize by scaling the residuals by the standard error from the regression. These results for model (9) are reported for all regions combined.

A necessary requirement for a valid error correction mechanism is co-integration in the long run relationship. Research by Pedroni (1997) suggests that the usual applications of DF and PP tests are inappropriate in order to test for co-integration in a panel setting. Therefore, in addition, we apply a test for co-integrating vectors in panel data.

4. The data

4.1. Data sources

The data are for ten of the standard regions of the United Kingdom with the dominant South East region divided into London and the rest of the South East (see Figure 1) and come from a variety of sources.[5] Real rent data were provided by the Investment Property Databank (IPD), an independent performance measurement and analysis service. They are appraisal-based series and, from 1981, represent the estimated open market rental values of over 12,000 properties on the IPD database. From 1971–1980 the rent series are from a

Figure 1. The standard regions of the United Kingdom.

sample of properties. The IPD now covers most of the institutional investment market. The data are collected in a standardized and consistent manner. They are the best quality available and are the most representative of the institutional property market in the United Kingdom.

The regional economic activity variables were provided by the Northern Ireland Economic Research Centre (NIERC). NIERC obtained real output variables by using different sectoral and regional deflators. Other economic data are from U.K. government statistics. For the retail and office property estimations, we use, respectively, real consumer expenditure and financial and business services employment. In the latter case, we also tested a real output measure. These categories, of course, do not map one-to-one onto the users of the space.

Supply data create the greatest problem for this type of research. Full series for each property type and the English regions are available for total floorspace from Department of the Environment/Inland Revenue Floorspace Statistics for 1974–1986 (and with gaps from 1962). The series were not published again until 1994. The Department of the Environment Construction Industry Statistics provides data on new construction orders and construction completions by property type. The latter are not available for much of the period covered by the rent data but the former are available (for a discussion of these series and a comparison at the U.K. level, see Ball et al., 1998). For this study, the floorspace and new orders series were combined to produce a series measuring the existing stock of floorspace plus floorspace under construction (for details see Appendix 1).

All variables used have been log transformed.

4.2. Basic statistics: Unit root and co-integration tests

Means values and standard deviations of the variables used in the study are presented in Table A1 in Appendix 2. The statistics presented are for changes in the values of the particular variables rather than for their levels. Table A2 reports both DF/ADF and Phillips and Perron (PP) unit root tests indicating the orders of integration of the time series. The macroeconomic variables (consumers expenditure and finance and business services employment) are stationary in first differences ($I(1)$). A few rental series, appear to be $I(0)$, although these tests lack power in small samples. In a minority of cases, there is some discrepancy between results for DF and PP tests. Finally, using Levin and Lin (1993) panel unit root tests on all regions combined were conducted with the finding that all variables were $I(1)$ except office supply which was $I(0)$. This latter would be problematic if office supply was the dependent variable with some $I(1)$ independent variables. It is not a problem in the current setting where the independent variable has an order of integration equal to the highest order of integration of any of the other independent variables.

There is evidence of a single co-integrating vector for all property types in all regions except Yorkshire & Humberside retail and Scottish offices, for which there appear to be two. Caution is required, however, given the small sample sizes when examining each region individually.

Given that panel estimation is employed, panel co-integration methods are also used. These methods are based on work by Pedroni (1997, 1999) who computes critical values for co-integration tests when pooled time series cross sectional data are used. Specifically, seven diagnostic tests are constructed. These are: the panel v-statistic, the panel ρ-statistic, the panel t-statistics, equivalent to the PP and ADF tests for single time series. Also constructed are the group ρ-statistic and group t-statistics again equivalent to the PP and ADF statistics. The panel statistics pool the autoregressive coefficient across panel members while the group statistics are based on estimators that average the individually estimated coefficients for each member.

The panel co-integration tests were estimated using the RATS (Regression Analysis of Time Series) package and the procedure was set up in such a way that the program would report a normalized statistic that is distributed as $N \sim (0, 1)$ under the null hypothesis of no co-integration. The results are reported in Table A3. These results suggest that panel co-integration cannot be rejected for the retail and office markets.

5. Results

5.1. The general modeling approach

The model was estimated using EViews econometric software. Within each of the two property types, all regions were initially pooled and long-run and short-run models were estimated. Separate models were next estimated for each region to consider the robustness of the models and the differences in the coefficient values among regions. Through a process of iteration, final models were selected. Regions were then combined into a number of panels based on the similarities in the coefficients in both the long run and short run models. Thus, our determinant for combining regions was the similarity in their long run and short run demand and supply elasticities rather than the similarities in the intensity and timing of cycles.[6] Once appropriate panel splits and the final models had been estimated, hypotheses were tested on restrictions on the coefficients as set out in Section 3.3.

The long-run levels relationships were estimated using a fixed-effects (constants allowed to vary from region to region) pooled model.[7] In the second stage, difference regression models common intercepts (expected to be zero) were estimated. Heteroskedastic consistent estimates are reported. In all cases, the preferred long-run models contain only a single economic activity variable and a measure of own supply only.[8]

The possibility of an errors-in-variables problem was also investigated. In no case was there a significant relationship found between the error term and the regressors.

5.2. Retail

Table A4 presents the EViews outputs for the preferred model for the retail sector with economic activity and supply coefficients both allowed to vary across regions. Part (a) shows the long run model and part (b) shows the short run model.

In the long run model, consumer expenditure is always correctly signed and highly significant (p-values of 1 percent or less), while supply is always correctly signed and is significant at 5 percent or less for nine regions, at 10 percent for one, but insignificant in the West Midlands. In the short run model, change in consumer expenditure is always correctly signed and highly significant (0.6 percent or less). Change in supply is correctly signed and significant at 10 percent or less in only four regions (three of which are in the south), and wrongly signed and insignificant in two regions. Importantly, the error correction term is correctly signed and highly significant. The overall R^2 is 53 percent.

Comparing the coefficients in the individual regional models, the consumer expenditure coefficients in the long run model are generally not significantly different in paired tests (a one tailed z-test with a 5 percent critical value of $\pm$ 1.65): the North stands out, the consumption expenditures coefficient being significantly lower than that in five regions, four of which are London and the surrounding three southern regions.[9] The supply coefficients present a rather different picture. London has a significantly higher coefficient (p-value of 2 percent or below) than all regions except two of the southern regions closest to it (the South East and East Anglia), and these show up at 6 percent. The North is significantly lower than eight regions (at 1.5 percent or less for seven regions and at 6 percent for the eighth). However, the low Durbin–Watson statistic for the long run model means that caution is required in interpreting these tests on coefficients.

There are no significant differences for consumer expenditure in the shortrun model. The London supply coefficient has a larger magnitude than six other regions at 3.5 percent or less (five of these are northern), and than eight at 6.5 percent or less (six in the northern).

The overall conclusions from these results are: the North has a lower long run consumer expenditures coefficient that London and the three southern regions; short run consumer expenditure coefficients do not vary; and London supply coefficients, in both the long-run and short run models, are higher. On this basis, we now consider separate models for the North and London but combine the other nine regions. Table A5 presents the results of the tests for coefficient equality between panels. As there are no significant differences between the North and the ''Rest'' (all regions except the North and London) these are combined.

Tables 1 and 2 show our models for London and for ''all regions except London''.[10,11] Economic activity and supply are highly significant and correctly signed in both the long-run and short-run models. The adjusted R^2 in the short run models is 57 percent for London and 44 percent for other regions. The coefficients on consumer expenditures and the error correction are not significantly different between areas. The error correction coefficient shows that rents adjust to about 30 percent of the imbalance in the previous period.

When the first lag of rental change is added as a regressor, it is highly significant in the London model and substantially improves the adjusted R^2 (from 57 percent to 72 percent). However, when the second lag is added, it is insignificant and reduces the significance of the supply variable to 10 percent. For the ''all regions except London'' model, the first lag is significant but it makes supply insignificant. When the second lag is added, it is insignificant. Accordingly, our preferred London model has a one-period lag of the dependent variable as a regressor, but the other model does not.

The short-run supply coefficient is five times higher (four times when lagged rent is

Table 1. Retail model: London.

Variable	Coefficient	Standard Error	*t*-Statistic
Long run relationship			
Consumers expend.	1.58	0.27	5.78***
Supply	−3.48	0.56	−6.19***
Intercept	6.02	0.50	11.94***
Adjusted R^2	63.9 percent		
Log likelihood	30.72	F-statistic	24.95
DW	0.57	Prob (F-stat)	0.00
Short-run relationship			
Intercept	0.01	0.02	0.42
ΔConsumers expend.	1.55	0.38	4.06***
ΔSupply	−3.54	1.37	−2.58*
Error correction term	−0.36	0.15	−2.37*
Adjusted R^2	57.3 percent		
Log likelihood	40.13	F-statistic	12.64
DW	1.11	Prob (F-stat)	0.00
Short run relationship with lagged rent			
Intercept	0.01	0.01	1.77
ΔConsumers expend.	0.98	0.36	2.74*
ΔSupply	−3.10	0.96	−3.24**
Error correction term	−0.46	0.14	−3.25**
ΔRent(−1)	0.43	0.07	6.05***
Adjusted R^2	72.2 percent		
Log likelihood	46.5	F-statistic	17.87
DW	1.33	Prob (F-stat)	0.00

Notes. Δ refers to the "change in" the value of the variable; two-tailed test, * indicates significant at 5 percent; ** indicates significant at 1 percent; *** indicates significant at 0.1 percent.

added) for London, so rents are more sensitive to changes in supply. While the floorspace increase has been the smallest for all regions, and much smaller than the United Kingdom as a whole, it has been at a rate comparable to that of the surrounding South East region. It may be that in London, with higher land costs and more restricted supply, unit turnover is higher and thus, the impact of a given level of floorspace is greater. The constant in the "all regions except London" model is significantly negative suggesting that, with no change in demand or supply, rents would fall. This may be because of increasing efficiency of floorspace usage. Thus, for any given level of economic activity and price, the demand for space is falling. Overall, both the London and the "all regions except London" models are good.

5.3. *Offices*

Table A6 presents the preferred model for the office sector. It is again a parsimonious model with single measures of economic activity (financial and business services

Table 2. Retail model: all regions except London.

Variable	Coefficient	Standard Error	*t*-Statistic
Long run relationship			
Consumers expend.	1.11	0.07	14.97***
Supply	− 0.74	0.09	− 7.89***
Intercept			
South East	1.82	0.12	15.79***
South West	0.90	0.17	5.21***
East Anglia	0.20	0.24	0.82
East Midlands	0.73	0.19	3.81***
West Midlands	0.83	0.17	4.86***
North West	1.14	0.15	7.48***
Yorkshire & Humberside	0.88	0.17	5.21***
North	0.56	0.20	2.76**
Wales	0.46	0.21	2.13*
Scotland	0.96	0.17	5.53***
Adjusted R^2	99.5 percent		
Log likelihood	45.17	*F*-statistic	5434.2
DW	0.54	Prob (*F*-stat)	0.00
Short run relationship			
Intercept	− 0.01	0.01	− 2.51*
ΔConsumers expend.	1.46	0.12	12.36***
ΔSupply	− 0.53	0.18	− 2.87**
Error correction Term	− 0.23	0.05	− 4.41***
Adjusted R^2	43.9 percent		
Log likelihood	480.94	*F*-statistic	71.27
DW	1.66	Prob (*F*-stat)	0.00

Notes. Δ refers to the ''change in'' the value of the variable; two-tailed test, * indicates significant at 5 percent ** indicates significant at 1 percent *** indicates significant at 0.1 percent.

employment) and supply. In the long-run model, employment is always correctly signed and is significant at 5 percent except for London, West Midlands (11 percent) and Wales. Supply is always correctly signed and is significant at 5 percent except for the West Midlands (11 percent).

In the short-run model, employment is always correctly signed and is significant (4 percent or less) except in Wales. Supply is correctly signed in only five regions and is significantly positive in the North. The error correction is correctly signed and highly significant. The overall R^2 is 31 percent.

In the paired tests on the long-run employment coefficients, Scotland and Wales stand out as, respectively higher and lower, than two of the northern English regions. The latter can be explained by the insignificant coefficient for Wales. For supply, Wales is again different from most of the northern English regions because of its incorrect sign. London has a much higher supply coefficient than the other regions but, as the standard error is high, the differences are not significant. In the short-run model, the employment coefficients for the North West is higher than two other regions. London again has a much higher coefficient but the high standard error means the differences are not significant. For supply, the South East differs from most other regions, largely because it has a large negative coefficient (with a relatively low standard error giving significance at 6.5 percent) whereas most other regions have positive but insignificant coefficients.

On the basis of these results we consider separate models for London and Wales. Table A7 shows the results of the coefficient tests for these panels. London is significantly different from both Wales and the ''Rest'' for long-run supply and short-run employment. Accordingly, we estimate separate panels for London and the ''all regions except London''.

Tables 3 and 4 show our preferred models for London and for ''all regions except

Table 3. Office model: London.

Variable	Coefficient	Standard Error	*t*-Statistic
Long run relationship			
Finance and business Services employment	1.25	0.68	1.85
Supply	−2.78	0.74	−3.73***
Intercept	6.63	1.54	4.31***
Adjusted R^2	41.2		
Log likelihood	28.18	*F*-statistic	10.47
DW	0.38	Prob (*F*-stat)	0.00
Short run relationship			
Intercept	−0.12	0.05	−2.35*
ΔFinance and business Services employment	4.20	0.87	4.85***
ΔSupply	0.77	2.23	0.37
Error correction Term	−0.04	0.09	−0.50
Adjusted R^2	39.8 percent		
Log likelihood	16.11	*F*-statistic	6.75
DW	1.13	Prob (*F*-stat)	0.00
Short run relationship with lagged rent			
Intercept	−0.08	0.04	−2.02
ΔFinance and business Services employment	2.69	0.84	3.18**
ΔSupply	0.91	1.68	0.54
Error correction Term	−0.19	0.07	−2.73**
ΔRent(−1)	0.50	0.18	2.74**
Adjusted R^2	58.5 percent		
Log likelihood	21.72	*F*-statistic	10.18
DW	1.96	Prob (*F*-stat)	0.00

Note. Δ refers to the ''change in'' the value of the variable; two-tailed test, * indicates significant at 5 percent; ** indicates significant at 1 percent; *** indicates significant at 0.1 percent.

Table 4. Office model: all regions except London.

Variable	Coefficient	Standard Error	t-Statistic
Long run relationship			
Finance and business Services employment	0.59	0.14	4.32***
Supply	−0.78	0.15	−5.26***
Intercept			
South East	4.41	0.18	23.91***
South West	2.62	0.41	6.32***
East Anglia	1.92	0.54	3.59***
East Midlands	2.43	0.49	4.99***
West Midlands	2.68	0.43	6.29***
North West	3.10	0.37	8.37***
Yorks & Humb	2.69	0.43	6.24***
North	2.33	0.52	4.51***
Wales	2.03	0.56	3.64***
Scotland	3.19	0.34	9.48***
Adjusted R^2	99.5 percent		
Log likelihood	364.01	F-statistic	1765.09
DW	0.33	Prob (F-stat)	0.00
Short run relationship			
Intercept	−0.04	0.01	−6.14***
ΔFinance and business Services employment	1.14	0.16	7.05***
ΔSupply	0.24	0.21	1.13
Error correction Term	−0.11	0.03	−4.02***
Adjusted R^2	22.9 percent		
Log likelihood	432.03	F-statistic	27.59
DW	1.01	Prob (F-stat)	0.00

Notes. Δ refers to the ''change in'' the value of the variable; two-tailed test, * indicates significant at 5 percent; ** indicates significant at 1 percent; *** indicates significant at 0.1 percent.

London''. The long-run models both have significant and correctly signed coefficients. The short-run adjusted R^2 is 41 percent for London and 23 percent for the other regions. The short-run coefficients on employment are highly significant and correctly signed, and the London coefficient is almost four times higher (two and a half times when lagged rental change is added, see below). This suggests rents rise more sharply in response to employment growth compared to elsewhere. Because the London office market is dominated by the City and West End markets, where occupiers are major firms with locationally sensitive space requirements and new supply is difficult to produce quickly, this is not an unexpected result.

The supply coefficients are wrongly signed but insignificant. This suggests, perhaps implausibly, that rents are not affected by supply in the short run. This result is, however, consistent with the finding of much of the literature reviewed in Section 2. The error correction is correctly signed but insignificant for London. For the ''all regions except

London'' panel, it is correctly signed and highly significant but has a small magnitude (0.11) suggesting a long adjustment process. The constants are both significantly negative, suggesting increasing efficiency of floorspace use.

When the lag of rental change is added to the London model, it is significant and the adjusted R^2 rises from 40 percent to 65 percent. The ECM is now significant at the 1 percent level. Supply remains positive but is even less significant. When the second lag is added, it is insignificant and the ECM becomes insignificant. For ''all regions except London,'' the first lag is significant but its addition makes supply significantly positive. The second lag is insignificant. Accordingly, we include lagged rental change in the London model but omit it from the other model. Overall, the London model is reasonable, but the ''all regions except London'' model is poorer.

5.4. *Coefficient tests within the final models*

For each of the models, we test the two sets of restrictions on the coefficients (γ_1 and γ_2 in the long run model; α_1 in the short run model) laid out in Section 3.4.

(1) $\gamma_1\alpha_3 = -\alpha_1$ and $\gamma_2\alpha_3 = -\alpha_2$ (a Koyck specification).
(2) $\alpha_0 = 0, \alpha_1 = \gamma_1, \alpha_2 = \gamma_2, \alpha_3 = -1$ (the ECM reduces to the long-run relationship).

The results are summarized in Table 5. We can reject both hypotheses for all models. Thus, we have a dynamic adjustment process that cannot be simplified into a partial adjustment or adaptive expectations model. We require the full ECM specification. In all our models we have a partial adjustment to the estimated long-run relationship.

5.5. *Long-run elasticities and short-run adjustment*

Referring to equation (4a), the implied long run price elasticity is the inverse of the supply coefficient and the income elasticity is the negative ratio of the economic activity and supply coefficients. The resultant elasticities are shown in Table 6. In all cases, the London elasticities are lower in absolute value than those for the ''all regions except London'' panel. Overall, the retail and office elasticities are quite similar. The exception is the office income elasticity for which the retail figure is about twice that of offices.

Figure 2 shows the time pattern of responses to errors in the different markets. These responses depend on the coefficients on both the EC term and the lagged rental change. For the ''all regions except London'' models, where the lagged rental change does not appear in the short-run relationship, the response builds slowly over time, only approaching unity after a decade or two. In contrast, in the London markets where the lagged change in rent enters (positively), the response is sharply accelerated, being effectively completed within two (retail) and five (office) years. Returning to our interpretation of the EC term as reflecting the missing lagged vacancy rate, these

Table 5. Coefficient tests within the final models.

	$\beta_1^* \alpha_3 = -\alpha_1$	$\beta_2^* \alpha_3 = -\alpha_2$	$\alpha_0 = 0$	$\alpha_3 = -1$	$\alpha_1 = b_1$	$\alpha_2 = \beta_2$	$\alpha_1 = 0.5\beta_1$	$\alpha_2 = 0.5\beta_2$
Without lagged rent								
Retail								
London	2.56	– 1.67	0.42	4.24	– 0.07	– 0.04	1.62	– 1.21
Other	10.23	– 1.92	– 2.51	14.48	2.73	1.06	6.61	– 0.74
Offices								
London	4.78	0.40	– 2.35	10.80	2.68	1.51	3.25	0.92
Other	6.64	1.53	– 6.14	31.67	2.58	3.91	3.98	2.42
Industrials								
London	1.48	– 0.20	1.09	5.80	1.57	– 0.72	1.48	– 0.42
Other	6.38	– 1.68	1.93	20.36	3.07	– 0.55	4.91	– 1.18
With lagged rent (+)								
Retail								
London (+)	1.15	– 1.93	1.18	3.87	– 1.33	0.34	0.43	– 1.23
Other	10.23	– 1.92	– 2.51	14.48	2.73	1.06	6.61	– 0.74
Offices								
London (+)	3.11	0.61	– 2.02	11.31	1.32	2.00	1.90	1.25
Other	6.64	1.53	– 6.14	31.67	2.58	3.91	3.98	2.42
Industrials								
London (+)	1.11	– 3.10	1.00	7.97	1.22	– 2.65	1.08	– 2.13
Other (+)	4.45	– 3.23	1.66	15.28	1.15	– 1.75	3.04	– 2.49

Notes. The null hypotheses are shown in the first row and one-tailed *z*-tests are used.

Table 6. Price and income elasticities.

	Price	Income
Retail		
London	– 0.29	0.46
Other	– 1.34	1.45
Offices		
London	– 0.36	0.45
Other	– 1.29	0.76

responses suggest a far more rapid adjustment of real rents in the London market, than in the regional markets, to shocks.

6. Discussion and conclusion

The models we have presented use single economic activity and supply variables yet, in general, perform well in explaining market behavior. We are able to estimate co-

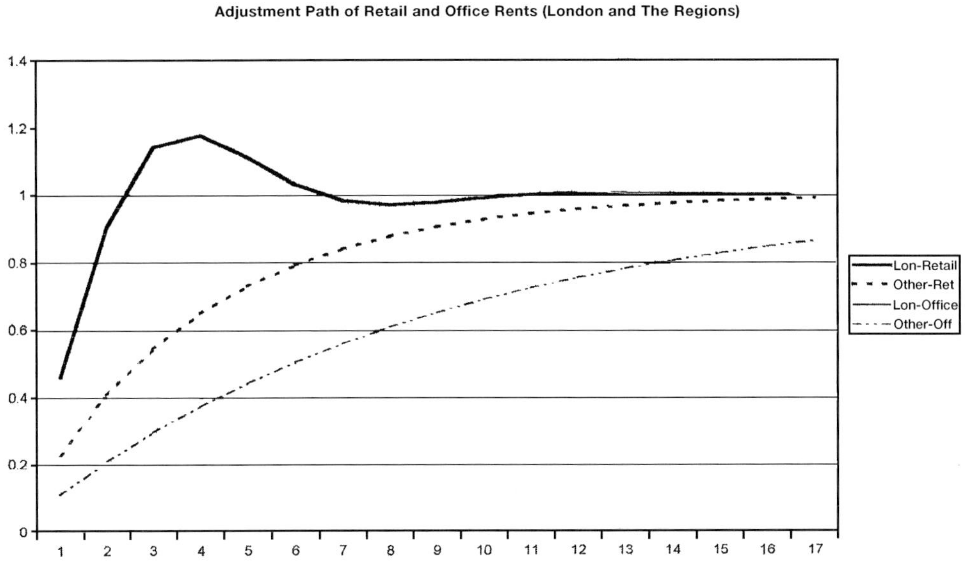

Figure 2. Adjustment path of retail and office rents (London and the regions).

integrating relationships and to use the error correction in the short-run adjustment model. The results are supportive of the error correction formulation: the correction is always highly significant and correctly signed. It always shows partial adjustment with the coefficient being less than unity. The use of lagged real rental change in the short run model has a significant effect in both the London models, resulting in estimates of more adjustment of real rents to shocks in London than in the regions.

The retail market is easiest to model, confirming previous work on "a single" U.K. market with a London factor. All variables are significant in both the long run and short run models. For the office market, supply is significant in the long run model (marginally in the case of London) but insignificant in both short run models. Such problems with office supply are common in the literature. Our economic activity variables are, respectively, consumer expenditures and financial and business services employment, which captures most of the user demand for offices.

We found no justification for separate regional models for areas other than London. This is most likely explained by our use of a different basis for comparison of the markets than in previous studies. Rather than the timing and magnitude of fluctuations in rents or returns, we are interested in property market responses to changes in economic activity and supply. Our firm conclusion is that, with the sole exception of London, the regional markets all behave in broadly the same way. They are driven by fundamental fluctuations in demand and supply and by lagged adjustments towards equilibrium. While the timing and intensity of shocks might vary between the North and South, the response of rents to given shocks is not statistically different.

Appendix 1: Supply data

As the construction completions data start only in 1980 and do not provide sufficient property type disaggregation, they cannot be used in the analysis. The floorspace statistics cover stock of a wide range of quality and were not published for the periods 1987–1993 and 1995 onwards. The Property Research Team of Prudential Portfolio Managers provided its estimates of missing years for some of the series, mainly the retail sector. The new orders series (in constant values) cover the full estimation period.

The floorspace data are not unproblematic. The published figures show (for England and Wales as a whole) percentage changes from 1984–1994 of +28 percent (offices), +22 percent (shops and restaurants) and −43 percent (factories). While the first two figures seem sensible, the fall in factory space, even with the dramatic changes in U.K. manufacturing in the period, seems high. An enquiry to the Department of Environment, Transport and the Regions produced the following explanation in a letter:

> [The] data are perceived as the most comprehensive source of floorspace data for England and Wales. However, since publishing the 1995 publication, several omissions have been identified—these were mainly industrial premises, but several large shops were also omitted. Only a small number of hereditaments were missing (around 1 percent) but these tended to be larger hereditaments. Care should therefore be taken in interpreting the statistics.

Initially it was hoped, for the available sample, to model change in supply as a function of the distributed lags of new orders with a constant rate of depreciation of stock. This could then be used the construct a series for the entire period 1971–1998. The following equation was estimated:

$$\Delta SU_t = \alpha_0 + \sum_{i=1} \alpha_i NO_{t+1-i} - dS_{t-1} \tag{A1}$$

where SU_t is the total stock, NO_t is the new construction orders and d is the constant rate of depreciation. Unfortunately the estimations typically produced poor models with insignificant coefficients, often with incorrect signs and of implausible magnitudes. A variation of the model with new orders divided by existing stock (to scale the supply) yielded similarly poor results. An alternative procedure was used to construct a series representing the total stock of floorspace plus new floorspace under construction. For each series, this proceeded as follows:

The floorspace series was interpolated and extrapolated using, respectively, average geometric growth in the periods 1974–1984 and 1984–1994.

The ratio of the change in the floorspace to new orders was calculated for each year. While there may be significant variations between the two series from year to year, on average this produces a factor to covert new orders (in constant values) to net additions to floorspace. It allows for both the increase in real value through time of a unit of construction work and a constant rate of depreciation of the stock. Particularly in the industrial market the depreciation is likely to have accelerated during the early 1980s but this proved impossible to model.

A time trend regression line was fitted to the ratio and used to construct a time varying conversion factor from value of new orders to floorspace. A simple linear trend was calculated as many of the industrial ratios were negative, thus making a log transformation impossible. Polynomial trends produced unconvincing results.

Starting with the floorspace figures for 1974, the converted new orders series was added each year to estimate a series for 1974–1998 (and subtracted to obtain data for 1970–1973). This means that the log differences of the new series are good estimates of market fluctuations. The new series was checked for its fit in 1984 and 1994. At worst the fit was within five per cent but was generally much lower.

No stock data are available for Scotland so it was assigned the 1974 floorspace of a comparable region and average growth rates applied for regions other than the South East.

Appendix 2: Detailed tables

Table A1. Summary statistics.

	Mean	St Dev	Mean	St Dev	Mean	St Dev
	London		South East		South West	
Retail rents	0.001	0.089	0.016	0.074	0.015	0.085
Office rents	−0.019	0.183	−0.016	0.091	−0.003	0.111
Consumers expenditure	0.022	0.032	0.029	0.029	0.031	0.028
Finance and business services employment	0.019	0.029	0.038	0.033	0.041	0.039
Retail supply	0.012	0.008	0.016	0.008	0.020	0.011
Office supply	0.018	0.013	0.027	0.014	0.035	0.028
	East Anglia		East Midlands		West Midlands	
Retail rents	0.012	0.102	0.013	0.088	0.018	0.089
Office rents	−0.004	0.111	−0.010	0.072	−0.004	0.111
Consumers expenditure	0.029	0.031	0.034	0.031	0.027	0.031
Finance and business services employment	0.038	0.032	0.036	0.033	0.029	0.026
Retail supply	0.021	0.021	0.017	0.018	0.017	0.009
Office supply	0.042	0.059	0.027	0.024	0.029	0.026
	North West		Yorks & Humberside		North	
Retail rents	0.021	0.082	0.005	0.068	0.014	0.058
Office rents	0.001	0.073	0.001	0.071	0.000	0.065
Consumers expenditure	0.024	0.030	0.028	0.025	0.022	0.032
Finance and business services employment	0.021	0.022	0.029	0.024	0.019	0.033
Retail supply	0.012	0.009	0.019	0.025	0.015	0.015
Office supply	0.015	0.012	0.025	0.019	0.015	0.021

Table A1. (*continued*)

	Mean	St Dev	Mean	St Dev
	Wales		Scotland	
Retail rents	0.013	0.076	0.022	0.102
Office rents	– 0.009	0.114	0.006	0.088
Consumers expenditure	0.025	0.026	0.024	0.028
Finance and business services employment	0.016	0.034	0.020	0.027
Retail supply	0.022	0.017	0.017	0.010
Office supply	0.024	0.025	0.033	0.015

Table A2. Order of Integration.

	A/DF	PP	A/DF	PP
	London		South East	
Retail rents	– 4.236 $I(0)$	– 2.705	– 3.294	– 2.861
Office rents	– 2.789 $I(0)$	– 2.694	– 2.822	– 2.634
Consumers expenditure	– 3.128	– 3.168	– 3.585	– 2.964
Finance and business services employment	– 3.066	– 2.666	– 5.328	– 4.548
Retail supply	– 2.958	– 4.775	– 2.963	– 5.243
Office supply	– 3.396	– 4.883	– 2.795	– 4.548
	South West		East Anglia	
Retail rents	– 3.545	– 3.149	– 3.749	– 3.913
Office rents	– 3.153	– 2.944	– 3.371	– 4.027 $I(2)$
Consumers expenditure	– 2.937	– 2.746	– 3.543	– 3.041
Finance and business services employment	– 4.170	– 3.255	– 2.631	– 3.243
Retail supply	– 3.906	– 3.127	– 4.372	– 5.263
Office supply	– 3.183	– 3.306 $I(0)$	– 4.955	– 6.560
	East Midlands		West Midlands	
Retail rents	– 3.371	– 3.438	– 3.354	– 3.928
Office rents	– 2.775	– 4.279 $I(2)$	– 2.638 $I(0)$	– 3.252
Consumers expenditure	– 4.452	– 2.904	– 4.580	– 2.702
Finance and business services employment	– 4.024	– 4.719	– 4.623	– 3.285
Retail supply	– 4.487	– 6.512	– 2.977	– 3.852
Office supply	– 4.839	– 5.828	– 5.474	– 6.521

Table A2. (*continued*)

	A/DF	PP	A/DF	PP
	North West		Yorks & Humberside	
Retail rents	– 5.152	– 3.316	– 3.583	– 3.179
Office rents	– 2.894	– 3.625	– 2.759	– 2.858
Consumers expenditure	– 3.701	– 3.092	– 4.712	– 2.808
Finance and business services employment	– 2.914	– 4.752	– 6.133	– 4.018
Retail supply	– 4.093	– 7.541	– 3.023	– 3.566
Office supply	– 4.465 $I(2)$	– 3.746	– 5.110	– 5.726
	North		Wales	
Retail rents	– 4.116	– 3.825	– 3.026	– 2.978
Office rents	– 3.593	– 3.029	– 3.348	– 3.068
Consumers expenditure	– 3.979	– 3.925	– 3.426	– 3.377
FBS employment	– 2.519	– 2.812	– 3.075	– 5.094
Retail supply	– 7.976	– 9.281	– 4.113 $I(2)$	– 3.464
Office supply	– 3.662	– 7.308	– 4.631	– 7.439
	Scotland		All Regions	
	A/DF	PP	(Levin & Lin procedure)	
Retail rents	– 3.826 $I(0)$	– 2.914 $I(0)$	– 5.561	
Office rents	– 4.149 $I(0)$	– 4.504 $I(0)$	– 5.907	
Consumers expenditure	– 4.566	– 3.631	– 5.959	
FBS employment	– 2.953	– 3.498	– 9.916	
Retail supply	– 5.804	– 5.708	– 3.170	
Office supply	– 3.905	– 6.944	– 1.059 $I(0)$	

All variables are $I(1)$ unless otherwise stated.

Table A3. Panel cointegration diagnostic statistics.

	Retail	Office
Panel v-statistic	2.953	1.016
Panel ρ-statistic	– 0.894	0.266
Panel t-statistic (non-parametric	– 1.714	– 0.319
Panel t-statistic (parametric)	– 1.915	– 0.112
Group ρ-statistic	0.263	1.594
Group t-statistic (non-parametric)	– 1.331	0.520
Group t-statistic (parametric)	– 1.927	0.493

Table A4. Separate retail regional models.

Variable	Coefficient	Standard Error	*t*-Statistic
Long run relationship			
Consumers expenditure			
London	1.58	0.28	5.75***
South East	1.66	0.36	4.61***
South West	1.47	0.14	10.35***
East Anglia	2.09	0.44	4.75***
East Midlands	1.24	0.35	3.54**
West Midlands	1.23	0.48	2.56**
North West	1.48	0.23	6.56***
Yorkshire & Humberside	1.49	0.31	4.86***
North	1.04	0.14	7.38***
Wales	1.56	0.07	22.34***
Scotland	1.64	0.61	2.70*
Supply			
London	−3.48	0.57	−6.15***
South East	−2.09	0.70	−2.99**
South West	−1.68	0.20	−8.23***
East Anglia	−2.14	0.62	−3.46**
East Midlands	−1.55	0.68	−2.28**
West Midlands	−0.48	0.56	−0.87
North West	−1.41	0.41	−3.47**
Yorkshire & Humberside	−1.38	0.36	−3.80***
North	−0.44	0.17	−2.57*
Wales	−0.98	0.07	−14.61***
Scotland	−1.37	0.83	−1.65
Fixed effects			
London	6.02	0.51	11.87***
South East	3.75	0.81	4.66***
South West	1.09	0.30	3.57**
East Anglia	−2.76	1.34	−2.06**
East Midlands	1.48	0.57	2.60**
West Midlands	−0.19	1.09	−0.18
North West	1.01	0.25	4.07***
Yorkshire & Humberside	0.43	0.70	0.62
North	0.41	0.38	1.09
Wales	−1.22	0.23	−5.23***
Scotland	−0.21	1.25	−0.16
Adjusted R^2	99.6%		
Log likelihood	507.99	*F*-statistic	2488.1
DW	0.71	Prob (*F*-stat)	0.00
Short run relationship			
Intercept	−0.01	0.01	−2.10**
ΔConsumers expenditure			
London	1.74	0.36	4.82***
South East	1.27	0.37	3.42**
South West	1.44	0.37	3.91***
East Anglia	1.81	0.58	3.14**
East Midlands	1.40	0.52	2.71*

Table A4. (*continued*)

Variable	Coefficient	Standard Error	*t*-Statistic
Short run relationship (*contd.*)			
ΔConsumers expenditure (*contd.*)			
West Midlands	1.61	0.31	5.21***
North West	1.59	0.29	5.44***
Yorkshire & Humberside	1.31	0.20	6.70***
North	1.08	0.24	4.61***
Wales	1.48	0.18	8.44***
Scotland	1.80	0.65	2.75**
ΔSupply			
London	−2.48	−1.02	−2.42**
South East	−0.72	0.84	−0.85
South West	−0.76	0.46	−1.64
East Anglia	−1.01	0.56	−1.79
East Midlands	−1.30	0.96	−1.35
West Midlands	−0.02	0.62	−0.03
North West	−0.69	0.70	−0.98
Yorkshire & Humberside	−0.42	0.18	−2.37*
North	0.01	0.50	0.01
Wales	−0.65	0.20	−3.32**
Scotland	−0.31	0.70	−0.45
Error correction term			
London	−0.31	0.14	−2.14*
South East	−0.35	0.15	−2.30*
South West	−0.41	0.23	−1.81
East Anglia	−0.52	0.21	−2.43*
East Midlands	−0.25	0.20	−1.26
West Midlands	−0.23	0.19	−1.23
North West	−0.47	0.18	−2.63*
Yorkshire & Humberside	−0.36	0.13	−2.87**
North	−0.45	0.14	−3.09**
Wales	−0.42	0.16	−2.57*
Scotland	−0.39	0.26	−1.49
Adjusted R^2	47.6%		
Log likelihood	548.45	*F*-statistic	9.13
DW	1.57	Prob (*F*-stat)	0.00

Notes. Δ refers to the ''change in'' the value of the variable; two-tailed test, * indicates significant at 5 percent; ** indicates significant at 1 percent; *** indicates significant at 0.1 percent.

Table A5. Retail panel coefficient tests.

	Coefficient	SE		London	REST
LT consumer	1.58	0.27	London		
Expenditures	1.13	0.08	REST	1.61	
	1.04	0.23	North	1.51	0.34
LT supply	– 3.48	0.56	London		
	– 0.84	0.11	REST	– 4.62***	
	– 0.44	0.29	North	– 4.81***	– 1.29
ST consumer	1.55	0.38	London		
Expenditures	1.55	0.14	REST	0.00	
	1.07	0.31	North	0.97	1.41
ST supply	– 3.54	1.37	London		
	– 0.46	0.20	REST	– 2.22*	
	– 0.33	0.73	North	– 2.06*	– 0.16
ECM	– 0.36	0.15	London		
	– 0.23	0.05	REST	– 0.82	
	– 0.46	0.19	North	0.42	1.17

Notes. In each case the null hypothesis is of coefficient equality and one-tailed z-tests are used. * indicates significant at 5 percent; ** indicates significant at 1 percent; *** indicates significant at 0.1 percent.
REST refers to all regions except London and the North.

Table A6. Separate office regional models.

Variable	Coefficient	Standard Error	t-Statistic
Long run relationship			
Finance and business services			
Employment			
London	1.25	1.15	1.09
South East	0.81	0.44	1.85
South West	1.49	0.85	1.75
East Anglia	1.11	0.58	1.90
East Midlands	1.50	0.65	2.29*
West Midlands	1.40	0.98	1.44
North West	1.48	0.28	5.37***
Yorkshire & Humberside	1.59	0.41	3.85***
North	1.07	0.19	5.54***
Wales	0.16	0.54	0.29
Scotland	1.90	0.41	4.62***
Supply			
London	– 2.78	1.26	– 2.20*
South East	– 2.04	0.60	– 3.38**
South West	– 1.62	0.94	– 1.73
East Anglia	– 1.14	0.52	– 2.20*
East Midlands	– 1.88	0.70	– 2.71*
West Midlands	– 1.36	0.95	– 1.43
North West	– 2.12	0.40	– 5.23***
Yorkshire & Humberside	– 1.87	0.48	– 3.94***

Table A6. (*continued*)

Variable	Coefficient	Standard Error	*t*-Statistic
Long run relationship (*contd.*)			
Finance and business services (*contd.*)			
Supply (*contd.*)			
North	– 1.77	0.26	– 6.92***
Wales	– 0.79	0.31	– 2.59*
Scotland	– 1.29	0.30	– 4.27***
Fixed Effects			
London	6.63	2.61	2.54*
South East	7.61	0.41	18.48***
South West	– 0.21	2.52	– 0.09
East Anglia	– 0.17	2.31	– 0.07
East Midlands	– 0.65	2.32	– 0.28
West Midlands	– 0.14	3.09	– 0.05
North West	1.47	0.58	2.52*
Yorkshire & Humberside	– 0.38	1.25	– 0.30
North	0.81	0.71	1.14
Wales	3.95	2.33	1.70
Scotland	– 1.59	1.27	– 1.25
Adjusted R^2	98.8%		
Log likelihood	417.26	F-statistic	947.56
DW	0.47	Prob (F-stat)	0.00
Short run relationship			
Intercept	– 0.04	0.01	– 6.69***
ΔFinance and business			
Services employment			
London	3.59	1.42	2.54*
South East	1.68	0.45	3.74***
South West	1.28	0.64	2.01
East Anglia	1.44	0.46	3.13**
East Midlands	0.97	0.20	4.73***
West Midlands	1.66	0.78	2.14*
North West	2.35	0.53	4.46***
Yorks & Humb	1.35	0.35	3.93***
North	0.81	0.22	3.73***
Wales	0.45	1.17	0.38
Scotland	1.97	0.67	2.93**
ΔSupply			
London	– 1.66	2.58	– 0.64
South East	– 1.29	0.70	– 1.82
South West	– 0.29	0.79	– 0.36
East Anglia	0.20	0.39	0.51
East Midlands	0.10	0.34	0.31
West Midlands	– 0.13	0.63	– 0.20
North West	– 0.60	0.52	– 1.16
Yorkshire & Humberside	0.37	0.25	1.52
North	0.71	0.37	1.91
Wales	0.16	1.11	0.14
Scotland	0.28	0.47	0.61

Table A6. (*continued*)

Variable	Coefficient	Standard Error	*t*-Statistic
Short run relationship (*contd.*)			
Error correction term			
London	−0.11	0.12	−0.85
South East	−0.17	0.08	−2.29
South West	−0.11	0.11	−0.99
East Anglia	−0.15	0.10	−1.47
East Midlands	−0.09	0.05	−1.79
West Midlands	−0.11	0.10	−1.11
North West	−0.13	0.10	−1.39
Yorkshire & Humberside	−0.14	0.06	−2.28**
North	−0.29	0.09	−3.13**
Wales	−0.23	0.16	−1.44
Scotland	−0.27	0.15	−1.81
Adjusted R^2	23.5%		
Log likelihood	465.63	*F*-statistic	3.75
DW	1.06	Prob (*F*-stat)	0.00

Notes. Δ refers to the "change in" the value of the variable; two-tailed test, * indicates significant at 5 percent; ** indicates significant at 1 percent; *** indicates significant at 0.1 percent.

Table A7. Office panel coefficient tests.

	Coefficient	SE		London	REST
LT services	1.25	0.68	London		
Employment	0.51	0.15	REST	1.06	
	0.16	0.50	Wales	1.30	0.68
LT supply	−2.78	0.74	London		
	−0.67	0.16	REST	−2.77**	
	−0.79	0.28	Wales	−2.49**	0.39
ST services	4.20	0.87	London		
Employment	1.18	0.17	REST	3.42**	
	0.12	0.76	Wales	3.55**	1.37
ST supply	0.77	2.23	London		
	0.29	0.22	REST	0.21	
	−0.71	1.15	Wales	0.59	0.86
ECM	−0.04	0.09	London		
	−0.11	0.03	REST	0.68	
	−0.28	0.13	Wales	1.47	1.27

Notes. In each case the null hypothesis is of coefficient equality and one-tailed *z*-tests are used. * indicates significant at 5 percent; ** indicates significant at 1 percent; *** indicates significant at 0.1 percent.

Acknowledgments

The authors would like to thank Angela Black, Ian McAvinchey, George Matysiak, Geoff Meen and Sotiris Tsolacos for advice on some of the finer points of current economietrics, and Peter Pedroni for allowing us to use his program for co-integrating vectors in panel data.

Notes

1. Originally we attempted to explain real industrial rents as well, but with little success. This is probably the consequence of extremely poor data on industrial space (see Appendix 1).
2. Tse and MacGregor (1999) propose a two-equation model of rents and vacancies based on adaptive exceptions.
3. A study that used panel data in an error correction framework is Hort (1998), who analyses a panel of house prices in twenty urban areas in Sweden.
4. Formally: A series with no deterministic trend and which has a stationary and invertible autoregressive moving average (ARMA) representation after differencing d times, but which is not stationary after differencing $d-1$ times, is said to be integrated of order d.

   The components of a vector x_t are said to be co-integrated of order d, b, if x_t is $I(d)$ and there exists a non zero vector α such that $\alpha^T x_t$ is $I(d-b)$, $d >= b > 0$. The vector α is called the co-integrating vector.

   In our models, we are looking for co-integrating relationships among variables that are individually integrated of order one, so the deviation from the equilibrium relationship is integrated of order zero, that is, it is stationary (Banerjee et al., 1993).
5. No rent data are available for Northern Ireland. A variety of changes have recently been made to regional boundaries but this study uses the old regions as rental data are currently available only for these.
6. This is in contrast to work on U.K. property market returns, where differences in the intensity and timing of cycles are crucial (see Hamelink et al., 2000, and Hoesli and MacGregor, 2000).
7. As we are using rental indices as the dependent variables and values as the independent variables, this was necessary to ensure a scaling factor.
8. Our initial strategy was to include three demand variables in each estimation: employment and output measures for the office market and consumer expenditure for the retail market. We expected that, in a competitive land market, there would be interactions among the property types. To avoid problems of collinearity, the second variable was orthogonalized with respect to the first, and the third with respect to the first and second. The estimation strategy was to start with consumer expenditure in the retail market and the better fit of employment and output in the office market. Each of the remaining variables was to be orthogonalized and added, with the most significant remaining to the third stage. In practice, at the second stage none of the orthogonalized variables was significant and correctly signed, although insignificance was by far the more common problem. Similarly, we tested both supply variables (again orthogonalized) in each estimation, but again the other supply variable was neither significant nor correctly signed. Thus, we are left with parsimonious models containing only single demand and supply variables.

   We also considered the possibility of a single competitive land market for both property types. We estimated models with retail and office rents as the dependent variables. Both demand variables and a combined retail and office supply variable were used as independent variables. These were poorer than the final models presented here for each sector. They had incorrectly signed or insignificant variables and most coefficients were significantly different between the models.
9. We use upper case letters for the names of regions (such as North) and lower case letters for broad geographical descriptions covering several regions (such as northern). Detailed results are available from the authors.
10. For all preferred models, the Durbin–Watson statistic suggests serial correlation in the long run models.

Given the use of levels in the long run relationship, this is to be expected. We can still add the co-integrating regression's residuals in the ECM, so long as they are $I(0)$, even if they are autocorrelated (in which case the only implication of autocorrelation is that we cannot make firm inferences about the coefficients in the original co-integrating relationship). If the residuals of the ECM are autocorrelated, it does not matter. The coefficient estimates in the (potentially) co-integrating term will still be unbiased and consistent provided that the residuals are $I(0)$.

11. Charemza and Deadman (1997) suggest that ''... the existence of autocorrlation ... [does] not necessarily imply that something [is] wrong with the model. It might [indicate] the fact that the valid model is an autoregressive distributed lag model with some common factor restrictions present. In this case, such autocorrelation can be regarded as a ''simplification'', not a nuisance (Hendry and Mizon, 1978).''

References

Ball, M., C. Lizieri, and B. D. MacGregor. (1998). *The Economics of Commercial Property Markets.* London: Routledge.

Banerjee, A., J. Dolado, J. W. Galbraith, and D. F. Hendry. (1993). *Co-integration, Error-Correction, and the Econometric Analysis of Non-Stationary Data.* Oxford: Oxford University Press.

Blank, D. M., and L. Winnick. (1953). ''The Structure of the Housing Market,'' *Quarterly Journal of Economics* 67, 181–203.

Charemza, W., and D. F. Deadman. (1997). *New Directions in Econometric Practice.* Cheltenham: Edward Elgar.

D'Arcy, E., T. McGough, and S. Tsolacos. (1997). ''National Economic Trends, Market Size and City Growth Effects on European Office Rents,'' *Journal of Property Research* 14(4), 297–308.

Dobson, S., and J. Goddard. (1992). ''The Determinants of Commercial Property Prices and Rents,'' *Bulletin of Economic Research* 44, 301–321.

Dougherty, C. D. (1992) *Introduction to Econometrics.* New York: Oxford University Press.

Engle, R. F., and C. W. J. Granger. (1987). ''Cointegration and Error Correction: Representation, Estimation and Testing,'' *Econometrica* 55, 251–276.

Fuller, W. A. (1976) *Introduction to Statistical Time Series.* New York: John Wiley.

Gabriel, S. A., and F. E. Nothaft. (1998). ''Rental Housing Markets and the Natural Vacancy Rate,'' *Journal of the American Real Estate and Urban Economics Association,* 16, 419–436.

Gardiner, C., and J. Henneberry. (1988). ''The Development of a Simple Regional Office Rent Prediction Model,'' *Journal of Valuation* 7(1), 36–52.

Gardiner, C., and J. Henneberry. (1991). ''Predicting Regional Office Rents Using Habit-persistence Theories,'' *Journal of Property Valuation and Investment* 9(3), 215–226.

Guissani, B., M. Hsia, and S. Tsolacos. (1993). ''A Comparative Analysis of the Major Determinants of Office Rental Values in Europe,'' *Journal of Property Valuation and Investment* 11(2), 157–173.

Hamelink, F., M. Hoesli, C. Lizieri, and B. D. MacGregor. (2000). ''Homogeneous Commercial Property Market Groupings and Portfolio Construction in the United Kingdom,'' *Environment and Planning A* 32, 323–344.

Harris, R. I. D. (1995). *Using Cointegration Analysis in Econometric Modelling.* London: Prentice Hall.

Hendershott, P. H. (1995). ''Real Effective Rent Determination: Evidence from the Sydney Office Market,'' *Journal of Property Research* 12(2), 127–135.

Hendershott, P. H. (1996). ''Rental Adjustment and Valuation in Overbuilt Markets: Evidence from the Sydney Office Market,'' *Journal of Urban Economics* 39, 51–67.

Hendershott, P. H., C. Lizieri, and G. A. Matysiak. (1999). ''The Workings of the London Office Market,'' *Real Estate Economies* 27(2), 365–387.

Hendry, D. F., and G. E. Mizon. (1978). ''Serial Correlation as a Convenient Simplification, Not a Nuisance: A Comment on a Study of The Demand for Money by the Bank of England,'' *Economic Journal* 88, 549–563.

Hetherington, J. (1988). ''Forecasting of Rents.'' In A. MacLeary, and N. Nanthakumaran (eds.) *Property Investment Theory* (pp. 97–107). London: E. & F. N. Spon.

Hoesli, M. C. Lizieri, and B. D. MacGregor. (1997). ''The Spatial Dimensions of the Investment Performance of UK Commercial Property,'' *Urban Studies* 34(9), 1475–94.

Hoesli, M., and B. D. MacGregor. (2000). *Property investment: The Principles and Practice of Portfolio Management*. Harlow: Pearson Education.

Hort, K. (1998). "The Determinants of Urban House Price Fluctuations in Sweden," *Journal of Housing Economics* 7(2), 93–120.

Key, T., B. D. MacGregor, N. Nanthakumaran, and F. Zarkesh. (1994). *Economic Cycles and Property Cycles, Main Report for Understanding the Property Cycle*. London: RICS.

Levin, A. C., and Lin. (1993). *Unit Root Tests in Panel Data: Asymptotic and Finite-Sample Properties*, mimeo.

McGough, T., and S. Tsolacos. (1995). "Forecasting Commercial Rental Values in the UK Using ARIMA Models," *Journal of Property Valuation and Investment* 13(5), 5–21.

Pedroni, P. (1999). "Critical Values for Cointegration Tests in Heterogeneous Panels with Multiple Regressors," *Oxford Bulletin of Economics and Statistics* 16(s1), 653–670.

Pedroni, P. (1997). *Panel Cointegration: Asymptotic and Finite Sample Properties of Pooled Time Series Tests with an Application to the PPP Hypothesis: New Results*, Working Paper, Indiana University.

Perron, P. (1988). "Trends and Random Walks in Macroeconomic Time Series: Further Evidence from a New Approach," *Journal of Economic Dynamics and Control* 12, 1361–1401

Phillips, P. C. B. (1987). "Time Series Regression with a Unit Root," *Econometrica* 55, 277–301.

Phillips, P. C. B., and P. Perron. (1988). "Testing for a Unit Root in Time Series Regressions," *Biometrika* 75, 335–346.

Pollakowski, H. O., S. M. Wachter, and L. Lynford. (1992). "Did Office Size Matter in the 1980s? A Time Series Cross-Sectional Analysis of Metropolitan Area Office Markets," *Journal of the American Real Estate and Urban Economics Association* 20(2), 303–324.

RICS. (1999). *The UK Property Cycle—a History from 1921 to 1997*. London: Royal Institution of Chartered Surveyors.

Rosen, K. T. (1984). "Towards a Model of the Office Building Sector," *Journal of the American Real Estate and Urban Economics Association* 12(3), 261–269.

Rosen, K. T., and L. B. Smith. (1984). "The Price Adjustment Process for Rental Housing and the Natural Vacancy Rate," *American Economic Review* 73, 779–786.

Shilling, J. D., C. F. Sirmans, and J. B. Corgel. (1987). "Price Adjustment Process for Rental Office Space," *Journal of Urban Economics* 22, 90–100.

Shilling, J. D., C. F. Sirmans, and J. B. Corgel. (1992). "Natural Office Vacancy Rates: Some Additional Estimates," *Journal of Urban Economics* 31, 140–143.

Silver, M., and M. Goode. (1990). "Econometric Forecasting Model for Rents in the British Retail Property Market," *International Journal of Management Science* 18(5) 529–539.

Smith, L. B. (1969). "A Model of the Canadian Housing and Mortgage Markets," *The Journal of Political Economy* 77, 795–816.

Smith, L. B. (1974). "A Note on the Price Adjustment Mechanism for Rental Housing," *American Economic Review* 64, 478–481.

Thompson, B., and S. Tsolacos. (1999). "Rental Adjustment and Forecasts in the Industrial Market," *Journal of Real Estate Research* 17(1/2), 151–168.

Tsolacos, S., G. Keogh, and T. McGough (1998). "Modelling Use, Investment and Development in the British Office Market," *Environment and Planning A* 30, 1409–1427.

Tse, R. Y. C., and B. D. MacGregor (1999). "Housing Vacancy and Rental Adjustment: Evidence from Hong Kong," *Urban Studies* 36, 1769–1782.

Wheaton, W. C. (1987). "The Cyclic Behavior of the National Office Market," *Journal of the American Real Estate and Urban Economics Association* 15(4), 281–299.

Wheaton, W. C., and R. G. Torto (1988). "Vacancy Rates and the Future of Office Rents," *Journal of the American Real Estate and Urban Economics Association* 16(4), 430–436.

Wheaton, W. C., R. G. Torto, and P. Evans (1997). "The Cyclic Behavior of the Greater London Office Market," *The Journal of Real Estate Finance and Economics* 15(1), 77–92.

Journal of Real Estate Finance and Economics, 24:1/2, 89–101, 2002

The Value of the Rent Control Option

DANNY BEN-SHAHAR
The Arison School of Business, The Interdisciplinary Center Herzliya, P.O. Box 167, Herzliya 46150, Israel
E-mail: danny@idc.ac.il

DAVID FELDMAN
Department of Business Administration, School of Management, Ben-Gurion University of the Negev, P.O. Box 653, Beer-Sheva 84105, Israel
E-mail: feldmand@bgumail.bgu.ac.il

DORON GREENBERG
Neger College, Hof Ashkelon 79165, Israel
E-mail: dorogre@post.tau.a-c.il

Abstract

In this paper, we combine direct arbitrage arguments and an option-pricing approach to develop a method of pricing the option for rent control. For a lump-sum payment of ''key money,'' a tenant acquires the right to rent a real estate unit for an exogenously determined controlled rent, as opposed to paying the free-market rent. The tenant may continue exercising this right as long as he or she lives. Alternatively, the tenant may sell the right to occupy the controlled rent unit and receive a fraction of the key money paid by the subsequent tenant. We value the equilibrium key money, in a representative agent's partial equilibrium, while endogenously determining the expected tenure duration in a controlled rent unit. We propose a procedure for valuing rent control options different from the representative agent's. Our analysis shows that under real-world levels of ''conditional life expectancy,'' the level of the fraction of the key money retained by a departing tenant has an insignificant effect on the expected tenure duration in a controlled rent unit and on the level of key money.

Key Words: rent control, option pricing, key money, tenure duration, conditional life expectancy

1. Introduction

This paper combines direct arbitrage arguments and an option-pricing approach to develop a method of pricing the option for rent control. We value the equilibrium key money, in a representative agent's partial equilibrium, while endogenously determining the expected tenure duration in a controlled rent unit. We analyze the results and propose a procedure for valuing rent control options different from the representative agent's. Under real-world levels of ''conditional life expectancy,'' the level of the fraction of the key money retained by a departing tenant has an insignificant effect on the expected tenure duration in a controlled rent unit and on the level of key money.

Although rent control policies worldwide have various forms and characteristics, most have two dominant features in common: rent payments are capped, and tenants ordinarily cannot be evicted. Hence, under the typical rent-control program, a tenant earns the right to periodically pay the controlled rent in exchange for housing services, along with the right to do so repetitively in the future. Put differently, at the beginning of every period, the tenant decides whether to extend the lease and thereby pay the controlled rent or to leave the dwelling unit.[1]

The rent control option has significant economic value. In fact, some rent-control systems permit tenants to transfer their right to reside under rent control in exchange for cash. In this case, the departing tenant transfers tenancy rights to a subsequent tenant, who, in return, delivers a lump-sum payment, referred to as key money. The departing tenant often shares this lump-sum payment with the landlord. Even in economies in which the payment of key money is legally restricted, it sometimes prevails in the black or gray markets.

The purpose of this paper is to evaluate the right to reside under rent control. One can view this right as a series of compounded call options. The underlying asset is housing services for the period, and the strike price is the controlled rent.

Our analysis combines arbitrage pricing considerations and an option-pricing approach. In essence, we value the key money. The value of the rent control option is a function of several variables: the level of the free market rent, the level of the controlled-rent, the rate of interest, the percentage of the key money received by a departing tenant (the residual goes to the landlord), the expected tenure duration, and tenants' life expectancy.

As the levels of both the free market rent and the controlled rent may change randomly over time, the value of the rent control option depends on the dynamic difference between the two. Hence, if we describe this difference as a stochastic process, the value of the rent control option would further depend on parameters of this process, including its volatility.

We first value the key money using no-arbitrage considerations. This, however, leaves us with the expected tenure duration undetermined. We view this duration as that of the representative tenant and then use an option-pricing approach to analyze the problem. When both approaches result in similar key money value and average tenure duration, we have a closure to the model.

The arbitrage-pricing conditions require that there will be no arbitrage in acquiring a dwelling unit in the free market and then renting it out under rent control. Nor should there be arbitrage in acquiring the right to a dwelling unit under rent control and leasing it in the free market. The option-pricing approach values the tenant's privilege, each period, to "leave" or "stay"; that is, to leave the rent controlled dwelling unit, get his or her fraction of key money, and start paying free market rent or to pay the controlled rent for the current period and postpone the leave-or-stay decision for next period.

Several authors apply option-pricing tools to evaluate lease contracts. Grenadier (1995) uses a real-option approach to value a variety of lease-based contingent claims. His work emphasizes the endogenous determination of the term structure of lease rates in a model consistent with general equilibrium, including specifications of market demand, demand shocks, and construction costs. Our approach is more closely related to that of McConnell and Schallheim (1983). Although they, too, do not specifically value the rent-control option, they do provide a framework for valuing asset-leasing contracts as a compounded option.

Our model may be applied to value the rent control option, while allowing a departing tenant to receive a fraction of an endogenously determined key money paid by a subsequent tenant. Moreover, by using an alternative valuation procedure, the model endogenously and simultaneously determines the expected tenure duration in a rent-controlled unit.

One can view a rent control contract as a form of limited ownership. Indeed, there is a partial equivalence between mortgage and rent control contracts: (1) the down payment on the mortgage is parallel to the key money for the rent control contract, (2) the mortgage payments are parallel to the controlled-rent payments, and (3) the net proceeds, after loan repayments at disposition, are equivalent to the portion of the key money received upon departing from the rental unit. Yet, there are two key differences: (1) the equity under the mortgage contract increases deterministically toward a fixed horizon, while the equity under rent control remains constant over time and is sold when the (ex-ante random) conditional life expectancy is sufficiently low; and (2) mortgage service payments are contracted at the initiation of the loan, while the level of rent control and the difference between the free-market rent and controlled rent are random.[2]

In Section 2 of this paper, we present the model in which we simultaneously determine the price of key money and the expected tenure duration. In Section 3, we present several simulation results. The paper ends with conclusions in Section 4.

2. The model

We define a ''free rent market'' as a market where dwelling units are leased for an exogenous fluctuating periodic ''free market rent.'' We define a ''controlled rent market'' as a market where dwelling units are available for an initial lump sum of ''key money'' followed by a flow of an exogenous periodic ''controlled market rent.'' A controlled rent contract allows the tenant, after paying the key money, to occupy the dwelling unit as long as he or she lives and pays the controlled market rent periodically. It also allows the tenant to transfer rights in the dwelling unit to another tenant for a lump sum of key money, a fraction of which goes to the landlord.

Suppose that free rent and controlled rent competitive markets coexist, without depreciation, taxes, and other transaction costs.[3] Then, a no arbitrage condition for homeowners implies that the cost of a dwelling unit should be equal to the value of ''selling'' it for key money and receiving the stream of controlled rent and future key money portions. If the value of a dwelling unit is the present value of the stream of future free market rent payments it would generate, the homeowner's no arbitrage condition must sustain the following condition:[4]

$$\mathrm{PV}\left(\sum_{t=0}^{\infty} RF_t\right) = P + \mathrm{PV}\left(\sum_{t=0}^{\infty} RC_t\right) + \sum_{j=1}^{\infty} \mathrm{PV}\Big((1-\alpha)P_{jt^*}\Big), \tag{1}$$

where $\mathrm{PV}(\cdot)$ is a present value operator, RF_t, RC_t, and P_t are the free market rent, controlled rent, and the value of key money, respectively, at period t; t^* is the expected tenure duration of a representative tenant in a controlled rent unit; P_{jt^*} is the value of key money j times t^* periods from time $t=0$; and α is the departing tenant's share in the key money paid by a succeeding tenant. To simplify notation, we omit a variable's time subscript when we refer to its current value; that is, its $t=0$ value.

Thus, Condition (1) asserts that one cannot generate arbitrage profits from purchasing a real estate unit and renting it out under a rent control program.

An equivalent condition from the perspective of a tenant who occupies a rent controlled dwelling unit for ''one cycle'' is as follows:

$$\mathrm{PV}\left(\sum_{t=0}^{t^*-1} RF_t\right) = P + \mathrm{PV}\left(\sum_{t=0}^{t^*-1} RC_t\right) - \mathrm{PV}(\alpha P_{t^*}). \tag{2}$$

Condition (2) asserts that the tenant's costs of renting in the free market are equal to his or her costs under controlled rent. In other words, the stream of free market rent payments (on the left-hand side of equation (2)) must equal the value of key money, plus the value of the stream of controlled rent payments, minus the value of the tenant's share in the key money that the succeeding tenant will pay (on the right-hand side of equation (2))—all in present value terms.

We now posit a flat term structure for the interest rate representing the appropriate risk for the cash flows involved and an interest rate r. In addition, we assume that $\mathrm{PV}(RC_t) = e^{-rt}RC$, $\mathrm{PV}(RF_t) = e^{-rt}RF$, and that $\mathrm{PV}(P_{t^*}) = e^{-rt^*}P$, where RF and P are the corresponding values when the present value operators are applied. In the first equation, we assume that RC_t is a constant equal to RC for every t. We lose no generality by this assumption because the value of the rent control option depends on the difference between the free-market rent and the controlled rent and not on their particular values. The second assumption implies that the expected value of the free market rent at any time in the future equals its current value. This is the case when the stochastic process of the free market rent is a Martingale. Similarly, the last assumption implies that the expected value of key money at a future date (which depends on the prevailing market rent) equals the time zero key money value, which is, once again, its expected value when the free market rent process is a Martingale.

Now equation (2) becomes

$$P = \frac{1 - e^{-rt^*}}{1 - \alpha e^{-rt^*}}\left(\frac{RF - RC}{1 - e^{-r}}\right). \tag{3}$$

Equation (3) expresses the no-arbitrage condition for the value of key money as a function of several relevant variables. The intuition underlying equation (3) is straightforward. When $\alpha = 1$—that is, when a departing tenant receives the entire lump sum of key money paid by a subsequent tenant—equation (3) is reduced to $P = (RF_t - RC)/(1 - e^{-r})$. Hence, the value of key money is the present value of the infinite sum of the difference between the periodical market rent and the periodical controlled rent. Moreover, since $\alpha = 1$ denotes the case where a departing tenant exclusively gets the entire key money paid by a subsequent tenant, the value of the key money is independent of t^*. When $\alpha = 0$, equation (3) becomes $P = (1 - e^{-rt^*})(RF - RC)/(1 - e^{-r})$. Then, when $t^* \to \infty$—that is when a tenant is expected to never vacate the dwelling unit—equation (3) once again becomes $P = (RF - RC)/(1 - e^{-r})$. Not surprisingly, this is identical to the case where $\alpha = 1$. The intuition is simple: as key money is paid more (less) frequently, the value of the key money must decrease (increase) to compensate for the housing costs.

To explicitly evaluate P given the variables on the right-hand side of equation (3), one should endogenously derive t^*, the expected tenure duration. The levels of the exogenous parameters α, RF_0, and RC simultaneously affect this optimal expected occupancy period, which in turn affects the value of P.

Because it is sufficient to model either the free-market rent or the controlled rent as a stochastic process, we choose to model RF_t as a stochastic process to more closely resemble the real world. We also assume that α is constant, which is occasionally the case in the real world. The tractability of the model, however, does not depend on these assumptions.

We develop a binomial tree[5] option-pricing approach as a complement to the arbitrage-pricing considerations that we summarized in equation (3). We claim that the key money P is the value of the right to rent a real estate unit and pay the controlled rent instead of the free market rent, and, in addition, to decide each period whether to extend this right or sell it. In other words, at each node of the binomial tree, the tenant faces a decision of whether to pay the controlled rent and thereby extend occupancy for another period, or to cease payments, vacate the unit, and receive a share of the key money paid by the subsequent tenant.

We use a discrete-time equivalent of an Ornstein–Uhlenbeck process to describe the dynamics of RF_t and follow the procedure developed in Nelson and Ramaswamy (1990).

Consider the Ornstein–Uhlenbeck process describing the evolution of the free market rent:

$$dRF_t = \delta(\gamma - RF_t)dt + \sigma dW_t, \tag{4}$$

where $\{W_t,\ t \geq 0\}$ is a Wiener process, $W_0 = 0$, and δ, γ, and σ are positive constants. This process reverts to the long-term mean γ, at a speed of adjustment δ, with an instantaneous standard deviation σ, for a given initial condition RF_0.

While we model a stochastic process for the free-market rent, the key money value is, in fact, generated from the difference between the free-market rent and the controlled rent. Thus, the choice of the process for the free-market rent should resemble the properties of this difference. In assuming the Ornstein–Uhlenbeck process, we assert that this difference is both stochastic and stable; that is, this difference exhibits continuous shocks but tends to revert to an asymptotic value. In addition, and in contrast to a random walk, its variance is bounded.

According to Nelson and Ramaswamy (1990), we define a binomial approximation to (4), such that the up step, RF^u_{t+1}, and the down step, RF^d_{t+1}, are

$$RF^u_{t+1} = RF_t + \sigma \quad \text{and} \quad RF^d_{t+1} = RF_t - \sigma, \tag{5}$$

the probability, q_t, of an up step, RF^u_{t+1}, is

$$q_t = \begin{cases} 0.5 + \delta(\gamma - RF_t)/2\sigma & \text{if} \quad 0 \le 0.5 + \delta(\gamma - RF_t)/2\sigma \le 1 \\ 0 & \text{if} \quad 0.5 + \delta(\gamma - RF_t)/2\sigma < 0, \\ 1 & \text{otherwise} \end{cases} \tag{6}$$

and the probability of a down step, RF^d_{t+1}, is $1 - q_t$.

Recall that P in equation (3) is the value of the rent control option for a representative tenant who enters a controlled rent real estate unit. The representative agent's expected tenure duration is t^* (t^* is determined endogenously). Now, when using the binomial option-pricing approach, we also value P_t (see equation (7) below), which is the value of the rent control option for a tenant already occupying a controlled rent dwelling unit, and is a function of the expected remaining tenure horizon.

We assume the existence of risk-neutral probabilities when we value the rent control option. Formally, at any node at time t, the value of the rent control option for a tenant occupying a controlled rent dwelling unit is

$$P_t = \max\left[RF_t - RC + \frac{q_t P^u_{t+1} + (1 - q_t)P^d_{t+1}}{e^r}, \alpha P(RF_t)\right], \tag{7}$$

where the probability q_t is defined in (6), RF_t, RC, α, and r are as defined earlier, max[•] is the maximum value operator, and P^u_{t+1} and P^d_{t+1} are time $t+1$ rent control option values following, respectively, an up or down move in the free market rent.

In the brackets on the right-hand side of equation (7), the term to the left of the comma is the value of the option to extend occupancy in the controlled rent dwelling unit by an additional period. It is equal to the difference between the current market rent and the controlled rent, plus the present expected value of the option in the next period. The term to the right of the comma is the tenant's share in the key money, substituted from equation (3a) below, which the tenant receives if he or she decides to vacate the unit.

We will now develop equation (3a), which is a modified version of equation (3), designed to reflect the mean-reversion property of the free rent process as specified by equation (4). We first argue that the mean of the free rent process at time s, $\mathrm{E}(RF_s)$, conditional on its time τ, $s > \tau$, realization, RF_τ, is

$$E(RF_s | RF_\tau) = \gamma + (RF_\tau - \gamma)e^{-\delta(s-\tau)}$$

(see, for example, Arnold, 1974: 134). The intuition underlying equation (8) is straightforward. For periods sufficiently close to the starting period (that is, when $s - \tau$ is small), the conditional mean is dominated by the initial condition RF_τ. However, as s grows, the conditional mean shifts from its initial condition, RF_τ, to the long-term mean γ

at an exponential rate of δ, the process' rate of adjustment. Applying equation (8) we can write the "mean-reversion equivalent" of equation (2),

$$\mathrm{PV}\left(\sum_{t=0}^{t^*-1}(\gamma + (RF-\gamma)e^{-\delta t})\right) = P + \mathrm{PV}\left(\sum_{t=0}^{t^*-1} RC_t\right) - \mathrm{PV}\big(\alpha P(\mathrm{E}(RF_{t^*}))\big). \tag{2a}$$

The difference between the left-hand sides of equations (2) and (2a) was explained in the previous paragraph. The explanation for the difference in the third term on the right-hand side of equation (2a) is that the random process that drives RF_t in equation (2) is a Martingale. Because the expected value of the free market rent at t^* is its value at $t = 0$, we assume that the key money at $t = 0$ and at t^* are the same. However, under the mean-reversion process used in equation (2a), a similar situation occurs only when RF_t at $t = 0$ is at its long-term mean γ. This might not be the case, and the key money at $t = 0$ and at t^* might differ because of different deviations of the free market rent from its long-term mean corresponding to those dates. Consequently, the mean-reversion equivalent of equation (3) is

$$P(RF, t^*) = \left(\frac{1-e^{-rt^*}}{1-e^{-r}}(\gamma - RC) + \frac{1-e^{-(r+\delta)t^*}}{1-e^{-(r+\delta)}}(RF-\gamma)\right) + \alpha e^{-rt^*} P(\mathrm{E}(RF_{t^*}), t^*). \tag{3a}$$

Note that when the free market rent is at its long-term mean (that is, when $RF = \gamma$), equation (3a) degenerates to equation (3). Next, assume that RF is only one step above the long-term mean. Then, one can assume that at t^* the free market rent process will already be at its long-term mean. The value of key money when the free market rent is at its long-term mean was determined earlier and can be substituted in the right-hand side of equation (3a). Then, one can solve for the value of the key money when the free market rent is a one-step deviation from its long-term mean. Now, one could repeat this procedure for a free market rent that is two steps away from its long-term mean. For this, one would use the value of the key money when the free market rent is at its long-term mean and the value of the key money when the free market rent is one step away from the long-term mean. One could repeat this procedure to produce values of key money for a grid of free market rent values.

Of course, the value of the rent control option under the two approaches—represented by P in equations (3a) and by P_t in equation (7)—must be identical when the time to maturity of the rent control option is t^*. Hence, we reach the solution to our problem by using equation (3a) to generate key money values for a given series of t^* and substituting these generated key money values into the right-hand side of equation (7). If the value of the key money produced by equation (7) coincides with that produced by equation (3a) and, in addition, if the expected tenure duration calculated *ex-post* from the solution to equation (7) matches the t^* plugged into equation (3a), we have a solution. The monotonic nature of the values in the problem results in a unique solution.

An interesting aspect of this model is that the *ex-ante* total number of periods in our binomial tree is affected by the representative tenant's life expectancy at any time-period of the tree. Particularly, at each node, we look at the tenant's remaining life expectancy and thereby determine the length of the tree. Because one's conditional life expectancy does not necessarily diminish by precisely one year when a calendar year passes, (it might diminish by either more or less than a year and sometimes might even increase), the length of the tree need not correspond to the representative tenant's *ex-ante* unconditional life expectancy when first occupying the rent control unit. We refer to such a tree as a ''conditional life expectancy tree.'' We differentiate it from a regular tree (the unconditional life expectancy tree), where the length of the tree equals the tenant's life expectancy upon taking occupancy in the controlled rent unit. It follows that the length of the ''conditional life expectancy'' tree is greater than that of the unconditional life expectancy tree. We assume that whenever the conditional life expectancy declines to one year, the tenant sells his or her rights to the controlled rent unit.

Moreover, in our rational expectations equilibrium, the endogenously determined t^* variable must hold both *ex-ante* and *ex-post*. Thus, by accounting for both the nodes on the binomial tree where the tenant selects to vacate the real estate unit and the probabilities of reaching those nodes, we calculate the value of t^*. The solutions to our problem show that the value of the *ex-post* calculated t^* equals the value of the parameter t^*, originally used in the pricing of P in equation (3a).

3. Analysis

We first examine the nodes of the binomial tree where the tenant chooses to vacate the real estate unit before the end of his or her ex-ante life expectancy. It turns out that while the number of departures along the tree depends on the particular parameters of the model, each of the early departures is contingent upon the value of the free market rent being sufficiently small compared to the controlled rent.

Intuitively, at every node of the tree, where RF is small compared to RC, the tenant must choose between two alternatives: (1) remaining in the controlled rent unit for one additional period and, thereby, losing the difference $RC - RF$ but gaining the value of having the option to stay or leave in the next period, and (2) moving out and, thereby, getting a share of the key money. Under both alternatives, the value of the option represents the long-term benefit of rent control relative to the free market rent, but the alternatives also provide these values with a gap of one period. Nonetheless, when RF and the ''conditional life expectancy'' are small enough, the cost associated with occupying the unit for one period is high enough to generate an incentive to vacate the unit.

Before analyzing the effect of the parameters on the attained equilibrium, it is important to note that except for σ, all of the model parameters simultaneously affect both equilibrium conditions expressed in equations (3a) and (7). Hence, a change in any one of these model parameters results in a new equilibrium, characterized by the couplet P and t^*. Put differently, we cannot perform a comparative statics analysis in its usual sense because any change in the value of a parameter causes a ''dynamic'' change in the equilibrium. In other words, the requirement that the value of one parameter changes while values of other parameters ''remain equal'' cannot be satisfied here.[6] Tables 1a and 1b list the equilibrium levels of P and t^* for a series of values of α and two different levels of the ''conditional life expectancy,'' T. Notice that while P consistently increases with α, the effect of α on t^* is ambiguous: when the ''conditional life expectancy'' (determining the length of the binomial tree) is sufficiently small (large), then t^* diminishes (increases) with α. This trend is robust with respect to changes in the other parameters' values in this model.

Intuitively, the greater the departing tenant's share in the key money paid by a subsequent tenant, the greater the value of the rent control option. However, notice from Tables 1a and 1b that the relative increase in P is more substantial as the ''conditional life expectancy'' falls. That is, while P in Table 1a increases from 11,055 (for $\alpha = 40$ percent) to 16,809 ($\alpha = 80$ percent)—a total increase of about 50 percent, it increases by less than 1 percent for the respective values of α in Table 1b (from 22,487 to 22,646). The intuition underlying this result is that the share in the key money, αP, is obtained only upon departure; however, when the ''conditional life expectancy'' grows large, the present value of the key money payment becomes less significant and the effect of α diminishes.

Finally, we test the effect of the parameter δ on the price of the rent control option. Recall that δ is the exponential rate of adjustment of RF_t to the long-term mean, γ. In Figures 1a, 1b, 2a, and 2b we present the change in the value of the rent control option as a function of the ''conditional life expectancy'', T, for two distinct values of δ and RF_0. In Figures 1a (2a) and 1b (2b) the initial value of the free market rent, RF_0, is below (above) its long-term mean.

Not surprisingly, we find that when RF_0 is below its long-term mean (as in Figures 1a and 1b, where $RF_0 = 2{,}400$ and $\gamma = 3{,}000$), the value of the rent control option both increases more rapidly with T and converges to a greater value when δ rises. This, of

Table 1. Equilibrium values of P and t^* for different values of α when (a) $T = 10$, (b) $T = 90$, $r = 4.5$ percent, $\sigma = 146$, $RF_0 = 3{,}000$, $RC = 2{,}000$, $\delta = 0.0625$, and $\gamma = 3{,}000$.

	α	P	t^*
(a)			
	0.4	11,055	9.999
	0.5	12,090	9.999
	0.6	13,338	9.999
	0.7	14,873	9.996
	0.8	16,809	9.995
(b)			
	0.4	22,487	89.957
	0.5	22,526	89.966
	0.6	22,566	89.969
	0.7	22,606	89.975
	0.8	22,646	89.978

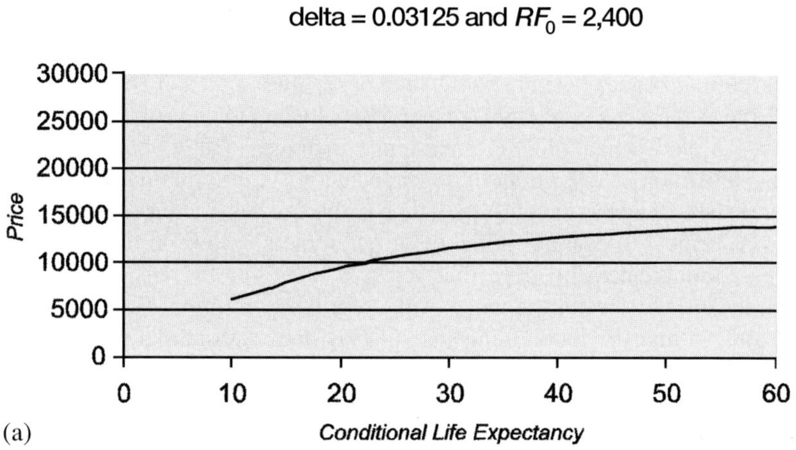

(a)

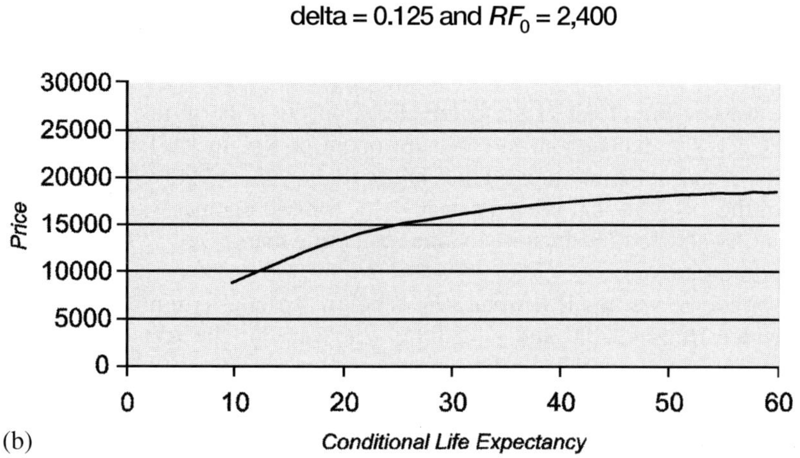

(b)

Figure 1. (a) The price of the rent control option as a value of the ''conditional life expectancy'', T, when $RF_0 = 2{,}400$, $\delta = 0.03125$, $\gamma = 3{,}000$, $RC = 2{,}000$, $\alpha = 0.5$, $r = 4.5$ percent $\sigma = 4.88$ percent. (b) The price of the rent control option as a value of the ''conditional life expectancy'', T, when $RF_0 = 2{,}400$, $\delta = 0.125$, $\gamma = 3{,}000$, $RC = 2{,}000$, $\alpha = 0.5$, $r = 4.5$ percent, $\sigma = 4.88$ percent.

course, follows the fact that the faster the relatively low free market rent adjusts to its higher long-term mean, the greater is the value of the option to rent control and the faster this value is reached, *ceteris paribus*.

Conversely, when RF_0 is above its long-term mean (as in Figures 2a and 2b, where $RF_0 = 3{,}600$ and $\gamma = 3{,}000$), the value of the rent control option, while increasing in T, both converges to a lower value and reaches that value faster when δ increases. Once again, this is a result of the faster adjustment to the long-term mean associated with a greater δ.

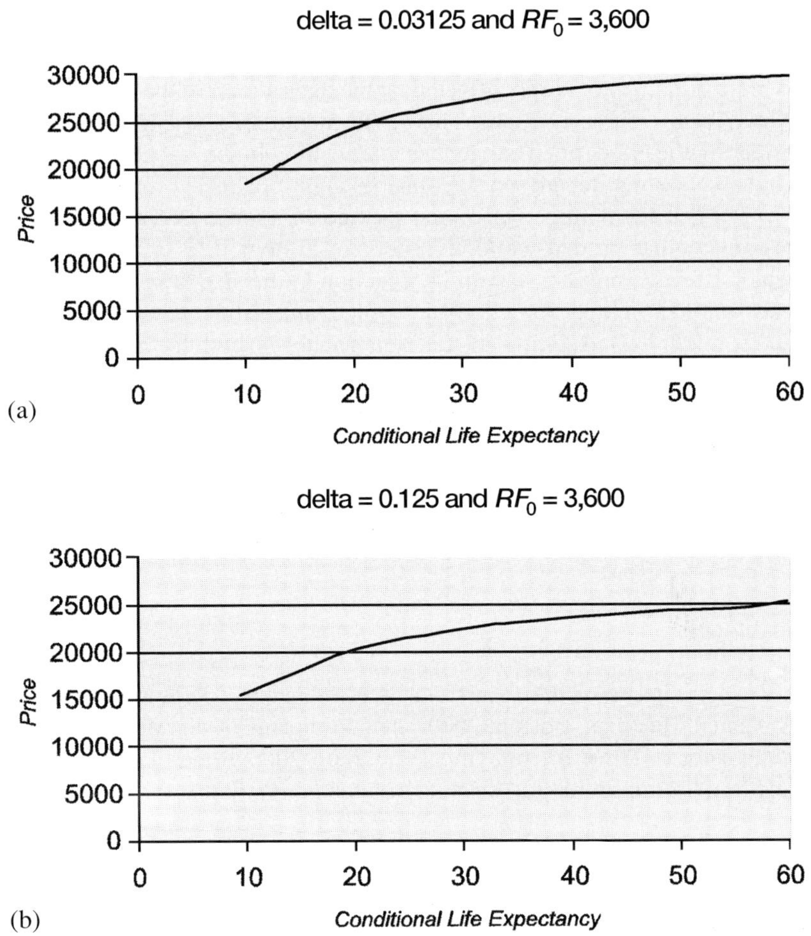

Figure 2. (a) The price of the rent control option as a value of the ''conditional life expectancy'', T, when $RF_0 = 3{,}600$, $\delta = 0.03125$, $\gamma = 3{,}000$, $RC = 2{,}000$, $\alpha = 0.5$, $r = 4.5$ percent $\sigma = 4.88$ percent (b) The price of the rent control option as a value of the ''conditional life expectancy'', T, when $RF_0 = 3{,}600$, $\delta = 0.125$, $\gamma = 3{,}000$, $RC = 2{,}000$, $\alpha = 0.5$, $r = 4.5$ percent, $\sigma = 4.88$ percent.

4. Summary and conclusion

We combine direct arbitrage arguments with an option-pricing approach to develop a method for valuing the rent control option. This method concurrently solves for the expected tenure duration in a controlled rent real estate asset.

While we assume that the free market rent evolves as an Ornstein–Uhlenbeck process, our suggested methodology applies to a wide class of diffusions. Also, if the data suggests it is worthwhile, a more sophisticated term structure model might replace our simplified assumption of a flat term structure.

An interesting result derived from the simulation of the model is that for a sufficiently long "conditional life expectancy," the equilibrium levels of both the key money and the expected tenure duration are hardly affected by the distribution of the key money between the departing tenant and the landlord. This result might become important, for instance, when considering the effect of an exogenous intervention in the fraction of the key money retained by a departing tenant on the tax revenues collected from controlled rent transactions or when attempting to affect the average duration in a controlled rent unit. Our results thus predict that for real-world levels of "conditional life expectancy," there will be only minor effects, implying that an intervention in the size of α is redundant.

There are several natural directions in which one might extend the model. Tax considerations might lead to significant additional analysis: both the implications of after-tax cash flows and of differential tax treatment for landlords and tenants. Furthermore, the exercise of the tenant's option to terminate the rent control contract might create a taxable effect to the landlord, which, in turn, might affect the landlord's optimal tax-deductible investments in the property. Another extension might further differentiate the risk adjustment to the cash flows. We believe, however, that empirical results should guide further analytical extensions.

Acknowledgments

We thank the participants of the Rent Control and Land Use Regulations session at the AREUEA Annual Meetings, Boston, 2000; the participants of the Maastricht-Cambridge Real Estate Finance and Investment Symposium, June, 2000; Robert Edelstein, Linda Hutz Pesante, and Ben Scafidi for helpful discussions; and Nir Parikman for research assistance.

Notes

1. Arnott (1995) provides a comprehensive review of rent control programs. Also, Malpezzi (1993) and Arnott and Mintz (1987) describe various rent control programs worldwide.
2. Even when the mortgage loan rate is variable, the changes in the mortgage service payments will not be perfectly correlated with the level of the controlled rent nor with the difference between the free-market rent and the controlled rent.
3. In fact, it is straightforward to incorporate transaction costs into the model, as long as they are deterministic over time.
4. Extracting arbitrage profits requires the existence of a liquid market for transferring future rent to a current lump sum, through, for example, housing management companies. Otherwise, the following equation will be a regular pricing relation.
5. The tree is binomial in the sense that each node yields two branches (see Cox et al., 1979). We do not restrict ourselves to the binomial distribution, however.
6. Consider, for example, the effect of changes in the fraction of the key money retained by a departing tenant, α, and examine the right-hand side of equation (7). Notice that a change in α has a direct effect on the term of the Maximum operator on the right-hand side. As can be seen from equation (3a), however, a change in α also has a direct effect on the value of the key money, P, which by itself affects the right-hand side of equation (7). It thus follows that a change in α simultaneously affects the equilibrium levels of the key money, P, and the expected tenure duration, t^*.

References

Arnold, L. (1974). *Stochastic Differential Equations: Theory And Applications*. New York: John Wiley and Sons.

Arnott, R. J. (1995). ''Time for Revisionism on Rent Control?'' *Journal of Economic Perspectives* 9, 99–120.

Arnott, R. J., and J. M. Mintz (ed.) (1987). *Rent Control: The International Experience*. Ontario: John Deutsch Institute.

Cox, J. C., S. A. Ross, and M. Rubinstein. (1979). ''Option Pricing: A Simplified Approach,'' *Journal of Financial Economics* 7, 229–263.

Grenadier, S. R. (1995). ''Valuing Lease Contracts: A Real-Options Approach,'' *Journal of Financial Economics* 38, 297–331.

Malpezzi, S. (1993). ''Can New York and Los Angeles learn from Kumasi and Bangalore? Costs and benefits of rent controls in developing countries,'' *Housing Policy Debate* 4, 589–626.

McConnell, J. J., and J. S. Schallheim. (1983). ''Valuation of Asset Leasing Contracts,'' *Journal of Financial Economics* 12, 237–261.

Nelson, D. B., and K. Ramaswamy. (1990). ''Simple Binomial Processes as Diffusion Approximations in Financial Models,'' *Review of Financial Studies* 3, 393–430.

Journal of Real Estate Finance and Economics, 24:1/2, 103–117, 2002

Initial Public Offerings: Evidence from the British, French and Swedish Property Share Markets

DIRK BROUNEN
Tinbergen Institute, The University of Amsterdam
E-mail: dirkb@fee.uva.nl

PIET EICHHOLTZ
Maastricht University, The University of Amsterdam and Kempen & Co.

Abstract

This paper investigates the underpricing and long-run performance of initial public offerings (IPOs), using a unique sample consisting of 54 British, French and Swedish property companies, which became publicly listed during the period 1984–1999. Similar to common stock IPOs, the European property share IPOs in our sample outperformed the benchmark on the first day of trading, on average with 2.55 percent. However, these property share IPOs tend to underperform their benchmark over the twelve-month period subsequent to the initial offering. We also examine explanatory factors such as issue size, the degree of debt financing, ex-ante uncertainty, and the underlying property types of the companies involved. The results are in line with those previously found for common stocks.

Key Words: IPO underpricing, equity issues, property companies

1. Introduction

Numerous studies have examined the performance of initial public offerings (IPOs) and documented the existence of short-run excess returns in combination with long-run underperformance. Ibbotson (1975) was among the first to report on the so-called ''underpricing'' of IPOs by documenting initial excess returns of 11.40 percent on U.S. common stock IPOs.[1] Studies on the long-run aftermarket price behavior, such as Ritter (1991) and Aggarwal and Rivoli (1990), showed that this initial outperformance appears to be a short-run phenomenon. The winner's curse theory, signaling-based models, and the theory that IPO performance is driven by fads have been used to attempt to explain this puzzling abnormal price behavior. However, numerous unanswered questions remain.

This paper tests implications derived from existing theories by studying a unique data set consisting of 54 European property companies from France, Sweden and the United Kingdom that became publicly listed during the period 1984–1999. We investigate whether the classical abnormal price behavior surrounding IPOs also exists in these

Author for correspondence: Dirk Brounen, The University of Amsterdam, Roetersstraat 11, NL-1018 WB Amsterdam.

European property share markets. Furthermore, we attempt to answer some of the research questions concerning the IPO-puzzle.

The paper is organized as follows. The next section discusses the related literature and states the theoretical implications that can be derived from this literature. Section 3 describes the sample collection procedures. In Section 4 we picture the institutional environments of the three national markets in our study. Section 5 gives an overview of the empirical results regarding the initial day price behavior. Section 6 reports our findings concerning the aftermarket price behavior, and Section 7 concludes.

2. Literature

A common explanation for the abnormal first day price behavior is the so-called ''winner's curse''. In Rock's (1986) model the IPO market contains two investors types; well-informed investors, who have superior knowledge about the true value of the issue and less-informed investors, who lack the special knowledge to correctly value the issue. This information asymmetry causes a ''lemons problem'' where the uninformed investors are left with the less successful IPOs. In order to keep badly informed investors interested in the IPO market, issuing firms are required to sell at a discount.[2] An explanatory factor directly derived from this winner's curse is the size of the issue. The larger the issue the more professionally it is likely to be managed and the more information about the true value will be available. This wider spread of information decreases the information asymmetry among investors. Because of this lower information asymmetry, these larger IPOs have less reason to underprice and are expected to show less initial outperformance.

A second factor that might explain the abnormal price behavior of IPOs is the degree of debt financing. Smith and Watts (1992) argued that firms with high growth potential will rely less on debt financing. This low reliance on debt financing is caused by their higher risk profiles, which make the debt market less accessible. When these growth companies go to the stock market during an IPO, the public will consider them more risky and will demand a higher risk premium in the form of more underpricing. Thus, we expect IPOs with the lowest debt ratios in our sample to be associated with the highest initial returns.

Another issue related to the underpricing of IPOs is the amount of uncertainty concerning the true value of the company involved. Alli et al. (1994) have examined this relationship by studying initial aftermarket price behavior of financial institutions. Since financial institutions are monitored by regulatory agents, the information asymmetry problem and the ex-ante uncertainty regarding true value should be less severe for financial institutions than for non-financial institutions. This proved to be the case. Because the value of property companies should reflect the value of their underlying property portfolio, we would expect property IPOs to be underpriced less severely than common stock IPOs.

A theory that could explain the long-run underperformance is the so-called ''fads theory''. Both Aggarwal and Rivoli (1990) and Ritter (1991) reported strong under-performance of IPOs after three years of -13.73 percent and -29.13 percent, respectively. Both studies point out that the abnormal price behavior of IPOs might be due to overoptimistic investors, who expect high excess returns, but sell the shares acquired in the IPO whenever their high expectations are not fulfilled in the longer run. This so-called fad causes extremely high demand in the early aftermarket, but at the same time drives the disappointed investors to sell their shares, thereby causing the long-run underperformance.

Some specific features of property shares should be taken into account. Wang et al. (1992) were the first to investigate the presence of IPO underpricing in a property share market. They reported a statistically significant average abnormal return of − 2.99 percent on the first day of trading for the U.S. REIT market. Ling and Ryngaert (1997) also investigated the U.S. REIT market and reported that REIT IPOs issued between 1991 and 1996 were underpriced, on average, by 3.60 percent. The differing results of these two studies imply that the question whether property share IPOs suffer from abnormal price behavior is still open.

Our paper extends the research of Wang et al. (1992) and Ling and Ryngaert (1997), by investigating European property share markets. Following Wang et al. (1992), we use the aftermarket standard deviation to quantify the ex-ante uncertainty surrounding the true value of the issue. We expect companies with high aftermarket standard deviations to be associated with higher initial day returns. Ling and Ryngaert (1997) also pointed out that the ex-ante uncertainty about the value of a new property issue could vary depending on the type of properties owned by the company. Retail property, for instance is often regarded as being more risky than residential property. Thus, we include property type as an additional factor that explains IPO price behavior.

3. Sample design

By combining the Global Property Research database with Bloomberg, Reuters and Datastream we found 72 property investment companies going public in the period 1984–1999 in Europe. The only countries in which the number of IPOs was large enough for meaningful statistical analysis were France, Sweden and the United Kingdom, which is why this study focuses on these three countries. After excluding spin-offs of existing listed companies and property developers we collected data concerning first day opening and closing prices and aftermarket returns for the remaining companies from Datastream, the *Financial Times* and from the property companies themselves. Furthermore, we asked the three national stock exchanges for assistance in locating the required data. These efforts resulted in a data set of 54 property share IPOs in the three largest European property share markets. Table 1 provides a distribution of the sample by country and by year. Besides the daily prices we also obtained information on the offering size, the pre-offer debt ratios, the aftermarket standard deviation and the underlying property type.

To adjust the property share returns for movements in the general property stock markets we used the GPR General National indices for the corresponding European countries. The GPR General National indices are total return indices of property shares, tracking the performance of all property investment companies in the corresponding

Table 1. Sample distribution by country and by year.

Country			Number of IPOs
A: Sample distribution by country			
France			17
Sweden			13
United Kingdom			24
Total: 54			
B: Sample distribution by year			
Year	Number of IPOs	Year	Number of IPOs
1984	1	1992	7
1985	1	1993	3
1986	1	1994	9
1987	1	1995	0
1988	1	1996	5
1989	10	1997	6
1990	3	1998	3
1991	2	1999	1
Total: 54			
C: Tax regimes			
France	33 percent		
Sweden*	28 percent		
United Kingdom*	23–31 percent		

*The exact corporate tax rate for U.K. property companies depends on profit level and company structure.

countries. These indices are available on a monthly basis, with December 1983 as base-month.

4. Institutional environments

The three European property share markets in our sample both differ and correspond in many respects. The U.K. market is the oldest and largest property share market in Europe, experiencing a relatively stable average annual return of 13.97 percent over the sample period. The companies in our sample are all pure equity property investors, who do not invest in mortgages. The institutional holdings in these companies vary drastically but are high compared to the Swedish and French markets. The majority of the U.K. IPOs in our sample date from the post-1992 period after the U.K. recovered from the real estate crisis of the early nineties. Listed property companies in the U.K. face corporate tax rates varying from 23 percent to 31 percent, depending on profit levels and company structure.

The Swedish property share market on the other hand is a lot younger and has been extremely turbulent over the sample period. As can be seen in Figure 1, an investment in a

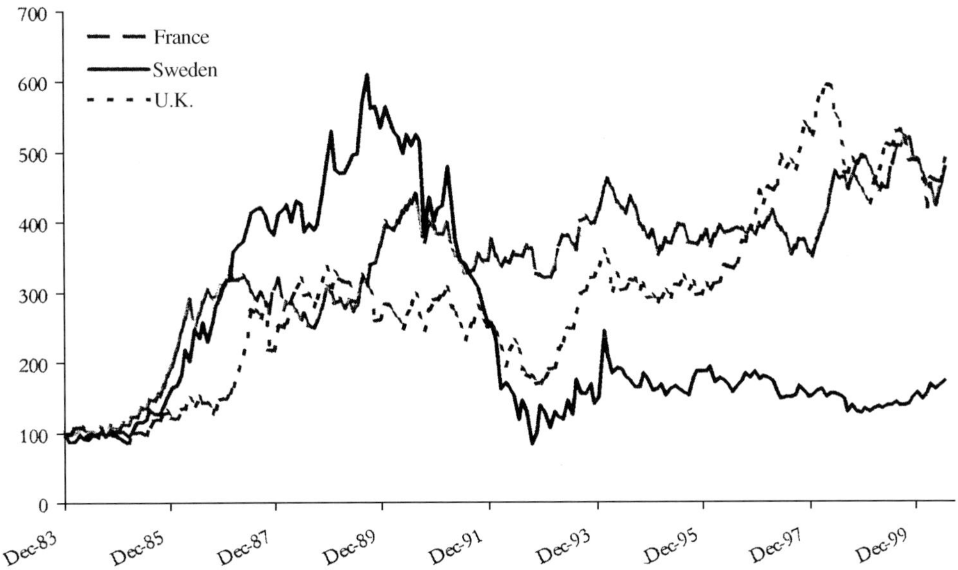

Figure 1. Market development of the French, Swedish and U.K. property share markets.

Swedish property share in 1984 would have surged sixfold in the following six years. However, this swift gain would have evaporated during the subsequent years. This volatile behavior is typical of the Swedish market, which has had many listings that were poorly structured in the late eighties. Several of these property companies had to leave the market in the early nineties when Sweden was struck by a recession. The institutional involvement in listed property companies in Sweden is relatively low compared to the U.K. and France. Swedish property companies face a corporate tax rate of 28 percent.

The third market of our study, the French market, has been the most stable over the sample period, yielding an average annual return of 11.71 percent. Most of the French IPOs in our sample are from the pre-1992 period, and the majority was strictly monitored by larger holding companies that ensured financing and thereby took away a lot of uncertainty for investors. The French property companies are subject to the national corporate tax rate of 33.33 percent.

5. Initial-day returns

5.1. Summary statistics

The initial day returns are calculated by dividing the difference between the offering price and the closing price by the offering price. To correct these raw first day returns for movements in the overall property share markets we subtracted the average daily GPR-General return of the corresponding country. The results are presented in Table 2.

Table 2. Initial day returns.

Sample	Initial Returns (percent)	GPR-General Returns (percent)	Initial Abnormal Returns (percent)	*t*-Statistic
Total	2.60	0.05	2.55*	3.26
Pre-1992	0.10	0.05	0.05	0.08
Post-1992	4.94	0.05	4.89*	4.18
U.K.	4.12	0.05	4.07*	3.62
France	0.82	0.05	0.77	0.61
Sweden	1.79	0.04	1.75	0.81

Notes. This table provides average returns for the first trading day for subsamples of property share IPOs and the average daily GPR-General index returns. The initial abnormal returns are calculated by taking the difference between the two. Initial abnormal returns marked with * are significant at the 5 percent level.

For the sample as a whole we find a statistically significant initial abnormal return of 2.55 percent, on average. This outcome conforms to the findings of Ling and Ryngaert (1997), who documented an initial abnormal return of 3.60 percent for the U.S. REIT market. Compared to the initial day returns of common stocks found in the literature, this 2.55 percent is rather modest, which supports the notion that the more transparent and therefore less risky property share issues are associated with significantly less underpricing than the more risky common stock IPOs. But although the extent of the underpricing is modest it is still significant and offers the investor an attractive return, even after correcting for transaction costs, which nowadays amount to approximately 40 basis points.

The move towards the European Monetary Union (EMU) in 1992 has had a significant impact on the European property share markets. Investors increasingly regard Europe as one market and have moved towards a more pan-European investment strategy, which has enhanced liquidity. However, given the fact that a French investor knows more about the French property market than about, say, the Swedish market, pan-European investment strategies are likely to increase differences in the level to which participating investors are informed concerning property share IPOs. This may cause property shares to be more susceptible to the winner's curse and exhibit stronger IPO underpricing. Indeed, we find the post-1992 IPOs in our sample to be underpriced by 4.89 percent, whereas the pre-1992 IPOs were not underpriced at all.

We also found initial day returns varying strongly across different countries. These cross-national differences can be explained by comparing differences in market structure and maturity. British IPOs produced a statistically significant initial abnormal return of 4.07 percent. The French IPOs, which are strongly monitored by holding companies hardly outperformed their benchmark on the first day of trading.

Table 3 reports the summary statistics on initial day returns for the full sample and for various subsamples. These subsamples are chosen to facilitate the investigation of the importance of different factors potentially affecting IPO underpricing: issue size, debt ratio, standard deviation, and sector specialization of the property portfolio. Initial abnormal returns are positive for each sub-sample. Table 3 shows that small issues are indeed associated with more underpricing than large issues. The average initial abnormal return for the small issues of 3.05 percent is significantly different from zero.

The table also shows that issues with lower debt ratios outperform the market index more strongly than issues with higher debt ratios. These differences confirm the implications derived from Smith and Watts (1992).

Ex-ante uncertainty appears to play a role in IPO underpricing. Issues belonging to the group with the highest aftermarket standard deviation are associated with high initial abnormal returns: 5.37 percent versus no significant first-day outperformance for the group with the lowest aftermarket standard deviation.

Finally, concerning the underlying property type, we discovered that specialized companies show a somewhat higher initial abnormal return than diversified companies, while they vary strongly among the different property types. Property companies specialized in managing retail property, for instance, yield an average initial day return of 4.39 percent, whereas companies specialized in office properties do not perform differently than the market index.

5.2. *Multivariate analysis of initial day returns*

The summary statistics of Table 3 suggest that small issues, issues with low debt ratios, and companies specialized in retail property entail more uncertainty about their true value and are therefore associated with higher initial day returns. But to truly isolate the impact of the different variables on the initial abnormal returns, multivariate regression analysis is needed. For every parameter we compute OLS-estimations of the coefficients, using the following model:

$$\begin{aligned}\text{IAR} = {} & \text{a} + \text{b}_1\text{Size} + \text{b}_2\text{Debt ratio} + \text{b}_3\text{Ex-ante uncertainty} + \text{b}_4\text{Specialized} \\ & + \text{b}_4\text{Retail} + \text{b}_5\text{Office} + \text{b}_6\text{Residential} + \text{b}_7\text{Post-1992} + \text{b}_8\text{UK} \\ & + \text{b}_9\text{Sweden} + \varepsilon. \end{aligned} \quad (1)$$

Table 4 reports the regression results. In order to minimize the influence of outliers we use a log specification for issue size, debt financing and aftermarket standard deviation. For these first three variables, the signs of the coefficients are consistent with the results reported in the summary statistics. Issues of lesser size, with smaller debt ratios and higher aftermarket standard deviations are indeed associated with more underpricing. The coefficients of the specialization dummy and the underlying property type are also in line with the results presented in Table 3. Finally, we look at the explanatory power of a post-1992 dummy variable and on two nationality dummies. The coefficient of the post-1992 dummy confirms our previous findings that the more recent IPOs are indeed associated with a higher initial day return. The signs of the coefficients of the nationality dummies give support to the national differences we reported in Table 2. The model has an adjusted R-squared of 65 percent.

Table 3. Summary statistics initial day returns.

Issue Size	Initial AR (percent)	*t*-Statistic	*N*
A: Size factor†			
Small, < 80 mln Euro	3.05*	2.82	25
Medium	2.87	1.44	10
Large, > 180 mln Euro	1.41	1.83	19
Debt Ratio			
B: Debt ratio factor‡			
High, > 0.49	2.02	1.70	18
Low, < 0.49	3.16*	2.18	36
Standard Deviation			
C: Ex-ante uncertainty proxy§			
High, > 3.00%	5.37	1.89	19
Medium	2.45*	2.83	21
Low, < 1.50%	0.69	0.98	14
D: Specialization/Property type factor ‖			
Diversified	1.97*	2.36	20
Specialized	2.26*	2.07	34
Office	−0.08	−0.09	13
Retail	4.39*	2.57	10
Residential	10.12*	3.02	5

†Size is measured in total capitalization of the tissue.
‡The debt ratio is computed by dividing the pre-offer total debt by the pre-offer market value of the firm.
§The ex-ante uncertainty proxy is equal to the standard deviation of the returns of the first 20 trading days.
‖ Specialization is determined by looking at the asset portfolio of the company. Companies having more than 80 percent of their total assets in one property type are considered specialized.
Initial abnormal returns marked with * are significant at the 5 percent level.

Table 4. OLS regression of initial abnormal returns on independent variables.

	Coefficients
Intercept	−0.07** (0.03)
Log of issue size	−0.00 (0.00)
Log (1 + percent debt financing)	0.05 (0.03)
Log of aftermarket standard deviation	2.31* (0.68)
Specialized dummy (yes = 1, no = 0)	0.01 (0.01)
Retail dummy (yes = 1, no = 0)	0.00 (0.02)
Office dummy (yes = 1, no = 0)	−0.02 (0.02)
Residential dummy (yes = 1, no = 0)	0.08* (0.02)
Post-1992 dummy (yes = 1, no = 0)	0.01 (0.02)
UK dummy (yes = 1, no = 0)	0.02 (0.02)
Sweden dummy (yes = 1, no = 0)	−0.02 (0.02)
R^2	0.65

Notes. The heteroskedasticity-consistent standard errors of the corresponding coefficient estimates are given between brackets. Coefficient estimates marked with * are significant at the 5 percent level, coefficient estimates marked with ** are significant at the 10 percent level.

Table 5. Cumulative abnormal returns.

	Total		France		Sweden		U.K.	
Period	CAR (%)	*t*-Statistic	CAR (%)	*t*-Statistic	CAR (%)	*t*-Statistic	CAR (%)	*t*-Statistic
Month 1	0.84	0.55	0.39	0.17	– 0.01	0.00	1.58	0.87
Month 2	1.38	0.56	– 1.78	– 0.77	0.57	0.12	3.82	0.84
Month 3	0.59	0.22	– 1.91	– 0.62	1.46	0.36	1.74	0.34
Month 4	– 0.96	– 0.36	– 1.78	– 0.39	– 4.06	– 0.82	1.18	0.27
Month 5	– 2.06	– 0.70	– 1.21	– 0.26	– 1.40	– 0.26	– 2.94	– 0.59
Month 6	0.27	0.08	– 1.94	– 0.41	8.53	1.16	– 2.61	– 0.52
Month 7	– 3.30	– 1.02	– 3.09	– 0.69	2.78	0.35	– 6.60	– 1.33
Month 8	– 2.45	– 0.80	– 4.86	– 1.05	2.13	0.27	– 3.29	– 0.75
Month 9	0.36	0.10	– 6.73	– 1.65	14.03	1.38	– 2.20	– 0.47
Month 10	1.03	0.29	– 3.15	– 0.73	17.40	1.89	– 4.81	– 0.97
Month 11	0.21	0.05	– 7.25	– 1.58	21.44	1.80	– 6.06	– 1.16
Month 12	– 1.29	– 0.29	– 12.62	– 2.52	18.89	1.49	– 4.53	– 0.87

Notes. The cumulative abnormal returns (CARs) are computed by applying the formula:

$$\mathrm{CAR}_t = \sum_{t=1}^{1}\left(\frac{1}{n}\sum_{i=1}^{n}\left(\frac{P_{it}-P_{it-1}}{P_{it-1}} - \frac{P_{bt}-P_{bt-1}}{P_{bt-1}}\right)\right),$$

where P_{it} is the price of the stock i on day t and P_{bt} is the price of the benchmark on day t.

6. Aftermarket returns

In addition to the short-run outperformance of IPOs, the literature also documents long-run underperformance. We now turn to that issue, using three separate methods for analysis. We first look at the mean cumulative abnormal returns[3] (CARs) for varying time periods. Secondly, we investigate buy-and-hold returns, and lastly, we look at wealth relatives.

The results of the CAR analysis are presented in Table 5 and show that the CARs for our sample as a whole decrease over a longer time period and lead to a negative twelve-month CAR of – 1.29 percent, on average. The initial outperformance documented for the first day of trading only lasts for three months. Furthermore, Table 5 shows that there are large differences between the national subsamples. British and French IPOs exhibit the traditional IPO price behavior by underperforming after the first year year, with – 4.53 percent and – 12.62 percent respectively. Swedish IPOs, on the other hand, outperformed considerably after twelve months. This difference can be explained by the fact that the Swedish property share market has been in a different phase than the more stable and mature French and British property share markets. The Swedish property share market has gone through rough times in the early nineties, leading to relatively low benchmark returns that were easily exceeded by the Swedish aftermarket IPO-returns.

Dissanaike (1994) has shown that the cumulation process involved in computing CARs can give biased outcomes. Therefore we also compute excess buy-and-hold returns for various time horizons. The outcomes of these computations are presented in Table 6.

Table 6. Excess buy-and-hold returns.

	Total		France		Sweden		U.K.	
Period	EBHR (%)	*t*-Statistic	EBHR (%)	*t*-Statistic	EBHR (%)	*t*-Statistic	EBHR (%)	*t*-Statistic
Month 1	0.88	0.58	0.39	0.17	0.12	0.03	1.58	0.87
Month 2	1.69	0.66	−2.17	−0.93	1.24	0.26	4.40	0.92
Month 3	0.58	0.21	−2.32	−0.72	1.95	0.43	1.72	0.33
Month 4	−1.43	−0.53	−2.16	−0.47	−4.65	−0.90	0.70	0.16
Month 5	−2.63	−0.90	−1.76	−0.36	−0.92	−0.17	−4.07	−0.83
Month 6	0.26	0.08	−1.31	−0.28	8.53	1.18	−3.02	−0.59
Month 7	−4.29	−1.29	−3.79	−0.83	0.92	0.11	−7.32	−1.48
Month 8	−3.96	−1.19	−5.81	−1.19	1.02	0.11	−5.37	−1.16
Month 9	−1.05	−0.28	−8.68	−2.04	14.60	1.45	−4.30	−0.85
Month 10	−0.95	−0.26	−4.30	−1.02	15.89	1.71	−7.56	−1.46
Month 11	−0.81	−0.18	−8.31	−1.95	24.64	2.03	−9.25	−1.65
Month 12	−0.55	−0.12	−10.76	−2.51	22.16	1.78	−5.83	−1.04

Notes. The excess buy-and-hold returns (EBHR) are calculated by applying the formula:

$$\text{EBHR} = \frac{1}{n}\sum_{i=1}^{n}\left(\frac{P_{i0}}{P_{it} - P_{i0}} - \frac{P_{b0}}{P_{bt} - P_{b0}}\right),$$

where P_{it} is the price of stock i on day t, P_{i0} is the initial day offering price of stock i, P_{bt} is the benchmark price on day t and P_{b0} is the initial day offering price of the benchmark.

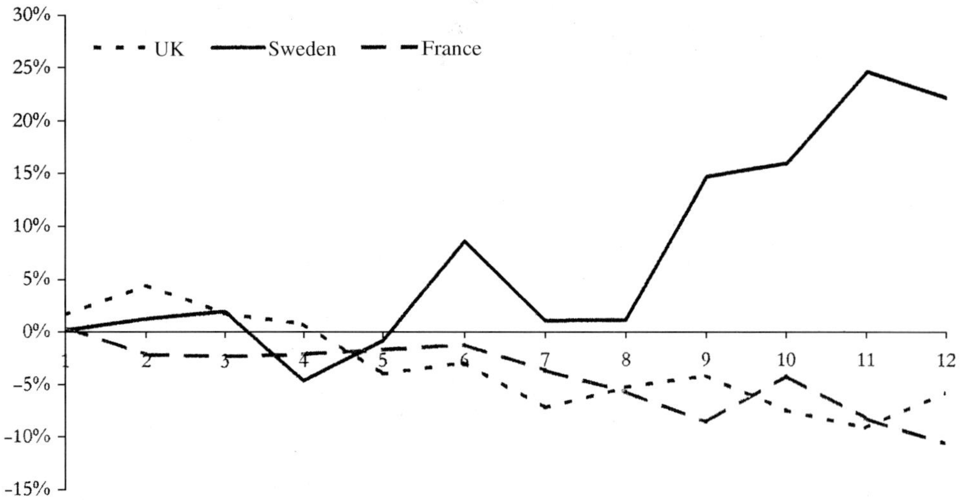

Figure 2. Aftermarket performance of the French, Swedish and U.K. property share IPOs in excess buy-and-hold returns.

Table 7. Wealth relatives.

	Company (%)	Benchmark (%)	Wealth Relative
A: Mean buy-and-hold returns			
Month 1	1.38	0.54	1.01
Month 2	4.16	2.47	1.02
Month 3	4.88	4.31	1.01
Month 4	4.33	5.77	0.99
Month 5	3.27	5.90	0.98
Month 6	6.61	6.98	1.00
Month 7	4.77	9.06	0.96
Month 8	5.27	9.23	0.96
Month 9	8.84	9.89	0.99
Month 10	5.99	6.94	0.99
Month 11	7.68	8.49	0.99
Month 12	6.28	9.07	0.97
B: Median buy-and-hold returns			
Month 1	0.00	0.94	0.99
Month 2	0.40	2.37	0.98
Month 3	2.12	5.37	0.97
Month 4	1.77	5.79	0.96
Month 5	1.53	6.35	0.95
Month 6	6.14	4.30	1.02
Month 7	2.64	3.55	0.99
Month 8	4.98	4.89	1.00
Month 9	2.21	5.24	0.97
Month 10	2.81	1.69	1.01
Month 11	1.11	5.67	0.96
Month 12	3.10	5.39	0.98

Note. The wealth relatives are computed by dividing 1 plus the buy-and-hold return of the property shares by 1 plus the corresponding buy-and-hold return of the GPR-General index.

Similar to the CARs the excess buy-and-hold returns also decrease strongly over time and the short-run outperformance is turned into a long-run underperformance. Again, as is illustrated in Figure 2, we find striking differences in the national subsamples where the British and French IPOs underperform and the Swedish IPOs ouperform in the long run.

Having calculated the excess buy-and-hold returns we can derive the wealth relatives both for the mean and for the median buy-and-hold returns. Table 7 presents these wealth relatives. In accordance with studies of Ritter (1991) and Gerbich et al. (1999) we find short-run wealth relatives slightly above one in combination with twelve-month wealth relatives significantly below one.

The results of all three methods indicate that the short-term outperformance we documented in Section 4 lasts only during the first few months of trading. For longer periods we find significant underperformance.

To further examine the relationship between short-term outperformance and long-run underperformance, we divide the European sample into subsamples based on the four

Table 8. Summary statistics of excess buy-and-hold returns.

Factor\Time	1	3	6	9	12
A Size†					
Small, < 80 mln Euro	−0.49%	−0.49%	−3.35%	−6.40%	−7.79%
	(−0.23)	(−0.11)	(−0.68)	(−1.12)	(−1.17)
Medium	2.76%	7.29%	4.22%	3.81%	12.20%
	(0.62)	(0.93)	(0.92)	(0.55)	(1.47)
Large, > 180 mln Euro	2.13%	−3.96%	1.35%	−0.71%	−2.01%
	(0.76)	(−1.00)	(0.18)	(−0.10)	(−0.23)
B Debt‡					
High, > 0.49	1.81%	−2.01%	−0.30%	−1.17%	−1.87%
	(0.70)	(−0.44)	(−0.07)	(−0.19)	(−0.30)
Low, < 0.49	0.64%	1.24%	2.63%	1.52%	1.96%
	(0.27)	(0.30)	(0.61)	(0.30)	(0.31)
C Aftermarket standard deviation§					
High, > 300 percent	2.74%	5.19%	4.71%	3.34%	5.90%
	(0.42)	(0.49)	(−0.49)	(−1.30)	(−1.43)
Medium	−0.06%	−4.24%	0.51%	2.03%	2.55%
	(−0.03)	(−1.15)	(0.11)	(0.34)	(0.34)
Low, < 1.50 percent	0.55%	2.50%	−3.28%	−7.68%	−8.74%
	(0.64)	(0.86)	(0.88)	(0.42)	(0.58)
D Specialization and property type ‖					
Diversified	2.95%	0.20%	−2.64%	−2.42%	−1.46%
	(1.30)	(0.06)	(−0.44)	(−0.32)	(−0.17)
Specialized	−0.38%	0.66%	1.97%	−0.16%	−0.13%
	(−0.16)	(0.14)	(0.42)	(−0.03)	(−0.02)
Office	1.93%	1.10%	−0.44%	−2.94%	0.13%
	(0.58)	(0.18)	(−0.07)	(−0.45)	(0.02)
Retail	−7.54%	−1.62%	0.34%	−9.33%	−16.71%
	(−2.07)	(−0.16)	(0.04)	(−1.32)	(−1.66)
Residential	7.04%	−1.85%	7.77%	16.05%	18.84%
	(1.50)	(−0.22)	(0.73)	(1.40)	(1.53)

Notes. Time periods are stated in months.
†Size is measured as capitalization of the issue.
‡The debt ratio is computed by dividing the pre-offer total debt by the pre-offer market value of the firm.
§The ex-ante uncertainty proxy is equal to the standard deviation of the returns of the first 20 trading days.
‖ Specialization is determined by looking at the asset portfolio of the company. Companies having more than 80% of their total assets in one property type are regarded specialized. The *t*-statistics are given between brackets.

variables we discussed before: issue size, degree of debt financing, aftermarket standard deviation and underlying property type. We calculate mean abnormal buy-and-hold returns for each of these subsamples and provide the results in Table 8. Comparing the results in this table with those given in Table 3 shows that initial day outperformance and long-run underperformance are closely related. For example, regarding the size factor we again find the smallest issues having the more abnormal price behavior: they exhibit a twelve-month excess buy-and-hold return of −7.79 percent, whereas the largest issues in our sample underperform their benchmark only mildly, with −2.01 percent, on average.

Table 9. OLS regression of twelve-month excess returns on independent variables.

	Coefficient
Intercept	– 0.45 (0.34)
Log of issue size	0.06 (0.05)
Log (1 + percent debt financing)	– 0.09 (0.39)
Log of aftermarket standard deviation	7.99 (5.06)
Specialized dummy (Yes = 1, no = 0)	0.15 (0.14)
Retail dummy (yes = 1, no = 0)	– 0.37** (0.18)
Office dummy (yes = 1, no = 0)	– 0.16 (0.15)
Residential dummy (yes = 1, no = 0)	– 0.01 (0.13)
Post-1992 dummy (yes = 1, no = 0)	– 0.11 (0.21)
UK dummy (yes = 1, no = 0)	0.16 (0.23)
Sweden dummy (yes = 1, no = 0)	0.19 (0.20)
R^2	0.20

Notes. The heteroskedasticity-consistent standard errors of the corresponding coefficient estimates are given between brackets. Coefficient estimates marked with ** are significant at the 10 percent level.

Furthermore, Table 8 shows that the companies with high debt ratios and low aftermarket standard deviation underperform their benchmark more severely than those with the low debt ratios and high aftermarket standard deviation.

Concerning the last factor, portfolio specialization, the general conclusion is that diversified companies seem to underperform more strongly than their specialized competitors.[4] But also among the specialized companies considerable differences in long-run performance exist. Companies specialized in residential properties tend to outperform in the long run, whereas companies specialized in retail property underperform significantly after twelve months. However, given the small sample sizes these results are offered with caution.

To isolate the impact of the individual factors, we also ran multivariate regressions on the twelve-month excess buy-and-hold returns and the identified factors. The results of these regressions, stated in Table 9, confirm the cross-sectional differences we reported in Table 8. The factors issue size, debt ratio and aftermarket standard deviation are positively related to the aftermarket price performance, whereas the results for the specialization dummy are mixed. The positive sign of the post-1992 dummy indicates that the more recent IPOs in our sample perform best in the longer run. The nationality dummy confirms our previous findings that nationality of the IPO does make a difference.

7. Conclusion and suggestions for further research

This paper documents the price behavior of 54 European property share IPOs. We find an overall excess return of 2.55 percent on the first trading and a modest underperformance after twelve months. Evidence presented in this paper is consistent with the winner's curse hypothesis of Rock (1986). Large issues, which are likely to be managed more professionally, are underpriced less and exhibit less abnormal long-run underperformance. Furthermore, we also found that IPOs with the highest aftermarket standard deviation, a proxy for the ex-ante uncertainty, are underpriced more severely and are associated with the best long-run performance. The modest size of the abnormal price behavior of the IPOs in our sample is consistent with theories that claim that less risky IPOs experience less severe abnormal price behavior.

The results also show that IPO underpricing of European property companies was much stronger after 1992 than before that year. This may well be caused by the fact that European integration, which gained speed in that period, has led to more pan-European property share investment. Our results suggest that stronger international involvement in IPOs has led to more information differences, and therefore to more influence of the winner's curse. An extension of this research could therefore be to investigate the relationship between the international involvement in IPOs and their underpricing.

Notes

1. For a broad discussion of empirical evidence regarding initial aftermarket price behavior of IPOs, see Smith (1986).
2. Keloharju (1993) and Michaeley and Shaw (1994) tested Rock's theory for the U.S. common stock market, and found strong support for the existence of a winner's curse.
3. For IPOs that are delisted prior to their three-year anniversary, the total return is calculated up to the delisting date.
4. This is in line with results for United States REITs documented by Eichholtz, Op 't Veld and Schweitzer (2000).

Acknowledgments

The authors thank David Ling, Hans op 't Veld, Kees Koedijk, Alireza Tourani Rad and an anonymous referee for their helpful comments and Caroline Vermue, the British, French and Swedish stock exchanges and Global Property Research for their assistance. All remaining errors are the responsibility of the authors.

References

Aggarwal, R., and P. Rivoli. (1990). "Fads in the Initial Public Offering Market?," *Financial Management* 19, 45–57.

Alli, K., J. Yau, and K. Yung. (1994). "The Underpricing of IPOs of Financial Institutions," *Journal of Business Finance and Accounting* 21, 1013–1030.

Dissanaike, G. (1994). "On the Computations of Returns in Tests of the Stock Market Overreaction Hypothesis," *Journal of Banking and Finance* 18, 1083–1094.

Eichholtz, P. M. A., H. Op 't Veld, and M. Schweitzer. (2000). "REIT Outperformance: Does Managerial Specialization Pay?," In S. Zenios, *The Performance of Financial Institutions*, Cambridge University Press.

Gerbich, M., M. Levis, and P. Venmore-Rowland. (1999). "Property Investment and Property Development Firm Performance Around Initial Public Offerings and Rights Offerings: U.K. Evidence," *Journal of Real Estate Finance and Economics* 18, 207–238.

Ibbotson, R. G. (1975). ''Price Performance of Common Stock New Issues,'' *Journal of Financial Economics* 2, 235–272.

Keloharju, M. (1993). ''The winner's curse, legal liability and the long-run price performance of initial public offerings in Finland,'' *Journal of Financial Economics* 34, 251–277.

Ling, D. C., and M. Ryngaert. (1997). ''Valuation Uncertainty, Institutional Involvement, and the Underpricing of IPOs: the Case of REITs,'' *Journal of Financial Economics* 43, 433–456.

Michaely, R., and W. H. Shaw. (1994). ''The Pricing of Initial Public Offerings: Tests of Adverse-Selection and Signaling Theories,'' *Review of Financial Studies* 7, 279–319.

Ritter, J. R. (1991). ''The Long-run Performance of Initial Public Offerings,'' *The Journal of Finance* 46, 3–27.

Rock, K. (1986). ''Why New Issues are Underpriced,'' *Journal of Financial Economics* 15, 187–212.

Smith, C. W. (1986). ''Investment Banking and the Capital Acquisition Process,'' *Journal of Financial Economics* 15, 3–29.

Smith, C. W., and R. Watts. (1992). ''The Investment Opportunity Set and Corporate Financing, Dividend, and Compensation Policies,'' *Journal of Financial Economics* 32, 263–292.

Wang, K., S. H. Chan, and G. W. Gau. (1992). ''Initial Public Offerings of Equity Securities: Anomalous Evidence Using REITs,'' *Journal of Financial Economics* 31, 381–410.

Journal of Real Estate Finance and Economics, 24:1/2, 119–142, 2002

Commercial Real Estate Return Performance: A Cross-Country Analysis

DAVID C. LING

ANDY NARANJO

Department of Finance, Insurance, and Real Estate, Warrington College of Business, University of Florida, Gainesville, FL 32611-7168

E-mail: ling@upi.edu; naranjo@dale.cba.ufl.edu

Abstract

This paper investigates the return performance of publicly traded real estate companies. The analysis spans the 1984–1999 time period and includes return data on over 600 companies in 28 countries. The return data reveal a substantial amount of variation in mean real estate returns and standard deviations across countries. Moreover, standard Treynor ratios, which scale country excess returns by the estimated beta on the world wealth portfolio, also reveal substantial variation across countries in excess real estate returns per unit of systematic risk. However, when we estimate Jensen's alphas using both single and multifactor specifications, we detect little evidence of abnormal, risk-adjusted returns at the country level. We do, however, find evidence of a strong world-wide factor in international real estate returns. Furthermore, even after controlling for the effects of world-wide systematic risk, an orthogonalized country-specific factor is highly significant. This suggests that real estate securities may provide international diversification opportunities.

Key Words: real estate return performance, risk-adjusted real estate returns, international real estate returns, international asset pricing

1. Introduction

A global real estate securities market has slowly developed over the last two decades. At year-end 1999, the market value of publicly traded real estate companies was approaching $400 billion. This public market provides a vehicle for investors to construct international commercial real estate portfolios without the burden of acquiring, managing, and disposing of direct property investments in far-away countries with unfamiliar legal, political, and market structures.[1] However, to sustain and increase the flow of investment capital into the international real estate securities market, performance benchmarks and relative performance measurement are vital. This paper investigates the return performance of publicly traded real estate companies. The analysis spans the 1984–1999 time period and includes return data on over 600 companies in 28 countries.

At the simplest level, performance analysis consists of comparing historical returns and their variances. However, a key problem with this simple unconditional approach is that it

Author for Correspondence: David Ling, Andy Naranjo, Department of Finance, Insurance, and Real Estate, Warrington College of Business, University of Florida, Gainesville, FL 32611-7168.

does not explicitly consider the risks associated with the returns. In order to obtain more accurate risk-return characteristics, and to examine why a specific performance level occurred, more precise estimates of risk are needed. To date, the most widely used approach to risk adjustment has been the use of single-beta models such as the capital asset pricing model (CAPM).[2]

Although the single-beta approach is a positive first step toward controlling for systematic sources of return variation when assessing return performance, there is a growing consensus that single-beta models provide an inadequate description of security pricing. For example, several studies have uncovered multiple sources of systematic risk that are priced in U.S. commercial real estate markets (e.g., Chan et al., 1990; Ling and Naranjo, 1996, 1999; Ling et al., 2000; and Karolyi and Sanders, 1999).[3] In an international context, several studies have found that continental and country specific factors, such as exchange rate risk, are additional sources of systematic risk (e.g., Eichholtz et al., 1998 and Liu and Mei, 1996). Therefore, to appropriately measure both domestic and international real estate return performance, it is necessary to adequately control for country specific sources of systematic risk.

To form a base-line, we first examine the *ex post* return performance of each country's real estate securities using a single-beta asset pricing model. Our proxy for the world wealth portfolio (i.e., systematic risk) is the total return on a broad-based index of international stocks. The estimated (Jensen's) alphas from these regressions provide direct evidence of abnormal risk-adjusted return performance. In addition, the estimated beta coefficients and coefficients of determination provide evidence on the extent to which country specific real estate returns respond to a global market risk factor. If returns on real estate securities in country i are heavily influenced by a worldwide risk factor, this may suggest that investors already diversified internationally with stocks will gain little additional diversification benefits by investing in the real estate securities of country i.

In a second specification of our asset pricing model, we add a country specific factor to the ex post real estate return regressions. This additional variable is designed to proxy for the effects of systematic risk factors in each country that are independent of worldwide systematic risk. More specifically, this risk factor is the change in each country's stock market index that is orthogonal to movements in the world wealth portfolio. Once again, Jensen's alphas from the estimation of these two-factor models are examined for evidence of abnormal return performance by country.

Although our country-wide regressions provide a clear indication of the absolute and relative performance of each country's value-weighted real estate index, this level of aggregation may mask significant within-country variation in performance across property companies. To address this issue, we separately calculate the mean return and estimate our two-factor model for each of the companies that comprise the GPR database.

Our results can be summarized as follows. The data reveal a substantial amount of variation in mean real estate returns and standard deviations across countries. Moreover, standard Treynor ratios also reveal substantial variation across countries in excess real estate returns per unit of systematic risk. However, when we estimate Jensen's alphas using single and multifactor specifications, we detect little evidence of abnormal returns at the country level. Similar to Case et al. (1999), we find evidence of a strong worldwide factor in international real estate returns. However, even after controlling for the effects of worldwide systematic risk, our orthogonalized country-specific factor is significant in 91 percent of the country regressions. This suggests that real estate securities may provide international diversification opportunities.

The disaggregated results reveal significant variation in raw firm returns both across and within countries. This suggests significant firm specific risk exists in international real estate securities markets, even after controlling for world and country specific effects. Thus, diversification benefits may be available to international investors from investing in a limited number of countries. This may reduce the cost of constructing diversified international portfolios to the extent that there are up-front fixed costs associated with analyzing the legal, political, and market risks of individual countries. However, although the disaggregated total return data reveal significant variation across companies within countries, only a handful of companies produced statistically significant abnormal returns (alphas).

We perform several tests to examine the robustness of our results with respect to estimation methodology and to the asset pricing restrictions imposed. First, to avoid generated regressors and associated problems, we reestimate our two-factor models using simultaneous equation estimation procedures. Second, we also reestimate both the single- and two-factor models after imposing appropriate asset pricing restrictions. These conditional Jensen's alphas are then compared to our earlier unconditional estimates. In both cases, we find that our excess performance results are virtually unchanged.

In Section 2 we present the conceptual framework for our study and describe the regression models used to analyze cross-country performance. Section 3 describes the data and presents various descriptive statistics such as unconditional mean returns and standard deviations. Section 4 contains the empirical regression results using country-level data, while our disaggregated (firm-level) results are presented in Section 5. Several robustness checks are performed and discussed in Section 6, and the last section offers some concluding comments.

2. Research methodology

A widely used framework for estimating excess (risk-adjusted) returns is Jensen's CAPM approach. To implement this approach in our international context, we estimate the following OLS regression:

$$R_{it} - R_{ft} = \alpha_i + \beta_{iw}[R_{wt} - R_{ft}] + e_{it}, \tag{1}$$

where: R_{it} is the U.S. dollar-weighted return on country i's real estate index in time period t, R_{ft} is the U.S. risk-free rate in time period t, α_i is a constant, β_{iw} is the return sensitivity (exposure) of country i's real estate returns to returns on the world wealth portfolio, R_{wt} is the U.S. dollar-weighted total return on the world wealth portfolio in time period t,

$R_{wt} - R_{ft}$ is the expected risk premium associated with an investment in the world wealth portfolio, and e_{it} is an error term.

Each country's alpha, α_i, represents the constant periodic return the investor is able to earn above (or below, if negative) the return on an unmanaged portfolio of international stocks (i.e., a buy-hold strategy) having identical market (systematic) risk. Thus, if the estimated alpha value from this *ex post* return regression is positive and statistically significant, the country level index of real estate returns is judged to have outperformed a buy-hold international strategy. Conversely, if the estimated alpha coefficient is negative and statistically significant, the real estate index has underperformed a passive buy-hold international strategy.

Jensen's model assumes there is but one source of systematic risk in the economy—that is, exposure to fluctuations in the value of the world wealth portfolio. However, as noted earlier, several recent studies have documented the existence of multiple systematic risk factors in both domestic and international stock, bond, and commercial real estate markets. Thus, Jensen's and other single-factor performance evaluation models may be mis-specified due to the existence of an omitted variable(s). The potential ramification of this mis-specification is that apparent excess return performance may simply reflect the risk premium(s) investors have earned for exposure to additional sources of systematic risk. However, because these additional risk factors are omitted from single-factor models, the return compensation attributable to these risk exposures may be erroneously picked up in the intercept and error terms, leading to incorrect return performance inferences.

In studies of U.S. real estate markets, the most common approach to specifying multifactor models of asset prices is to use macroeconomic factors and/or other variables that have been shown in prior studies to carry *ex ante* risk premiums.[4] The use of prespecified factors is not possible in the current study for several reasons. Most importantly, identifying a set of consistently "priced factors" in each country is problematic due to the length and breadth of the available real estate data for each country. Moreover, many of the "usual suspects" (i.e., changes in interest rates, term structure slopes, industrial production, national consumption, etc.) are not available in a consistently measured and timely fashion across the countries in our sample.[5]

To circumvent these international data limitations, we employ a two-factor variant of the model used by Liu et al. (1990). This two-factor model serves as a general specification for other multifactor asset-pricing models through the use of two portmanteau variables that proxy for latent asset pricing risks including country-related macroeconomic state variables, predetermined factors, and institutional factors. The estimation of this model requires a two-step procedure. First, for each country in our sample, we estimate the following OLS regression

$$R_{it}^{s} - R_{ft} = \alpha_i^{s} + \beta_{iw}^{s}[R_{wt} - R_{ft}] + e_{it}^{s}, \tag{2}$$

where R_{it}^{s} is the U.S. dollar-weighted return on country i's stock index in time period t and e_{it}^{s} are the unexplained residuals (i.e., the orthogonal component). These residuals represent the portion of each country's stock returns not explained by movements in the world wealth portfolio. This unexplained variation serves as a portmanteau variable that proxies for latent country-related macroeconomics state variables and predetermined factors such as changed in interest rates and term structure slopes growth rates in industrial production, per capita consumption, size related effects, and exchange rate risk. These residuals also capture the effects of the myriad institutional factors that can vary significantly across continents and countries and that standard asset pricing models generally ignore.[6,7]

To estimate a multifactor specification of the unconditional real estate asset-pricing model, we add this orthogonalized country-specific risk factor to the *ex post* real estate return regressions and estimate the following equation:

$$R_{it} - R_{ft} = \alpha_i + \beta_{iw}[R_{wt} - R_{ft}] + \beta_{iR}\, e^{s}_{it} + u_{it}. \tag{3}$$

As before, β_{iw} is the estimated return sensitivity of country i's real estate return index to return on the world wealth portfolio. β_{iR} is the estimated exposure of country i's real estate return index to returns on the orthoganalized country specific risk factor. If β_{iR} cannot be distinguished from zero, we conclude that the country specific risk factor does not increase the explanatory power of the model, once we have controlled for worldwide systematic risk. Once again, the estimated constants (Jensen's alphas) from this two-factor model can be examined for evidence of superior risk-adjusted return performance.

Because return-influencing events in real estate markets are decidedly local in nature, we anticipate that our estimates of β_{iR} will be statistically significant. However, with the gradual emergence of international real estate capital flows during our study period, real estate markets have generally experienced increased openness and competition. This suggests that the relative influence of the world index on real estate returns may have increased over the study period.

3. Data

The international real estate securities data used in this study are obtained from the Global Real Estate Securities Database of Global Property Research (GPR), a Netherlands-based firm. This database contains prices, market capitalization, dividends, and company characteristics of real estate companies listed on the stock exchanges of more than 30 countries on a monthly basis since 1984. This unique database contains the history of some 600 real estate companies—both currently listed companies and those that have been delisted. The GPR index is constructed to be representative of the movements in the worldwide real estate securities market. In December 1999, the aggregate GPR index contained return information on 434 companies in 30 countries. The market value of these securities was $362.7 billion.[8]

Most of the GPR times-series began in January 1984, and we currently have data through December 1999. The GPR database is consistent across countries with respect to the inclusion criteria of companies, the treatment of initial public offerings, and the distinction between property development and property investment companies. The GPR country indices are available on both a market value-weighted and equally-weighted basis, although we primarily use the market-weighted indices in this study.[9]

The country-level and world capital market equity indices (i.e., country and world wealth portfolio proxies) are compiled by Morgan Stanley Capital International (MSCI) and are obtained from Datastream.[10] The MSCI indices are the most widely used country and world indices by international money managers for asset allocation decisions and performance measurement. They are also widely used by academic researchers because of their consistency, extensive market coverage, and historical availability dating back to 1970. The MSCI total return indices (with dividend reinvestment) are value-weighted and composed of stocks that broadly represent each market.[11] Non-nationals can also readily purchase the stocks in these indices. All the returns are calculated in excess of the U.S. Treasury bill closest to 30 days to maturity on the last trading day of the month. These interest rate data are from Ibbotson and Associates.

3.1. Advantages and limitations of the data

Although the GPR database is constructed to representative of the universe of publicly traded real estate companies, it is important to note that returns on these securities may not accurately reflect returns in private real estate markets, which is where the majority of commercial real estate in most countries is valued and exchanged. Eichholtz and Hartzell (1996), Giliberto and Mengden (1996), and others argue that property share prices are likely to be more volatile than the underlying real estate assets for several reasons. First, because these public real estate firms are operating companies, their share prices are sensitive to the market's changing assessment of the quality and vision of the management team. Second, because the securities are publicly traded, they are exposed to the arbitrage forces of the public market. Nevertheless, there is an obvious link between the performance of real estate in the public and private markets.

Several authors who have investigated international real estate portfolio issues have used time series of rents and capitalization rates, instead of property share return data, in their research (e.g., Goetzman and Wachter, 1996, and Case et al., 1999). The advantage of such an approach is that the database may contain information on a larger sample of the commercial real estate stock in a given market or country. The disadvantages of this approach reflect the problems of infrequent trading and the lack of a central marketplace for privately held and traded assets. Moreover, rents and capitalization rates in different countries are hard to compare, given the international variation in rental contracts.[12] Real estate stock indices have the advantage that they are publicly traded, transaction-based, transparent, and reported on a frequent basis (Lizieri et al., 1998). For these reasons, we limit our analysis to publicly traded property shares.[13]

3.2. Descriptive statistics

Table 1 provides descriptive statistics for the full sample period from 1984–1999. On average, the aggregate GPR index was comprised of 277 firms over the 192 sample months. However, many of the country-level returns must be interpreted with caution due to the small number of companies that comprise the index in some countries. In fact, the return indices in 12 of the 20 countries in the 1984–1999 sample are calculated with an average number of companies less than 10. The last two columns in Table 1 reveal that six

Table 1. Summary statistics for commercial real estate returns across countries: annualized monthly percent returns in U.S. dollars: 1984–1999.

	Mean Return	Std. Dev.	Treynor Ratio	Treynor Ratio Rank	Monthly Obs.	Ave. No. of Firms in Index	Ave. Mkt. Value (U.S. $m.)	Market Value Rank
Australia	14.9	18.0	1.37	6	192	15	6,066	8
Belgium	7.5	17.6	0.63	12	156	2	442	16
Canada	− 7.9	27.0	− 1.31	19	192	6	2,942	11
France	11.4	17.0	0.89	8	192	35	12,768	6
Germany	8.0	12.1	1.55	2	192	14	18,807	5
Hong Kong	28.8	41.6	1.50	4	192	22	28,773	3
Ireland	20.4	36.8	2.00	1	175	1	144	19
Italy	12.5	27.2	0.89	7	192	4	871	15
Japan	15.5	39.7	0.51	15	192	17	34,393	1
Malaysia	14.1	57.4	0.53	14	168	5	1,040	13
Netherlands	7.2	13.1	0.34	17	192	7	6,089	7
New Zealand	3.3	27.3	− 0.41	18	144	3	264	18
Norway	18.9	33.2	1.51	3	192	2	330	17
Singapore	22.3	45.1	0.83	9	192	5	5,570	9
Spain	12.0	33.1	0.62	13	154	2	884	14
Sweden	9.3	36.9	0.41	16	192	4	1,202	12
Switzerland	9.3	13.8	1.41	5	192	16	4,656	10
United Kingdom	12.5	22.8	0.71	11	192	41	19,817	4
United States	10.9	15.1	0.73	10	192	71	33,515	2
Aggregated GPR	11.4	17.2	0.51	—	192	277	181,773	—
World Stock Portfolio	15.9	14.4	—	—	—	—	—	—
U.S. Benchmarks								
Large Cap Stocks	17.7	14.8	—	—	—	—	—	—
Small Cap Stocks	13.1	17.8	—	—	—	—	—	—
L–T Gov. Bonds	11.2	9.7	—	—	—	—	—	—

Notes. The international real estate securities data are from the Global Real Estate Securities Database of Global Property Research (GPR). For the country real estate returns, we use the market-weighted GPR country indices which have been converted into U.S. dollars. The GPR database is consistent across countries with respect to the inclusion criteria of companies, the treatment of initial public offerings, and the distinction between property development and property investment companies. The GPR index is constructed to be representative of the movements in the worldwide real estate securities market. The country level and world capital market return indices are value-weighted equity indices (in U.S. dollar terms) constructed by Morgan Stanley. We obtain these data from Datastream. The U.S. benchmark data are from Ibbotson and Associates. The Treynor ratios are calculated using each country's beta with respect to the world portfolio (the beta estimates are shown in Table 4).

countries dominate the aggregate GPR index. On average, Japan accounted for \$34.4 billion, or 18.9 percent, of the market value of the aggregate index. Japan's average contribution to the aggregate index was closely followed by the U.S. with an average market capitalization of \$33.5 billion. Hong Kong (15.8 percent), the United Kingdom (10.9 percent), Germany (10.3 percent), and France (7.0 percent) followed in importance. The remaining countries each contributed less than 4 percent, on average, to the market value of the aggregate GPR index.

The first and second columns of Table 1 contain the annualized mean monthly return and standard deviation, converted into U.S. dollars. For example, the U.S. posted an average annual return of 10.9 percent over the 1984 to 1999 period with a standard deviation of 15.1 percent. On a market-weighted basis, GPR's collection of publicly traded real estate companies produced an 11.4 percent annual return with a standard deviation of 17.2 percent. There was, however, a great deal of variability around the 11.4 percent aggregate return. For example, Hong Kong and Singapore produced total returns in excess of 20 percent per year, while Canada severely underperformed with an annual return of − 7.9 percent per year.

Based on univariate return statistics, international real estate securities underperformed relative to the world wealth portfolio (proxied by Morgan Stanley's world index of international stocks) over the 1984–1999 period. The world wealth/stock portfolio produced both a higher mean annual return than real estate securities (15.9 percent vs 11.4 percent) and a lower standard deviation (14.4 percent vs 17.2 percent) From the perspective of a U.S.-based investor, the GPR index also underperformed relative to U.S. stock and bond markets on a raw return per unit of total risk basis. For example, large cap U.S. stock provided an average annual return of 17.7 percent and a standard deviation of 14.8 percent (a return per unit of risk ration of 1.19). This compares favorably with the return/risk ratio of 0.66 (11.4 percent/17.2 percent) produced by the value-weighted aggregate real estate securities index. With a return/risk ratio of 1.15 (11.2 percent/9.8 percent), the U.S. long-term government bond index also outperformed the aggregate GPR index. The aggregate return/risk performance of international real estate companies more closely approximated the returns on the U.S. small cap index (13.1 percent/17.8 percent = 0.73).

The absolute and relative performance of international real estate securities varies significantly across our sub-periods. Although the aggregate GPR index produced a mean annual return of 11.4 percent over the full sample period, the average return during the 1984–1989 period was 26.4 percent (see Table 2). This exceeds the corresponding 22.5 percent average return on the world wealth portfolio. In addition, the aggregate GPR index significantly outperformed the three U.S. benchmarks on a return per unit of risk basis during 1984–1989.

The average market capitalization of Japanese real estate companies accounted for 37.4 percent of the aggregate index during the 1984–1989 period. This is especially significant because the Japanese securities produced an average return of 48.5 percent during this period. Hong Kong securities, which on average contributed 9.4 percent of the aggregate capitalization of the index during this period, produced an average return of 38.4 percent per year. Thus, nearly 50 percent of the market capitalization of the aggregate index was

Table 2. Summary statistics for commercial real estate returns across countries: Annualized monthly percent returns in U.S. dollars: 1984–1989.

	Mean Return	Std. Dev.	Treynor Ratio	Treynor Ratio Rank	Monthly Obs.	Ave. No. of Firms in Index	Ave. Mkt. Value (U.S. $m.)	Market Value Rank
Australia	18.0	22.6	1.41	12	72	7	1,734	10
Belgium	21.5	27.7	2.73	4	36	2	211	16
Canada	18.1	23.5	1.13	15	72	5	2,877	8
France	25.3	20.7	2.28	7	72	15	4,784	6
Germany	15.3	13.8	0.05	18	72	10	5,561	5
Hong Kong	38.4	39.6	2.21	8	72	17	7,934	4
Ireland	26.1	43.9	1.92	9	55	1	24	20
Italy	28.0	28.7	2.72	5	72	3	412	14
Japan	48.5	47.8	2.35	6	72	10	31,640	1
Malaysia	24.0	56.5	1.39	13	48	4	390	15
Netherlands	17.3	12.4	2.84	3	72	5	2,836	9
New Zealand	18.9	39.9	−48.38	19	24	2	79	18
Norway	33.8	34.0	4.17	2	72	1	136	17
Singapore	28.6	46.0	1.34	14	72	3	1,009	11
Spain	33.0	44.7	1.66	10	34	1	483	13
Sweden	32.2	25.3	5.67	1	72	2	662	12
Switzerland	13.3	15.9	1.61	11	72	14	3,548	7
United Kingdom	21.0	26.9	1.12	16	72	36	11,566	2
United States	15.7	15.5	1.00	17	72	38	9,316	3
Aggregate GPR	26.4	19.5	1.66	—	72	171	84,660	—
World Stock Portfolio	22.5	15.2	—	—	—	—	—	—
U.S. Benchmarks								
Large Cap Stocks	17.2	15.6	—	—	—	—	—	—
Small Cap Stocks	8.9	18.4	—	—	—	—	—	—
L–T Gov. Bonds	15.2	11.9	—	—	—	—	—	—

Notes. The international real estate securities data are from the Global Real Estate Securities Database of Global Property Research (GPR). For the country real estate returns, we use the market-weighted GPR country indices which have been converted into U.S. dollars. The GPR database is consistent across countries with respect to the inclusion criteria of companies, the treatment of initial public offerings, and the distinction between property development and property investment companies. The GPR index is constructed to be representative of the movements in the worldwide real estate securities market. The country level and world capital market return indices are value-weighted equity indices (in U.S. dollar terms) constructed by Morgan Stanley. We obtain these data from Datastream. The U.S. benchmark data are from Ibbotson and Associates. The Treynor ratios are calculated using each country's beta with respect to the world portfolio (the beta estimates are shown in Table 4).

contributed by two countries that averaged better than 38 percent annual returns. However, these two Asian economies were not alone in producing large, and volatile, real estate returns. In fact, no country represented in the index generated an average return of less than 13 percent and most were significantly higher, albeit with, in most cases, significant volatility.

The boom in global real estate security prices came to an end during the 1990s. The total return to the aggregate GPR index averaged just 2.4 percent per year (see Table 3). Aggregate return volatility, however, was only slightly lower (15.2 percent) than during

Table 3. Summary statistics for commercial real estate returns across countries: annualized monthly percent returns in U.S. dollars: 1990–1999.

	Mean Return	Std. Dev.	Treynor Ratio	Treynor Ratio Rank	Monthly Obs.	Ave. No. of Firms in Index	Ave. Mkt. Value (U.S. $m.)	Market Value Rank
Argentina	19.6	43.4	0.69	6	77	1	396	22
Australia	13.0	14.6	1.32	2	120	20	8,666	7
Austria	1.8	13.0	−13.35	28	120	4	604	18
Belgium	3.5	13.1	−0.59	20	120	2	511	20
Canada	−23.4	28.1	0.01	15	120	7	2,981	12
Denmark	1.9	17.0	−1.30	25	61	1	136	28
France	3.0	13.8	−0.35	17	120	47	17,559	6
Germany	3.7	10.8	−1.64	27	120	16	26,755	4
Hong Kong	23.1	42.8	1.12	4	120	24	41,276	2
Indonesia	−1.9	71.0	−0.64	21	117	3	386	23
Ireland	17.8	33.3	2.15	1	120	1	199	26
Italy	3.1	26.0	−0.23	16	120	5	1,147	15
Japan	−4.3	32.8	−0.46	19	120	21	36,045	3
Malaysia	10.1	57.9	0.27	12	120	5	1,300	14
Mexico	−0.4	69.4	−0.40	18	75	2	557	19
Netherlands	1.1	13.2	−0.84	23	120	9	8,041	9
New Zealand	0.2	24.1	−0.87	24	120	3	301	25
Norway	10.0	32.6	0.51	9	120	2	446	21
Philippines	11.6	46.5	0.44	10	99	2	4,033	11
Portugal	−7.7	32.2	0.00	26	120	2	177	27
Singapore	18.5	44.7	0.60	7	120	6	8,307	8
South Africa	16.0	31.7	0.79	5	31	5	369	24
Spain	6.0	29.1	0.14	14	120	2	998	16
Sweden	−4.5	41.9	−0.82	22	120	5	1,525	13
Switzerland	6.9	12.4	1.27	3	120	17	5,320	10
Thailand	16.6	165.2	0.25	13	105	1	675	17
United Kingdom	7.4	19.9	0.33	11	120	44	24,767	5
United States	7.9	14.9	0.52	8	120	90	48,035	1
Aggregate GPR	2.4	15.2	−0.24		120	340	240,040	—
World Stock Portfolio	11.8	13.8	—	—	—	—	—	—
U.S. Benchmarks								
Large Cap Stocks	18.0	13.3	—	—	—	—	—	—
Small Cap Stocks	15.7	17.4	—	—	—	—	—	—
L–T Gov. Bonds	8.8	8.2	—	—	—	—	—	—

Notes. The international real estate securities data are from the Global Real Estate Securities Database of Global Property Research (GPR). For the country real estate returns, we use the market-weighted GPR country indices which have been converted into U.S. dollars. The GPR database is consistent across countries with respect to the inclusion criteria of companies, the treatment of initial public offerings, and the distinction between property development and property investment companies. The GPR index is constructed to be representative of the movements in the worldwide real estate securities market. The country level and world capital market return indices are value-weighted equity indices (in U.S. dollar terms) constructed by Morgan Stanley. We obtain these data from Datastream. The U.S. benchmark data are from Ibbotson and Associates. The Treynor ratios are calculated using each country's beta with respect to the world portfolio (the beta estimates are shown in Table 4).

the booming 1980s. The average annual return to the world wealth portfolio also declined significantly from 22.5 percent in 1984–1999 to 11.8 percent in the 1990s. However, this 11.8 percent return exceeded by a factor of five the return on the aggregate GPR index. The poor performance of the GPR index is even more pronounced when compared to the average returns produced by U.S. large cap stocks (18.0 percent) and small cap stocks (15.7 percent) during the 1990s.

The average number of firms in the aggregate index increased significantly to an average of 340 in the 1990s. The corresponding average market capitalization was $240 billion. The U.S. replaced Japan as the largest contributor of market capitalization to the aggregate index—accounting for 20 percent, on average, of the aggregate index during this period. The U.S. was followed by Hong Kong (17.2 percent), Japan (15.0 percent), Germany (11.1 percent), and the United Kingdom (10.3 percent).

3.3. Treynor ratios

The means and standard deviations reported in the first columns of Tables 1–3 clearly indicate that international real estate returns have been quite volatile. However, modern portfolio theory posits that only systematic risk, not total risk, is priced in competitive capital markets. Thus, from the perspective of an investor seeking to build a diversified portfolio of international real estate securities, a more appropriate measure of risk is the extent to which returns in a particular country are likely to co-vary with returns on the world wealth portfolio (WWP). To address this question, monthly returns in excess of the U.S. Treasury bill rate for each country were regressed on the world wealth portfolio's excess return (see equation (1)). The betas from these *ex post* regressions measure the degree of (worldwide) systematic risk in each country's real estate securities. The mean excess return in each country was then divided by the WWP beta to produce a standard Treynor ratio for each country, and for the aggregate GPR index, for the full sample and both sub-periods.[14] The Treynor ratios, and the relative ranking of each country based on its Treynor ratio, are displayed in columns 3 and 4 of Tables 1–3.

The Treynor ratio for the aggregate GPR index was 0.51 over the 1984–1999 period. The ratio ranged across countries from 2.0 to -1.31. Two countries with large real estate securities markets, Germany and Hong Kong, performed very well, ranking second and fourth, respectively. The U.S. ratio of 0.73 put it squarely in the middle of the 20 countries for which we had adequate data to calculate returns for the 1984–1999 time period.

The Treynor ratio for the aggregate GPR index was 1.66 in the 1984–1989 period, which is reflective of the general real estate boom that affected most, but not all, real estate markets during this period. With a ratio of 1.00, the U.S. ranked 17 out of 20 countries. This poor relative performance was caused by the significant downturn that hit most U.S. real estate markets in the mid-to-late 1980s. In sharp contrast to the 1980s, the Treynor ratio for the aggregate GPR index was -0.24 percent in the 1990s. This reflects the severe real estate recession that began in the U.S. in the 1980s and finally swept across many international markets during the 1990s. Many U.S. commercial real estate markets began to recover in the early 1990s and most were booming by the late 1990s. Thus, the U.S.

managed a Treynor ratio of 0.52 during the 1990s, which placed it eighth out of 28 countries.

4. Regression results

4.1. Single-factor model

The Treynor ratio permits us to rank the relative excess return performance of countries based on a measure systematic risk. However, it does not allow us to determine whether real estate securities provided investors with positive (or negative) risk-adjusted (i.e abnormal) returns. To address this issue, we estimate both the single-factor and two factor return regressions for our three sample periods.[15] An estimated alpha significantly different from zero indicates abnormal return performance.

Table 4 displays the regression results obtained for using a single risk factor—the world stock portfolio—to measure *ex post* return performance. The first panel in Table 4 presents results from the full sample period. The second and third panels display results for our two sub-periods. Coefficient estimates for α_i and β_{iw}, along with the adjusted R^2, are reported in the first row for each country. The statistics are in parentheses, with significance at the 10 percent level indicated by an asterisk (*).

When the aggregate value-weighted GPR monthly index is regressed on a constant and the world wealth portfolio, the estimated alpha for the full sample period is -0.321 per month, or 3.85 percent per year (see the last row of Table 4). However, because the t-statistic is -1.391, we cannot reject the null hypothesis that the risk adjusted abnormal return on the aggregate GPR index is zero. Although the estimated alphas for numerous countries are large, the standard errors of the estimates preclude us from concluding the abnormal performance is statistically significantly different from zero. The only exception during 1984–1999 is Canada.

It is interesting to note that the beta with respect to the world wealth portfolio is 0.933 for the aggregate GPR index, strongly indicating that a value-weighted portfolio of publicly available international real estate securities was comparable in (systematic) risk to the world wealth portfolio over the full sample period. Moreover, returns on the WWP explain 61 percent of the variation in aggregate GPR returns. The country specific betas are all positive and statistically significant and the adjusted R^2s range from 0.019 (Germany) to 0.338 (Japan). These results suggest that a worldwide systematic risk factor explains a significant proportion of the cross-section of international real estate returns.

The single-index results are similar for our two sub periods with respect to the number of countries that produce statistically significant abnormal returns. During the 1948–1989 time period, only Sweden's abnormal return of 1.608 per month (or 19.30 percent per year) is distinguishable from zero at the 10 percent level of significance. During the 1990–1999 period, Canada, Japan, The Netherlands, and Portugal produced negative excess returns (alphas) that are statistically significant.

The beta with respect to the WWP for the aggregate GRP index is 0.968 in the 1984–1989 period and 0.887 in the 1990s. These results, coupled with the beta of 0.933 for the

Table 4. Single-factor performance of commercial real estate returns monthly percent excess returns in U.S. dollars.

	1984–1999			1984–1989			1990–1999		
	α_i	β_{iw}	Adj. R^2	α_i	β_{iw}	Adj. R^2	α_i	β_{iw}	Adj. R^2
Argentina	—	—	—	—	—	—	−0.399	1.788	0.255
							(−0.310)	(5.165)*	
Australia	0.281	0.562	0.199	0.061	0.643	0.175	0.381	0.507	0.227
	(0.816)	(6.944)*		(0.084)	(4.013)*		(1.107)	(5.971)*	
Austria	—	—	—	—	—	—	−0.250	0.019	−0.008
							(−0.715)	(0.217)	
Belgium	−0.012	0.300	0.057	0.769	0.458	0.054	−0.254	0.221	0.047
	(−0.030)	(3.208)*		(0.582)	(1.728)*		(−0.740)	(2.613)*	
Canada	−1.890	0.862	0.209	−0.160	0.817	0.270	−2.893	0.847	0.169
	(−3.691)*	(7.156)*		(−0.223)	(5.219)*		(−4.226)*	(5.008)*	
Denmark	—	—	—	—	—	—	−0.451	0.201	0.005
							(−0.681)	(1.137)	
France	0.026	0.541	0.209	0.643	0.667	0.231	−0.383	0.428	0.179
	(0.082)	(7.163)*		(0.997)	(4.727)*		(−1.144)	(5.166)*	
Germany	0.091	0.129	0.019	0.414	0.207	0.039	−0.128	0.061	−0.002
	(0.355)	(2.154)*		(0.859)	(1.965)*		(−0.442)	(0.853)	
Hong Kong	0.789	1.283	0.195	1.055	1.181	0.196	0.669	1.353	0.186
	(0.991)	(6.850)*		(0.836)	(4.280)*		(0.647)	(5.293)*	
Indonesia	—	—	—	—	—	—	−1.410	0.866	0.019
							(−0.738)	(1.810)*	
Ireland	0.720	0.630	0.056	0.299	0.851	0.076	0.826	0.503	0.036
	(0.896)	(3.366)*		(0.172)	(2.333)*		(0.941)	(2.319)*	
Italy	0.037	0.639	0.111	0.898	0.643	0.105	−0.472	0.612	0.100
	(0.067)	(4.982)*		(0.933)	(3.054)*		(−0.716)	(3.753)*	
Japan	−0.474	1.601	0.338	1.514	1.470	0.209	−1.597	1.644	0.484
	(−0.689)	(9.901)*		(1.001)	(4.443)*		(−2.538)*	(10.577)*	
Malaysia	−0.470	1.409	0.126	−0.058	1.061	0.078	−0.546	1.608	0.141
	(−0.384)	(4.982)*		(−0.025)	(2.228)*		(−0.379)	(4.516)*	
Mexico	—	—	—	—	—	—	−1.212	0.982	0.011
							(−0.509)	(1.341)	
Netherlands	−0.192	0.348	0.145	0.456	0.299	0.122	−0.556	0.367	0.143
	(−0.747)	(5.759)*		(1.097)	(3.296)*		(−1.704)*	(4.555)*	
New Zealand	−0.439	0.389	0.031	1.006	−0.020	−0.045	−0.679	0.449	0.059
	(−0.665)	(2.357)*		(0.402)	(−0.030)		(−1.080)	(2.890)*	
Norway	0.475	0.729	0.096	1.523	0.535	0.044	−0.071	0.847	0.123
	(0.705)	(4.600)*		(1.292)	(2.074)*		(−0.087)	(4.183)*	
Philippines	—	—	—	—	—	—	−0.668	1.375	0.121
							(−0.510)	(3.781)*	
Portugal	—	—	—	—	—	—	−1.447	0.720	0.088
							(−1.752)*	(3.519)*	
Singapore	−0.038	1.664	0.279	0.025	1.345	0.186	0.041	1.904	0.344
	(−0.047)	(8.631)*		(0.017)	(4.156)*		(0.042)	(7.924)*	
South Africa	—	—	—	—	—	—	−0.638	1.173	0.317
							(−0.447)	(3.802)*	
Spain	0.092	0.905	0.151	1.275	1.325	0.213	−0.234	0.738	0.119
	(0.129)	(5.298)*		(0.642)	(3.154)*		(−0.322)	(4.109)*	

Table 4. (*continued*)

	1984–1999			1984–1989			1990–1999		
	α_i	β_{iw}	Adj. R^2	α_i	β_{iw}	Adj. R^2	α_i	β_{iw}	Adj. R^2
Sweden	−0.345	0.729	0.077	1.608	0.370	0.036	−1.364	0.946	0.090
	(−0.455)	(4.094)*		(1.821)*	(1.916)*		(−1.271)	(3.565)*	
Switzerland	0.129	0.220	0.048	0.096	0.323	0.082	0.111	0.142	0.017
	(0.448)	(3.243)*		(0.176)	(2.713)*		(0.337)	(1.747)*	
Thailand	—	—	—	—	—	—	−1.987	3.993	0.077
							(−0.430)	(3.098)*	
United Kingdom	−0.105	0.805	0.255	−0.198	1.034	0.331	−0.134	0.635	0.189
	(−0.250)	(8.128)*		(−0.252)	(6.016)*		(−0.278)	(5.331)*	
United States	−0.075	0.585	0.308	−0.214	0.709	0.479	−0.039	0.496	0.206
	(−0.281)	(9.260)*		(−0.538)	(8.141)*		(−0.109)	(5.624)*	
Aggregate	−0.321	0.933	0.608	0.336	0.968	0.562	−0.721	0.887	0.650
	(−1.391)	(17.192)*		(0.729)	(9.605)*		(−2.976)*	(14.828)*	

Notes. t-statistics in parentheses. * denotes significance at the 10 percent level or below.
For each of the three sample periods and for each country, we estimate the following model:

$$R_{it} - R_{ft} = \alpha_i + \beta_{iw}[R_{wt} - R_{ft}] + e_{it},$$

where R_{it} is the return in U.S. dollars on country i's real estate total return index in time period t, R_{ft} is the U.S. T-bill rate in time period t, α_i is a constant (Jensen's alpha), β_{iw} is the return sensitivity (exposure) of country i's real estate returns on the world equity portfolio, R_{wt} is the total return in U.S. dollars on the world equity portfolio from Morgan Stanley in time period t, and e_{it} is an error term.

full sample, strongly suggest that a value-weighted portfolio of publicly available international real estate securities has been comparable in systematic risk to the WWP. This, is turn, suggests that international stock investors who are seeking to diversify their portfolios by adding real estate securities may want to hold those securities in proportions different from their relative contributions to the aggregate GPR index.

4.2. *Two factor model*

The results from estimating our two-factor model (equation (3)) are displayed in Table 5, with results for the 1984–1999 period contained in the first panel. Several results from this estimation are worth noting. First, the country alphas are little changed by the addition of the country specific risk factor. For example, the estimated alpha for the U.S. is now −0.083 per month, versus −0.075 in the single-factor model. A simple average of the 20 country alphas is now −0.097, versus −0.074 in the single-factor model. Although the estimated alphas remain virtually unchanged, the alphas for Hong Kong (0.799) and The Netherlands (−0.944) are now statistically significant at the 10 percent level.

A comparison of the WWP betas in the single- and two-factor models reveals they are remarkably invariant with respect to the addition of the country specific factor during the

Table 5. Multi-index performance of commercial real estate returns monthly percent excess returns in U.S. dollars.

	1984–1999				1984–1989				1990–1999			
	α_i	β_{iW}	β_{iR}	Adj. R^2	α_i	β_{iW}	β_{iR}	Adj. R^2	α_i	β_{iW}	β_{iR}	Adj. R^2
Argentina	—	—	—	—	—	—	—	—	−0.430	1.782	0.850	0.533
									(6.501)*	(6.717)*		
Australia	0.285	0.561	0.594	0.649	0.086	0.568	0.578	0.674	0.402	0.567	0.632	0.604
	(1.251)	(10.466)*	(15.578)*		(0.187)	(5.626)*	(10.395)*		(1.634)	(9.289)*	(10.605)*	
Austria	—	—	—	—	—	—	—	—	−0.190	0.018	0.110	0.017
									(0.207)	(2.001)*		
Belgium	−0.010	0.301	0.385	0.132	0.724	0.407	0.205	0.040	−0.214	0.274	0.456	0.203
	(−0.026)	(3.347)*	(3.765)*		(0.543)	(1.473)	(0.709)		(−0.684)	(3.510)*	(4.897)*	
Canada	−1.893	0.861	0.830	0.345	0.068	0.787	0.709	0.401	−3.064	0.866	0.952	0.331
	(−4.064)*	(7.859)*	(6.356)*		(0.105)	(5.545)*	(4.035)*		(−4.982)*	(5.707)*	(5.409)*	
Denmark	—	—	—	—	—	—	—	—	−0.471	0.207	0.482	0.135
									(1.257)	(3.118)*		
France	0.027	0.543	0.492	0.401	0.534	0.591	0.522	0.447	−.0308	.0479	.0417	0.312
	(0.096)	(8.256)*	(7.828)*		(0.975)	(4.904)*	(5.325)*		(−1.004)	(6.262)*	(4.867)*	
Germany	0.089	0.130	0.201	0.097	0.359	0.204	0.239	0.165	−0.110	0.064	0.142	0.025
	(0.364)	(2.258)*	(4.161)*		(0.798)	(2.078)*	(3.410)*		(−0.383)	(0.910)	(2.056)*	
Hong Kong	0.799	1.283	1.296	0.892	1.219	1.224	1.201	0.913	0.559	1.311	1.360	0.885
	(2.743)*	(18.724)*	(34.992)*		(2.944)*	(13.510)*	(24.099)*		(1.435)	(13.612)*	(26.615)*	
Indonesia	—	—	—	—	—	—	—	—	−0.995	0.709	1.110	0.601
									(−0.817)	(2.324)*	(12.939)*	
Ireland	0.719	0.630	0.051	0.053	0.287	0.842	−0.015	0.059	0.455	0.258	0.633	0.100
	(0.894)	(3.360)*	(0.617)		(0.163)	(2.256)*	(−0.142)		(0.531)	(1.150)	(3.054)*	
Italy	0.026	0.641	0.736	0.489	0.409	0.620	0.774	0.494	−0.217	0.644	0.707	0.468
	(0.062)	(6.593)*	(11.872)*		(0.562)	(3.910)*	(7.402)*		(−0.428)	(5.137)*	(9.056)*	
Japan	−0.429	1.600	1.302	0.640	−0.444	1.791	1.747	0.548	−0.916	1.530	1.050	0.773
	(−0.844)	(13.406)*	(12.613)*		(−0.378)	(7.052)*	(7.313)*		(−2.174)*	(14.759)*	(12.214)*	
Malaysia	−0.479	1.408	0.611	0.333	−0.022	1.163	0.119	0.073	−0.963	0.979	1.199	0.636
	(−0.448)	(5.700)*	(7.231)*		(−0.009)	(2.364)*	(0.862)		(−1.026)	(4.130)*	(12.650)*	
Mexico	—	—	—	—	—	—	—	—	−1.087	0.998	0.790	0.158
									(−0.490)	(1.436)	(3.670)*	
Netherlands	−0.191	0.349	0.273	0.193	0.468	0.288	0.148	0.131	−0.560	0.392	0.396	0.227
	(−0.765)	(5.938)*	(3.502)*		(1.131)	(3.168)*	(1.317)		(−1.808)*	(5.098)*	(3.706)*	
New Zealand	−0.944	0.260	0.752	0.380	0.243	0.508	0.889	0.440	−1.182	0.241	0.698	0.342
	(−1.779)*	(1.961)*	(8.971)*		(0.132)	(1.004)	(4.477)*		(−2.227)*	(1.813)*	(7.167)*	
Norway	0.479	0.731	0.523	0.202	1.368	0.472	0.566	0.173	0.036	0.896	0.502	0.213
	(0.756)	(4.908)*	(5.118)*		(1.246)	(1.962)*	(3.446)*		(0.047)	(4.662)*	(3.805)*	
Philippines	—	—	—	—	—	—	—	—	−0.725	1.355	0.593	0.285
									(−0.615)	(4.132)*	(4.808)*	

Table 5. (continued)

	1984–1999				1984–1989				1990–1999			
	α_i	β_{iW}	β_{iR}	Adj. R^2	α_i	β_{iW}	β_{iR}	Adj. R^2	α_i	β_{iW}	β_{iR}	Adj. R^2
Portugal	—	—	—	—	—	—	—	—	− 1.460	0.715	0.438	0.145
									(− 1.825)*	(3.620)*	(2.965)*	
Singapore	0.024	1.652	1.427	0.815	0.477	1.649	1.415	0.811	− 0.249	1.636	1.446	0.816
	(0.057)	(16.919)*	(23.429)*		(0.668)	(10.476)*	(15.230)*		(− 0.483)	(12.752)*	(17.333)*	
South Africa	—	—	—	—	—	—	—	—	− 0.744	1.137	0.488	0.499
									(− 0.607)	(4.297)*	(3.337)*	
Spain	0.085	0.905	0.652	0.258	1.263	1.374	0.157	0.192	− 0.222	0.629	0.897	0.372
	(0.126)	(5.667)*	(4.757)*		(0.628)	(3.100)*	(0.399)		(− 0.361)	(4.126)*	(6.937)*	
Sweden	− 0.369	0.727	0.733	0.194	1.559	0.450	0.397	0.110	− 1.416	0.798	0.969	0.230
	(− 0.522)	(4.374)*	(5.335)*		(1.837)*	(2.390)*	(2.613)*		(− 1.434)	(3.245)*	(4.717)*	
Switzerland	0.138	0.220	0.451	0.249	0.233	0.326	0.401	0.227	0.023	0.134	0.506	0.281
	(0.538)	(3.649)*	(7.190)*		(0.465)	(2.982)*	(3.755)*		(0.080)	(1.932)*	(6.621)*	
Thailand	—	—	—	—	—	—	—	—	− 1.558	3.841	2.047	0.324
									(− 0.393)	(3.481)*	(6.181)*	
United Kingdom	− 0.115	0.808	1.081	0.597	0.118	0.827	1.091	0.706	− 0.255	0.783	1.058	0.466
	(− 0.370)	(11.083)*	(12.686)*		(0.227)	(7.125)*	(9.491)*		(− 0.653)	(7.954)*	(7.854)*	
United States	− 0.082	0.586	0.609	0.448	0.210	0.648	0.738	0.732	− 0.199	0.519	0.490	0.275
	(− 0.343)	(10.375)*	(6.977)*		(0.723)	(10.309)*	(8.191)*		(− 0.577)	(6.144)*	(3.483)*	

Notes. t-statistics in parentheses * denotes significance at the 10 percent level or below.

For each of the three sample periods and for each country, we use a two-step estimation procedure. In the first step, we regress excess country-wide stock returns (in excess of the risk-free rate) on the excess returns earned on world equity portfolio. In particular, we estimate the following regression:

$$R^s_{it} - R_{ft} = \alpha^s_i + \beta^s_{iw}[R_{wt} - R_{ft}] + e^s_{it},$$

where R^s_{it} is the total return on country i's stock index, R_{ft} is the U.S. T-bill rate, and R_{wt} is the total return on the world equity portfolio in time period t. The equity data are from Morgan Stanley. e^s_{it} are the unexplained residuals. These residuals represent the portion of each country's stock returns that are not explained by movements in the world wealth portfolio. In the second step, we include the orthogonalized country-specific risk factor (i.e., the orthogonalized residuals) as an explanatory variable in the real estate return regressions and estimate the following equation.

$$R_{it} - R_{ft} = \alpha_i + \beta_{iw}[R_{wt} - R_{ft}] + \beta_{iR}\, e^s_{it} + u_{it},$$

R_{it} is the return on country i's real estate total return index in time period t, and R_{ft} is the U.S. T-bill rate in time period t, β_{iw} is the estimated return sensitivity of country i's GPR index to returns on the world wealth portfolio (R_{wt}). β_{iR} is the estimated sensitivity of country i's GPR index to returns on the orthoganalized country specific risk factor (e^s_{it}). The estimated constants (α_i - Jensen's alphas) from these two-factor models can be used as evidence of superior risk-adjusted return performance.

1984–1999 period. However, the addition of the country specific factor has a significant effect on the ability of the regression model to explain the cross-section of real estate returns in each country. In all but one of the 19 countries represented in our 1984–1999 sample, the estimated coefficient on the country-specific risk factor is positive and highly significant. For example, the estimated coefficient on the U.S. factor is equal to 0.609 with a *t*-statistic of 6.977. Relative to the single-factor model, the inclusion of the U.S. risk factor increases the adjusted R^2 of the U.S. model from 0.308 to 0.448. The increase in explanatory power from adding a country-specific factor is even more pronounced in many other countries. Overall, the (equally-weighted) average R^2 for our 19 country sample in the 1984–1999 period increases from 0.152 to 0.388 with the addition of the country specific factor.

Interestingly, the effect of adding a country specific risk factor on the estimated alpha is more pronounced in our two sub-periods. For example, the estimated U.S. alpha during the 1984–1989 changes from -0.214 in the single-factor model to 0.210 in the two-factor model. Moreover, the estimated U.S. WWP beta moves from -0.538 in the single-factor model to 0.648 in the two-factor model. The estimated alphas also vary considerably between the single-and two-factor models in the 1990–1999 period. These frequently large shifts in the slope of the estimated regression line from one subperiod to the next suggest the *ex post* return regressions may be mis-specified when the country-specific factor is excluded.[16] Moreover, the mis-specification is more pronounced the shorter is the sample period. This result is intuitively appealing because it suggests the influence of international capital markets on within-country average real estate returns is more pronounced the longer is the sample period. However, these results should be interpreted with caution given that the estimated alphas, although frequently large in magnitude, are generally lacking in statistical significance in both the single-factor and two-factor models.

Despite the large (26.4 percent) annual average returns earned by the aggregate GPR index in 1984–1999, only two countries had estimated alpha coefficients significantly greater than zero: Sweden in the single-factor model and Hong Kong in the two-factor model. During the 1990s, Canada, Japan, The Netherlands, and Portugal significantly underperformed on a risk-adjusted basis in both the single- and two-factor models. It also is worth noting that the aggregate GPR index produced statistically significant negative abnormal returns in the 1990s. The estimated alpha in the single-factor specification is -0.721, or 8.65 percent annually (t-statistic $= 2.976$).

Looking at the regression explanatory powers (R^2s), we find that they are positively correlated with each country's share in the world portfolio (0.48), and this result is robust over our sub-periods. Interestingly, although there is a positive relation between the regression explanatory powers for each country and the number of firms in the index, this relation varies substantially over our sub-periods (0.56 for the 1980s and 0.10 for the 1990s), suggesting that the increase in the number of firms in the 1990s added potentially more idiosyncratic noise. It is important to note that this result is particularly relevant for the U.S. and for some of the smaller countries with few firms. Finally, the distribution of beta coefficients with respect to time and their relation to the regression R^2s is marginally positive, indicating a slight increase in country real estate sensitivity to world market movements.

5. Firm level performance by country

As discussed in the previous section, only a handful of country-level regressions produced statistically significant alphas, despite the significant variation in total returns across countries. However, aggregation to the country level may mask significant within-country variation in return performance across property companies. To examine this issue, we first calculate the mean return for each company in the GPR database. To be included in the company level sample, a total return for the firm must have been reported in at least 90 of the 120 months that comprise the 1990–1999 time period. As reported in Table 6, 202 companies in 14 countries satisfied our inclusion criterion.

For each of the 14 countries in this sub-sample, we report in Table 6 the average return for the firm with the highest, median, and lowest average total return, respectively, during the 1990s. For example, return data on 39 U.S. firms were available in at least 90 months during the 1990s. The mean company level returns ranged from a high of 33.6 percent per year to a low of − 6.3 percent. The annualized mean return for the median U.S. firm was 12.2 percent. Numerous other countries also display substantial variation in average returns across firms. For example, the average 1990s firm level return in the U.K. ranged form 74.5 percent to − 19.1 percent annually, with a median of 9.6 percent. Overall, the results in Table 6 strongly suggest that a great deal of company specific risk exists in international real estate securities. Moreover, these results suggest that strategic

Table 6. Summary statistics on average firm level returns across countries: annualized monthly percent total returns and standard deviations in U.S. dollars: 1990–1999.

		Average Returns					
	No. of Firms	High	Std. Dev.	Median	Std. Dev.	Low	Std. Dev.
Australia	3	5.6	11.3	4.0	25.4	3.2	11.2
Austria	10	33.6	25.5	12.4	16.2	6.3	17.1
Canada	3	8.5	37.8	− 11.3	28.1	− 26.1	55.5
France	29	25.2	45.3	7.4	21.8	− 24.0	39.8
Germany	14	5.3	13.9	3.8	10.4	− 11.1	36.4
Hong Kong	20	36.3	50.1	19.3	47.0	− 15.8	76.7
Italy	4	14.4	46.5	2.0	34.0	1.4	33.4
Japan	19	3.5	57.5	− 4.0	54.2	− 11.9	36.6
Malaysia	3	26.0	82.9	20.3	75.2	8.1	56.3
Netherlands	7	9.7	12.8	1.6	14.5	− 5.1	22.9
Singapore	4	27.2	48.9	13.9	43.9	8.1	45.4
Switzerland	15	9.4	13.9	8.1	14.2	4.4	31.5
United Kingdom	32	74.5	276.4	9.6	26.8	− 19.1	44.2
United States	39	33.6	49.2	12.2	21.4	− 6.3	28.9

Notes. To be included in the company level sample, a total return for the firm must have been reported in at least 90 of the 120 months that comprise the 1990–1999 time period. The firm level international real estate securities data are from the Global Real Estate Securities Database of Global Property Research (GPR). The GPR database is consistent across countries with respect to the inclusion criteria of companies, the treatment of initial public offerings, and the distinction between property development and property investment companies.

diversification both across and within countries may result in more risk reduction at the international portfolio level than would be accomplished with a strategy of holding a portfolio in each country that mimics a value-weighted real estate securities index.

Although the disaggregated total return data reveal significant return variation across companies within countries, it does not necessarily follow that a significant number of firms earned positive or negative risk-adjusted returns. To examine *ex post* performance, we separately estimate our two-factor model (equation (3)) for each of the 202 companies in our firm-level sample. These results are reported in Table 7. The number of positive and negative firm level alphas in each country is based on statistically significant alphas (at the 10 percent level).

The lack of statistically significant alphas in Table 7 is noteworthy. Of the 202 firms in this sub-sample, only nine produced positive abnormal returns. Twenty-four companies produced negative abnormal returns. However, 17 of these are Japanese firms—a country that experienced a severe commercial real estate recession during the 1990s. Despite the exceedingly poor relative performance of U.S. real estate stocks in 1998 and 1999, none of the 39 U.S. companies produced negative returns on a risk-adjusted basis.

Despite the apparent lack of company level abnormal return performance in most countries, the results in Table 7 should be interpreted with caution for several reasons. First, it is well known that the noise embedded in firm level total return data makes it difficult to reject the null hypothesis of no abnormal return performance. Second, the results assume that the assumptions of our asset pricing model are valid. In particular, these results are predicted on the assumption that all systematic risk in each country is proxied by movements in our two risk factors. Finally, our estimations were performed without imposing standard asset pricing restrictions. This latter issue is addressed in the following section.

6. Robustness checks

In estimating Jensen's alphas with our two-factor model, we used a two-step regression procedure. A potential problem with this approach is that the second regression used to estimate Jensen's alphas contains a generated regressor (i.e., the orthogonal component) with a potential errors-in-variables problem. To assess the effects of this potential problem, for each country, we used non-linear simultaneous equation regression procedures to jointly estimate both equations associated with the two-step regression procedure (see Pagan, 1984). We find that the results reported in Table 5 are virtually unchanged for each country.

An additional potential concern is that the models that we have estimated are unconstrained versions of the corresponding asset pricing models. In particular, we have not imposed the asset pricing restrictions implied by each of the models. For instance, in the two-factor model, we estimate:

$$R_{it} - R_{ft} = \alpha_i + \beta_{iw}[R_{wt} - R_{ft}] + \beta_{iR} e^s_{it} + u_{it}. \tag{3}$$

Table 7. Firm level multi-index performance of commercial real estate returns: Monthly percent excess returns in U.S. dollars: 1990–1999.

	No. of Firms in Sample	Number of Firms with + Alphas	Number of Firms with − Alphas	High-Low Range of Signif. Alphas
Australia	10	2	0	0.25
Austria	3	0	0	—
Canada	3	0	2	1.25
France	29	0	2	1.53
Germany	14	0	0	—
Hong Kong	20	2	1	4.08
Italy	4	0	0	—
Japan	20	0	17	1.41
Malaysia	3	0	0	—
Netherlands	7	0	1	—
Singapore	4	0	0	—
Switzerland	15	0	0	—
United Kingdom	32	0	1	—
United States	38	5	0	1.38
Totals	202	9	24	

Notes. The number of positive and negatives alphas are based on the number of significant firm level alphas (at the 10 percent level). The alphas are based on the two-factor model described below.

To be included in the company level sample, a total return for the firm must have been reported in at least 90 of the 120 months that comprise the 1990–1999 time period. The firm level international real estate securities data are from the Global Real Estate Securities Database of Global Property Research (GPR). The GPR database is consistent across countries with respect to the inclusion criteria of companies, the treatment of initial public offerings, and the distinction between property development and property investment companies.

For each firm in each country, we use a two-step estimation procedure. In the first step, we regress excess country-wide stock returns (in excess of the risk free rate) on the excess returns earned on world equity portfolio. In particular, we estimate the following regression:

$$R_{it}^{s} - R_{ft} = \alpha_i^{s} + \beta_{iw}^{s}[R_{wt} - R_{ft}] + e_{it}^{s},$$

where R_{it}^{s} is the total return on country i's stock index, R_{ft} is the U.S. T-bill rate, and R_{wt} is the total return on the world equity portfolio in time period t. The equity return data are from Morgan Stanley. e_{it}^{s} are the unexplained residuals which represent the portion of each country's stock market returns that are not explained by movements in the world stock portfolio. In the second step, we include the orthogonalized country-specific risk factor (i.e., the orthogonalized residuals) as an explanatory variable in the following firm level real estate return regressions:

$$R_{it} - R_{ft} = \alpha_i + \beta_{iw}[R_{wt} - R_{ft}] + \beta_{iR}\bar{e}_{it}^{\,s} + u_{it},$$

R_{it} is the return on firm i (in country i) in time period t, and R_{ft} is the U.S. T-bill rate in time period t. β_{iw} is the estimated return sensitivity of firm i to returns on the world wealth portfolio (R_{wt}). β_{iR} is the estimated return sensitivity of firm i to returns on the orthoganalized country specific risk factor (e_{it}^{s}). The estimated firm level constants (α_i - Jensen's alphas) from these two-factor models can be used as evidence of superior risk-adjusted return performance.

Equation (3) is the unconstrained version of the following two-factor asset pricing model,

$$R_{it} - R_{ft} = -\lambda_0\beta_{iw} + \lambda_2\beta_{iR} + \beta_{iw}[R_{wt} - R_{ft}] + \beta_{iR}\, e^{s}_{it} + u_{it}, \tag{4}$$

where λ_0 is the zero-beta excess rate of return (the return in excess of the risk-free rate) and λ_2 is the risk premia corresponding to the second factor. Note that the risk premia corresponding to the market factor falls out of the estimating equation (see Liu et al., 1990, and Ling and Naranjo, 1996, 1999). The model corresponding to (4) is derived by substituting the expected returns asset pricing equation into the returns generating equation implied by the asset pricing model. From equations (3) and (4), we can see that the constraint in equation (4) is on the intercept (alpha) in equation (3): $\alpha_i = -\lambda_0\beta_{iw} + \lambda_2\beta_{iR}$.

In order to estimate the parameters in equation (4) for each country, it is necessary to simultaneously estimate pricing equations for at least as many portfolios (firms) as there are risk factors. In simultaneously estimating equation (4) within each country, we would ideally like to use portfolio level data to reduce the idiosyncratic noise associated with using firm level data. Unfortunately, with the exception of a couple of markets, we do not have a sufficient number of firms within each market to construct various real estate portfolios. We, therefore, are restricted to using the firm-level data to estimate equation (4). Moreover, for several of the countries, there were an insufficient number of firms to estimate equation (4). For the remaining countries, however, we again find that the excess performance results are very similar to those reported in Table 5.[17]

7. Concluding remarks

The diversification potential associated with investing internationally has received increased attention in recent years from both academics and practitioners. However, the risks and uncertainties of direct real estate investments in foreign countries have generally outweighed the possible reductions in portfolio risk from international diversification.

Over the last two decades, a global real estate securities market has slowly developed. Compared to private markets, this growing public market provides a vehicle for investors to construct international commercial real estate portfolios without the significant burden of acquiring, managing, and disposing of direct property investments in far-away countries with unfamiliar legal, political, and market structures. However, little is currently known about the return performance and diversification potential of the international real estate securities market. This paper investigates the return performance of publicly traded real estate companies. The analysis spans the 1984–1999 time period and included return data on over 600 companies in 28 countries.

Our results can be summarized as follows. The return data reveal a substantial amount of variation in mean real estate returns and standard deviations across countries. Moreover, standard Treynor ratios also reveal substantial variation across countries in excess real estate returns per unit of systematic risk. However, when we estimate Jensen's alphas using single and multifactor specifications, we detect little evidence of abnormal returns at the country level. To the extent these results are generalizable, they suggest investors should concern themselves with the covariance structure of returns across countries and not attempt to pick ''winners.'' Similar to Case et al. (1999), we find evidence of a strong worldwide factor in international real estate returns. However, even after controlling for the effects of worldwide systematic risk, an orthogonalized country-specific risk factor is highly significant in the vast majority of the ex post return regressions. This suggests that real estate securities may provide international diversification opportunities. This conclusion is further supported by our analysis of firm level return data.

Acknowledgment

We thank Piet Eichholtz, Pat Hendershott, Charles Ward, two anonymous referees, and participants at the 2000 Maastricht-Cambridge Property Investment Symposium for valuable comments and suggestions. We also thank Elvan Aktas for valuable research assistance and Piet Eichholtz and Hans Op 't Veld of Global Property Research for assistance with the data. Additionally, we thank the Real Estate Research Institute for providing funding support for this project.

Notes

1. See Eichholtz and Koedijk (1996) for a detailed discussion of the evolution and importance of international real estate securities markets.
2. See, for example, Glascock (1991), Glascock and Hughes (1995), Gyourko and Kiem (1992), Hartzell and Mengden (1987), Kuhle et al. (1987), and McIntosh et al. (1991).
3. In terms of other capital markets, several researchers have also shown that there are multiple risk factors in equity and bond returns. See, for example, Chen et al. (1986), Ferson and Harvey (1991), and Fama and French (1993).
4. See, for example, Ling and Naranjo (1996, 1998).
5. Historical bond data to measure the default premium, for instance, are unavailable across most of the countries in our sample.
6. Institutional factors can take many forms and shapes. Geurts and Jaffe (1996) list and discuss 16 variables that can be linked with the economic consequences of the institutional framework.
7. A potential alternative specification is to use a continental factor in place of the country or world factor. However, at a theoretical level, there is no clear justification for a continental factor. Moreover, an additional concern is that the use of a continental factor imposes the assumption that the countries within each continent are integrated, whereas the two factors that we use allow for the returns to fluctuate with respect to domestic influences (potentially segmented events) and world influences (potentially integrated events) (see Ling and Naranjo, 1999). Lastly, to the extent the continental effects are not correlated with the world influences, they are subsumed in the country factors that we employ.
8. We have chosen to include the broadest possible set of countries (all 30 countries when possible). It is important to note that the retention of specific countries does not have a consequential effect on our overall results since our analysis is not aggregated across countries.
9. The GPR Index includes companies for which the market capitalization is over 50 million in U.S. dollars for two consecutive months. Companies are included for which at least 75 percent of revenues is derived from

investment activities or a combination of investment and development activities. The Index includes office, residential, retail, industrial, health care, hotel, and diversified real estate companies. If a company derives more than 75 percent of its revenue from one country, not being the country of its primary listing, the company is placed in the index of the country in which the assets are located. Dividends are included in the index at the ex-dividend date and are assumed to be reinvested in the index. See Eichholtz et al. (1998) for more details.

10. Ideally, the world wealth portfolio should include the whole range of instruments: real estate, stocks, bonds, commodities, and so on. Unfortunately, these data are not generally available on a global basis and the market size of them is not known precisely. However, given common fluctuations in the factors that comprise the world wealth portfolio, it is likely that our market portfolio proxy is highly correlated with the ''true'' world portfolio. Furthermore, to the extent that there are measurement errors, these are likely to be mitigated with the two-factor specification that we employ.
11. For example, there is a 99 percent correlation between the MSCI U.S. return and the value-weighted return calculated by the Center for Research in Security Prices at the University of Chicago.
12. See Corgel et al. (1992) and Geurts and Jaffe (1996) for an expanded discussion of these international differences.
13. Additional studies that investigate international real estate securities include Asabere et al. (1991), Barkham and Geltner (1995), and Liu et al. (1997). Because our focus is on the performance of real estate securities, and not on the links between the securities and the underlying commercial real estate, we do not attempt to remove the effects of leverage from the real estate stock indices.
14. Treynor ratios are discussed in Chapter 21 of *Commercial Real Estate Finance and Investment*, David Geltner and Norm Miller, Prentice Hall, forthcoming.
15. It is important to note that we include the single-factor results for comparison with the Treynor ratios that were calculated from the single-index model and for comparison purposes with earlier studies that employ single-factor models.
16. As a further robustness check, we also tried various leads and lags of the two factors. The leads and lags of the two factors were not significant when the contemporaneous factors were included in the regressions.
17. Over the 1990–1999 sample period, for instance, we could obtain estimates of equation (4) for Australia, Canada, France, Germany, Hong Kong, Japan, The Netherlands, Switzerland, U.K., and the U.S.

References

Asabere, P., R. Kleiman, and C. McGowan. (1991). ''The Risk-Return Attributes of International Real Estate Equities,'' *Journal of Real Estate Research* 6, 143–152.

Barkham, R., and D. Geltner. (1995). ''Price Discovery in American and British Property Markets,'' *Real Estate Economics* 23, 21–44.

Case, B., W. Goetzman, and K. G. Rouwenhorst. (1999). ''Global Real Estate Markets—Cycles and Fundamentals,'' mimeo, Yale School of Management.

Chan, K. C., P. H. Hendershott, and A. B. Sanders. (1990). ''Risk and Return on Real Estate: Evidence From Equity REITs,'' *AREUEA Journal* 18(4), 431–452.

Chen, N., R. Roll, and S. Ross. (1986). ''Economic Forces and the Stock Market,'' *Journal of Business* 59, 383–403.

Corgel, J. B., A. J. Jaffe, and R. T. Lie. (1992). ''Modeling in the Economics of Leasing Provisions: Some Cross-Cultural Comparisons of European Contracts,'' Mimeo, Cornell University.

Eichholtz, P. M. A., and D. J. Hartzell. (1996). ''Property Shares, Appraisals and the Stock Market: An International Perspective,'' *Journal of Real Estate Finance and Economics* 12, 163–178.

Eichholtz, P. M. A., and K. G. Koedijk. (1996). ''The Global Real Estate Securities Market,'' *Real Estate Finance* 13(1), 76–82.

Eichholtz, P. M. A., R. Huisman, K. Koedijk, and L. Schuin. (1998). ''Continental Factors in International Real Estate Returns,'' *Real Estate Economics* 26(3), 493–509.

Fama, G., and K. R. French. (1993). ''Common Risk Factors in the Returns on Stocks and Bonds,'' *Journal of Financial Economics* 33, 23–49.

Ferson, W., and C. Harvey. (1991). ''The Variation of Economic Risk Premiums,'' *Journal of Political Economy* 99, 385–415.

Geurts, T. G., and A. J. Jaffe. (1996). ''Risk and Real Estate Investment: An International Perspective,'' *The Journal of Real Estate Research* 11(2), 117–130.

Gilerberto, S. M., and A. Mengden. (1996). ''REITs and Real Estate: Two Markets Reexamined,'' *Real Estate Finance* 13(1), 56–60.

Glascock, J. (1991). ''Market Conditions, Risk, and Real Estate Portfolio Returns: Some Empirical Evidence,'' *Journal of Real Estate Finance and Economics* 4(4), 367–373.

Glascock, J., and W. T. Hughes. (1995). ''NAREIT Identified Exchange Listed REITs and Their Performance Characteristics,'' *Journal of Real Estate Literature* 3, 68–83.

Goetzman, W., and S. Wachter. (1996). ''The Global Real Estate Crash: Evidence from an International Database,'' mimeo, Yale School of Management.

Gyourko, J., and D. B. Keim. (1992). ''What Does the Stock Market Tell Us About Real Estate Returns?'' *Journal of the American Real Estate and Urban Economics Association* 20, 457–485.

Hartzell, D. J., and A. E. Mengden. (1987). *Another Look at Equity Real Estate Investment Trust Returns.* New York: Salomon Brothers, Inc.

Karolyi, G. A., and A. B. Sanders. (1999). ''The Variation in Economic Risk Premiums in Real Estate Returns,'' *Journal of Real Estate Finance and Economics* 17, 245–262.

Kuhle, J. L, C. H. Walther, and C. H. Wurtzeback. (1987). ''The Financial Performance of Real Estate Investment Trusts,'' *The Journal of Real Estate Research* 1(1), 67–75.

Ling, D. C., and A. Naranjo. (1996). ''Economic Risk Factors and Commercial Real Estate Returns,'' *Journal of Real Estate Finance and Economics* 14, 283–307.

Ling, D. C., and A. Naranjo. (1999). ''The Integration of Commercial Real Estate Markets and Stock Markets,'' *Real Estate Economics* 27(3), 483–516.

Ling, D. C., A. Naranjo, and M. Ryngaert. (2000). ''The Predictability of Equity REIT Returns,'' *Journal of Real Estate Finance and Economics* 20(2), 117–136.

Liu, C. H., D. J. Hartzell, and M. E. Hoesli. (1997). ''International Evidence on Real Estate Securities as an Inflation Hedge,'' *Real Estate Economics* 25(2), 193–222.

Liu, C. H., and J. Mei. (1996). ''The Predictability of International Real Estate Markets, Exchange Risk, and Diversification Consequences,'' *Real Estate Economics* 26, 3–39.

Lizieri, C., S. Satchell, E. Worzala, and R. Dacco. (1998). ''Real Interest Regimes and Real Estate Performance: A Comparison of U.K. and U.S. Markets,'' *Journal of Real Estate Research* 16(3), 339–355.

McIntosh, W., Y. Liang, and D. L. Tompkins. (1991). ''An Examination of the Small Firm Effect Within the REIT Industry,'' *The Journal of Real Estate Research* 6(1), 9–17.

Pagan, A. (1984). ''Econometric Issues in the Analysis of Regressions with Generated Regressors,'' *International Economic Review* 25: 221–247.

Journal of Real Estate Finance and Economics, 24:1/2, 143–165, 2002

Rational Delays: The Case of Real Estate

STEPHEN DAY CAULEY
The Richard S. Ziman Center for Real Estate, Anderson School at UCLA, 110 Westwood Plaza, Los Angeles, CA 90095
E-mail: scauley@agsm.ucla.edu

ANDREY D. PAVLOV
Simon Fraser University 8888 University Dr. Burnaby, BC V5A 1S6, Canada
E-mail: apavlov@anderson.ucla.edu

Abstract

Real estate markets, for both commercial real estate and single family homes, typically respond to a large negative demand shock with a period during which the volume of transactions and liquidity of real estate declines. Explanations for these periods have focused on overly optimistic owners, imperfections in real estate markets and/or minimum down payment requirements. These are important characteristics of real estate markets, but they do not provide a satisfying explanation for the long-term declines in the number of transactions and liquidity of real estate that frequently follow negative demand shocks. This paper presents estimates, for a specific real estate market (Los Angeles single family dwellings), of the option-like value of an owner's interest in a property. Our estimates imply that when an owner has little or negative equity, the value of waiting to sell is likely to exceed the net carrying cost. Consequently, the option value of a potential seller's interest may eliminate the possibility of an otherwise mutually advantageous transaction.

Key Words: real estate liquidity, real options, demand shocks, home values

1. Introduction

Real estate markets, for both commercial real estate and single family homes, typically respond to a large negative demand shock with a period during which the volume of transactions and the liquidity of real estate declines. Explanations for these periods have typically focused on overly optimistic owners and/or imperfections in real estate markets. More recently, Stein (1995) developed a model for single family homes, where a minimum down payment requirement can result in a decline in the volume of transactions following a negative demand shock. In his model, sellers are ''locked-in'' to their existing homes because a decline in equity in their existing home, in conjunction with a minimum down-payment requirement, precludes them from purchasing a new home. While all of the above are important characteristics of real estate markets, they do not provide a satisfying explanation for the long-term declines in the volume of transactions and liquidity of real estate that frequently follow negative demand shocks. We show that decreases in the liquidity of housing could occur in the absence of any of these factors. The inability to insure against post-shock price uncertainty can be sufficient to preclude the possibility of an otherwise mutually advantageous transaction.

In the absence of deficiency judgments (e.g., a non-recourse loan), an owner's interest in a property is equivalent to a portfolio comprised of the property, a mortgage loan (a liability) and a put option that gives the owner the right to sell the property to the mortgagee at a price equal to the mortgage loan balance (i.e., default on the loan). Alternatively, excluding the possibility of mortgage loan prepayment prior to sale, the owner's interest can be thought of as a call option written on the house by the mortgagee, where the exercise price of the option is the mortgage loan balance.

We hypothesize that, following a large negative demand shock, the value of the option is large enough to preclude otherwise mutually advantageous transactions.[1] To date there have been no estimates, for commercial real estate or for single family homes, of the option value incorporated in levered ownership of real estate. High quality transaction data is available for single family dwellings. For this reason we use actual transaction data for the affluent western portion of Los Angeles County to estimate this value, assuming different exercise prices (i.e., loan-to-value ratios), for a ''motivated'' seller of a typical ''West-Side'' home. Our estimates imply that when an owner has little or negative home equity the value of waiting to sell is likely to exceed the net carrying cost. Consequently, the option value of a potential seller's interest may eliminate the possibility of an otherwise mutually advantageous transaction. While these estimates are for single family homes in a specific real estate market, they suggest that the option value of the owner's interest, in conjunction with minimum down payment requirement, may explain the decline in asset liquidity that follows a negative demand shock.

The remainder of this paper is divided into sections that: (1) describe home ownership as a complex derivative security, (2) describe how we estimate the value of this derivative, and (3) present our estimates of the option value for a motivated seller of a typical West Side home.

2. Home ownership as an option

As was previously noted, the levered purchase of a home can be thought of as the purchase of a complex derivative security (i.e., an American call option).[2] The down payment, due at purchase, is the cost of buying the option, and the monthly principal and interest payments are costs necessary to ''maintain'' the option. The option is exercised when a home is sold and the outstanding loan balance is paid. Mortgage loan default is equivalent to letting the option expire. The purchasers' losses are limited to their initial investment, but their potential gains are not. The value of a home to an individual (e.g., reservation price for a seller or the maximum bid price for a potential buyer) would be determined by the value of the housing services provided and the value of the option inherent in home ownership.

For organized financial markets, the characteristics of an option that is sold (written) are the same as the characteristics of an option that is purchased. This need not be true for the sale of an owner's equity interest in a home. For example, following a large negative demand shock, minimum down-payment requirements frequently result in the exercise price of the option that is being sold (i.e., the seller's mortgage loan balance) being greater than the exercise price of the option that would be bought (i.e., the maximum mortgage loan for a buyer).[3] For example, if a house with a mortgage loan balance of $400,000 (e.g., it was originally purchased for $500,000) was sold for $400,000 the exercise price of the option being sold would equal the loan balance of $400,000. Whereas, with a minimum down-payment requirement of 20 percent, the exercise price of the option that is bought is $320,000. Thus, as is shown below, the time value of the option representing the seller's interest is more valuable than the one contained in the best possible financing contract obtainable by the buyer. In contrast, following a positive demand shock, potential buyers can own an option with the same exercise price (and therefore value) as the option being sold (i.e., the seller's loan balance).[4] We contend that this asymmetry in the exercise price of the option being bought and sold can explain differences in real estate markets responses to positive and negative demand shocks.

The sale of a home and undertaking an investment project are irreversible actions that can be delayed. A rapidly growing body of literature analyzes investments as options. This approach has shown that the ability to delay an irreversible action can affect the value and timing of that action. Consequently, the ability to delay the sale of a home can affect a seller's reservation price because the seller would have to be compensated for the value of the option of delaying the sale that is being given up (i.e., the value of the potential for increases in bid prices).[5]

Papers by Kester (1994), Mason and Merton (1985), Trigeorgis and Mason (1987), and Copeland et al. (1991) heuristically discuss investments as options. Tourinho (1979) showed that natural resource reserves can be viewed as options to produce the resource and should be valued accordingly. Dixit and Pidyck (1994) show that the basic investment option is analogous to a call option on a stock. Mason and Merton (1985) and McDonald and Siegel (1985) also examine similarities between financial options and investment decisions. Brennan and Schwartz (1985) develop this connection further by allowing firms to open, close, and mothball a mine that produces a natural resource whose price fluctuates over time.

Kau and Kim (1994) and Cornell et al. (1996) used option-pricing theory to value the option to default on a mortgage loan. Both papers conclude that it may be optimal to delay default by making a loan payment when the market value of the property is less than the mortgage loan balance (i.e., the option is ''out-of-the-money''). As was previously mentioned, Cornell et al. (1996) recognize that the value of the option to default may result in declines in volume following a negative demand shock. These papers did not include empirical estimates of the value of the option to default.

3. Estimating the option value of real estate ownership

In this section we describe the technique we use to estimate the option value of a seller's interest in a home. The perspective we take is that of a ''motivated'' seller. The seller's motivation is the amount by which the monetary or psychic costs associated with owning the house for an additional period of time exceed the value of the housing services they would receive from the property. To simplify our analysis we will assume the seller receives no services from the house (e.g., the house is vacant).[6] In this case the seller's reservation price would equal the mortgage loan balance plus the net value of the option, (i.e., the value of the option minus one month carrying costs of the house). Because most sellers receive valuable housing services, our estimates would provide lower bounds on the price a motivated seller must be offered before a mutually agreeable transaction is possible.

Estimating the value of a complex American style derivative, such as a motivated seller's interest in a home, has been traditionally accomplished by finite difference or binomial techniques. Longstaff and Schwartz (2001) present a relatively simple method, the least-squares Monte-Carlo (LSMC) approach, for the valuation of American options by simulation. Their approach combines the principles of risk-neutral valuation with least-squares regression to estimate the value of complex American options. We utilize this technique to value the option inherent in a seller's interest in his home (Appendix B provides a detailed description of our application of their method).

Underlying our implementation of the LSMC approach is the assumption that home prices V are described by the following stochastic process:

$$\frac{\mathrm{d}V}{V} = (r - s)\,\mathrm{d}t + \sigma\,\mathrm{d}z, \tag{1}$$

where r is the relevant risky rate of return for residential real estate, s is the net service flow from owning an home, σ is the volatility of home prices, and $\mathrm{d}z$ is the standard Wiener process.[7] In this formulation, a negative demand shock is the occurrence of a z that is negative and large in absolute value.

Under the risk-neutral metric, the above model of home prices is replaced by:

$$\frac{\mathrm{d}V}{V} = (r_f - s)\,\mathrm{d}t + \sigma\,\mathrm{d}z, \tag{2}$$

where r_f is the risk-free rate of return.

Going from a risky to a risk-neutral world will result in the correct value of a derivative based upon a traded security because the expected return and discount rate used to evaluate the cash flows are adjusted accordingly (Hull, 1997). A home is not a traded security held solely for investment purposes. For this reason, risk-neutral valuation may overestimate the value of the option inherent in home ownership. To protect against this bias we have been extremely conservative in our implementation of the LSMC methodology.

The LSMC method starts by simulating price paths for the underlying asset (e.g., the house). In our implementation of the LSMC we generate price paths for a home for 60 months into the future.[8] The simulated price paths are then used to estimate, by least squares, the pay-off for in the money options (i.e., the bid price is greater than the loan balance) conditional upon the home value at each point in time. This estimates the expected value of continuation. The value of the option is then estimated by assuming that a "motivated" risk-neutral seller acts optimally given the holding costs. The value of the option that represents the owner's interest equals the expected present value (at the risk free rate) of the cash flows associated with optimal exercise of the option (i.e., sale of the house or default on the mortgage loan). The data needed to simulate the price paths are the risk free rate of interest, the volatility of the rate of appreciation of residential real estate, σ, and the value of the net service flow s.

3.1. Estimating the volatility of real estate appreciation rates

Unlike financial markets, real estate markets do not provide all of the data needed to calculate the value of the option that represents the owner's interest in a home. Specifically, the heterogeneity of properties and infrequent trading result in the absence of reliable estimates of the historical volatility of residential real estate appreciation.[9] To calculate this statistic we need to first estimate the time series of rates of appreciation of the underlying asset. We use the following semi-log hedonic home value model to estimate this series:[10]

$$\ln(\text{Value}_{it}) = \text{Constant} + \sum_{t=2}^{T} \beta_t S_t + \alpha' C_i, + \varepsilon, \tag{3}$$

where Value_{it} is the price paid for home i sold at time t, C_i is a vector of physical characteristics that describe the home, S_t is a matrix of indicator variables for the time of sale, and β_t is the marginal time effect (i.e., monthly). T is the total number of months in the sample and ε is an error term with zero expectation.[11] Thus β_t is an estimate of the rate of appreciation for time period t. The mean of the vector β provides an estimate of the expected monthly rate of home appreciation. By calculating the standard deviation of the estimates of β_t, we obtain an estimate of the volatility of the monthly rate of appreciation. We will refer to this as the "naïve" estimate of the volatility. This estimate is "naïve" because it is uncertain as to what extent the estimated standard deviation is due to errors in estimating the rates of appreciation rather than actual variation in the rate of appreciation. Below we show that the "naïve" estimate has an upward bias and we provide a bias-corrected estimate of volatility.

3.2. Data and parameter estimates

To estimate the mean and standard deviation of the month-to-month rate of appreciation for a home we use transaction data. The data comes from Data Quick—a company specializing in assembling and providing publicly available data. The underlying data are extracted from the office of the Los Angeles County Recorder. We have included all transactions that occurred between January 1985 and September 1997 in the affluent West Side of Los Angeles County (i.e., the shaded area of Figure 1), a total of 15,354 observations.[12] This region was chosen because it is relatively homogeneous, a large number of transactions occur every month, and the authors are very familiar with the area

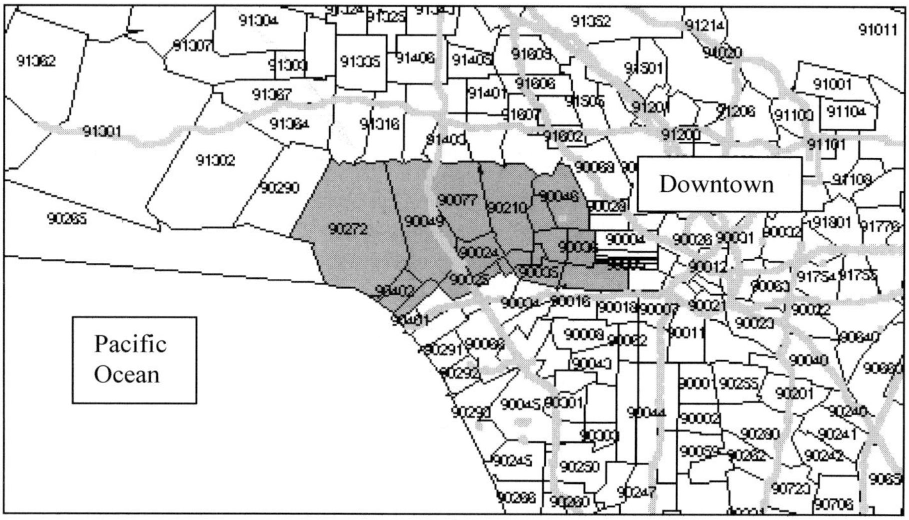

Figure 1. Los Angeles the West-Side.

(UCLA is located at the center of the area).[13] Table 1 provides summary statistics describing the transactions that occurred during the thirteen-year period. Inspection of this table reveals that this is one the most expensive areas in the U.S. The median transaction price was approximately $470,000 for a three-bedroom and two-bathroom house.

Tables 2 and 3 report the parameter estimates and implied appreciation rates obtained by estimating equation (3). The parameter estimates presented in Table 2 have the expected signs and are consistent with those obtained from previous research. From Table 3 we can see that our model estimated an average monthly appreciation rate of 0.38 percent with a standard deviation of more than six percent. These are our ''naïve'' estimates of the mean and volatility of home value appreciation.

Figure 2 depicts the time series of estimates of the value (January $1985 = 100$) of a typical West Side home implied by the parameter estimates of equation (3).[14] As can be seen from this figure, the late 1980s and early 1990s were a boom/bust period for Southern California home values. Between 1985 and 1991 home values increased by more than 140 percent. Then they dropped by almost fifty percent during the early 1990s. At the

Table 1. Descriptive statistics for transactions 1/1985–9/1997.

$N = 15{,}354$	Trans. Value	Square Feet	Number Bedrooms	Number Bathrooms	Pool (0, 1)	Garage (0, 1)	House Age	Lot Size
Mean	575,460	2,300	3.17	2.38	0.21	0.81	52	9,840
Median	475,000	2,036	3	2	0	1	56	7,500
St. Dev.	374,005	1,022	0.99	1.23	0.41	0.40	19	6,210

Table 2. Parameter estimates.

$N = 15{,}354$ $R^2 = 0.66$	Square feet	Square feet^2	Number Bedrms	Number Bathrms	Pool (0, 1)	Garage (0, 1)	House Age	House Age^2	Lot Size	Lot Size^2
Estimate	0.0004	– 0.23E-7	– 0.0174	0.0602	0.1010	0.1167	0.0181	– 0.0002	0.0001	– 0.44E-9
St. Error	≈ 0	≈ 0	0.0040	0.0039	0.0078	0.0073	0.0007	≈ 0	≈ 0	≈ 0

Table 3. Implied monthly rates of appreciation.

Average Appreciation Rate	Standard Deviation of the Appreciation Rate	Median Appreciation Rate	Skewness of the Appreciation Rate
0.0038	0.0619	0.0028	0.3263

beginning of 1998 home values were comparable to 1987 levels.[15] During the entire period month-to-month variations in the estimated rate of appreciation were large relative to the mean.

3.3. *Bias-corrected estimate of the volatility*

As was noted above, the ''naïve'' estimate of volatility contains an upward bias because the estimated rates of appreciation (returns) used to calculate it are subject to sampling error. In particular, the estimated return $\hat{\beta}_t$ can be represented as mean (expected) rate of appreciation plus an incremental return for period t, plus sampling error:

$$\hat{\beta}_t = r + \delta_t + \eta_t, \tag{4}$$

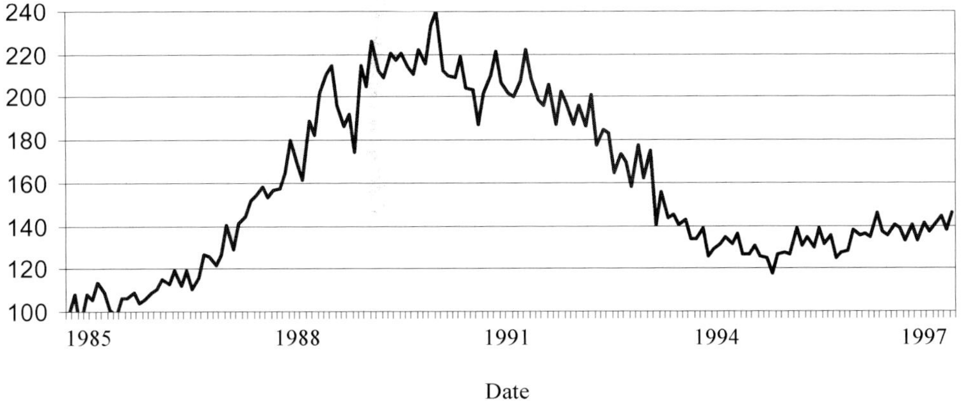

Figure 2. Index of home values (January 1985 = 100).

where $\hat{\beta}_t$ is the estimated return at time t, r is the expected return, δ_t is the realized incremental return at time t, (thus $r + \delta_t$ is the true return for period t), and η_t is the sampling error contained in $\hat{\beta}_t$.

In terms of our model, the estimate of the volatility of price appreciation should equal the standard deviation of the monthly incremental returns:

$$\text{std}(\delta_t)^2 = \frac{1}{T-1}\sum(\delta_t)^2. \tag{5}$$

Because we do not observe the incremental monthly returns, we approximate their standard deviation with the standard deviation of β_t, the estimated rates of appreciation:

$$\text{std}(\hat{\beta}_t)^2 = \frac{1}{T-1}\sum(\hat{\beta}_t - \hat{\beta})^2. \tag{6}$$

Appendix A provides a formal argument that the standard deviation of the estimated rates of appreciation contains an upward bias. Using an estimate of this bias, we compute a bias-corrected estimate of the standard deviation as follows:

$$\text{std}(\delta_t)^2 = \text{std}(\hat{\beta}_t)^2 - \frac{1}{T}\sum \text{std}(\eta_t)^2. \tag{7}$$

To implement the bias-correction we need an estimate of the standard errors η_t. An estimate comes directly from the regression model (3). Under the standard linear regression assumptions, each $\hat{\beta}_t$ is normally distributed with an easily estimable variance. In our example, all of the assumptions of standard linear regression model are unlikely to be satisfied. In particular, the errors may be correlated which can result in underestimating the standard errors of the parameter estimates. In response to this potential problem we compute bootstrap standard deviations of the estimated rates of return $\hat{\beta}_t$. To this end, we draw 500 samples with replacement from the original data and estimate model (3) with each sample. Following the bootstrap literature (Efron and Tibshirani, 1998) we use the estimated returns from each sample to approximate the estimation variance of each monthly return $\hat{\beta}_t$.

Given the bootstrap estimates of the variance of the returns $\hat{\beta}_t$, we compute the bias-corrected estimate of the volatility. Table 4 reports the estimate of the bias and the bias-corrected estimate of volatility.

Our best estimate of the volatility of the monthly appreciation rates is the bias-corrected estimate of 0.0237. Consequently, our best estimate of the option value will be based upon its value. Notice that the ''naïve'' estimate is more than two and one-half times the bias-corrected estimate. Given the relationship between the volatility of the underlying asset and the value of an option, the naïve estimate would have substantially over estimated the option value of a motivated seller's interest in their home.

Table 4. Bias-corrected estimate of the volatility of the monthly appreciation rates.

"Naïve" Estimate of the Volatility	Estimate of the Bias of the Naïve Estimate	Bias-Corrected Estimate
0.0619	0.0382	0.0237

3.4. Lower bound estimates of home value volatility

Recall we hypothesized that, following a large negative demand shock, the option value representing a seller's interest in their home may exceed the costs of delaying a sale. Since the greater the asset volatility, the greater the option value of a home, it is useful to estimate a lower bound for the volatility of the monthly appreciation rates. In this way we will ensure that our conclusion is not due to sampling error.

In addition to point estimates of the rates of return, β_t, model (3) allows us to construct confidence intervals around these estimates. As described above, we have used bootstrap resampling to estimate non-parametric confidence intervals around each $\hat{\beta}_t$. We use these confidence intervals (corresponding to 90 percent confidence level) to estimate a lower bound on the standard deviation of the monthly rate of return. The approach we take is extremely conservative, in that it is likely to substantially under-estimate the true volatility of home values. We start by generating a time series of "proxy" monthly returns that are based upon the confidence intervals around each $\hat{\beta}_t$. The proxy returns are based upon the assumption that the true return lies within the respective confidence interval at the point closest to the estimated mean, over all $\hat{\beta}_t$, monthly returns (i.e., 0.38 percent per month). The proxy return for a month is determined as follows: if the estimated mean monthly return (EMMR) lies within the confidence interval for a month, then the proxy return for the corresponding month is set equal to the EMMR (0.38 percent). If the EMMR is below the lower confidence bound, then the proxy return is set equal to the lower confidence bound for the corresponding month's estimate. Finally, if the EMMR is above the confidence interval, the proxy return is set equal to the upper confidence bound. Our lower bound estimate of home value volatility is the standard deviation of the proxy returns. Notice that if the EMMR lies within the confidence intervals for all estimated monthly returns, the estimated standard deviation will be zero. Figure 3 and Table 5 provide an example that illustrates how the lower bound estimate is obtained.

The squares in Figure 3 and the first row in Table 5 represent illustrative return estimates for four months (each corresponding to a β_t). These are the values that would be used to compute the "naïve" estimate of home value volatility. In addition to the return estimates, we have computed bootstrap confidence intervals around each of the estimates. The confidence intervals are depicted in the diagram and presented in the second and third rows of Table 5. The proxy return for a month is the value closest to the mean return that lies within the respective confidence interval. The triangles in the figure and the last row of Table 5 report the proxy returns. The first return estimate (January) is zero and the mean return lies within the confidence interval percentage is $(-2, 2)$. In this case, the return

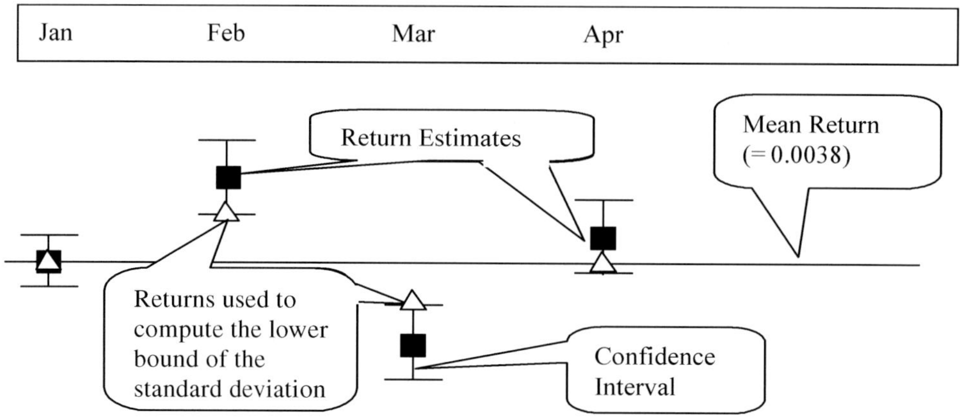

Figure 3. Computing the lower bound of the volatility.

used for the naïve estimate is zero, while the proxy return is the mean return, i.e., 0.38 percent. The return estimate for February is 10 percent with a 90 percent confidence interval of 7 and 13 percent. Since the mean return of 0.38 percent is below the lower confidence bound, the proxy return equals the point within the confidence interval closest to the mean return, i.e., the lower confidence bound of 7 percent. Thus, the naïve estimate is based on the 10 percent return for February and the proxy return is 7 percent. Similarly, for the third return (March) we use the point estimate of − 12 percent for the naïve estimate and − 7 percent for the proxy value. The last return reported in the diagram is 4 percent, which is above the mean return of 0.38 percent. Similarly to the first observation (January), the mean return lies within the confidence interval for the return, so we set the proxy value equal to the mean return.

The lower bound described above is extremely conservative. This approach minimizes the standard deviation of the returns subject to the constraint that each return is within its respective confidence interval. Table 6 reports our lower bound estimate of the volatility of monthly home value appreciation.

As expected, our lower bound estimate is substantially below both the naïve and the bias-corrected estimates. The lower bound estimate is less than a quarter of the "naïve" estimate and approximately 60 percent of the bias-corrected estimate of volatility.

Table 5. Example of estimating the lower bound on the standard deviation of the monthly returns.

	Jan	Feb	Mar	Apr	Estimated Std Deviation
Return Estimate	0	0.1	− 0.12	0.04	
Upper confidence bound for each return	0.02	0.13	− 0.07	0.09	
Lower confidence bound for each return	− 0.02	0.07	− 0.17	− 0.01	
Return used for the "naïve" estimates	0	0.1	− 0.12	0.04	0.09
Proxy return used for the lower bound	0.0038	0.07	− 0.07	0.0038	0.06

Table 6. Lower bound estimates of the volatility of the monthly home value appreciation rates.

Method	Estimated Volatility
''Naïve'' estimate	0.0619
Bias-corrected estimate	0.0237
Lower bound estimate	0.0150

3.5. Net service flow from owning a home

The net service flow from owning a home *s* is the difference between the market value of the housing services provided by the house and its carrying costs. The market value of the services is not observable and there is no generally agreed upon method of estimating its value.[16] The rental cost of a house provides a lower bound on the market value of these services (it's a lower bound because ''pride of ownership'' has a value). Consequently, the difference between the rental cost of a ''typical'' house and the user cost of the corresponding house provides us with a lower bound estimate for *s*. Using rental data provided by local real estate brokers and the methodology presented in Gabriel, Mattey, and Wascher (1999) to estimate the user cost of home ownership, we obtain estimates of the net value of housing services *s* that are negative and very close to zero. Alternatively a very conservative estimate (in terms of option value) would be obtained if we assumed the net value of the housing services provided the owners a 10 percent rate of return on their (typically 20 percent) equity investment. This assumption is very conservative because, while there is substantial risk associated with the market value of the home, there is less risk associated with the value of the housing services provided by a home. The above assumptions translate into a net value of housing services *s* of 2 percent per year. The actual net service flow from owning a typical West Los Angeles home is almost certain to lie closer to 0 than 2 percent per year. Consequently, we provide estimates of the time value of the option using both values.

4. Option values implied by the estimates of home value volatility

As described earlier, the motivated seller's interest in their home can be represented as a complex American call option on that home. To value the option-like interest of the homeowners we make the following assumptions:

- The current owners are motivated to sell and derive no valuable housing services from owning the home;
- The mortgage loan is a 8 percent interest, fully amortizing loan with 23 years to maturity.[17];
- Refinancing to obtain a lower interest rate is not possible,

- The option expires in 5 years (i.e., the loan has a balloon payment in 5 years) and the potential seller can exercise the option at the end of each month (i.e., when the next payment is due);
- There are no costs associated with mortgage loan default;
- The risk-free interest rate is 5 percent;
- The marginal income tax rate for the potential sellers is 30 percent, this results in an after-tax interest cost of 5.6 percent per year;[18]
- Property taxes are determined by California Proposition 13 so that they equal 1 percent of the original purchase price;
- There are no other costs the homeowners incur to keep the home;
- The current maximum net bid price for the home is $400,000, this is the estimated value of the ''typical'' West Side home as of the end of 1997.[19]

In addition, we assume there are no transaction costs associated with the sale of a house. Transaction costs in excess of 6 percent are common when a home is sold. With a transaction cost this large, a potential buyer would have to bid $425,530 for the seller to be offered a net price of $400,000. The effect of transaction costs can also be seen by the fact that for a home bought with 20 percent equity, the bid prices would have to go down by only 15 percent for the owner's interest to be equivalent to an at-the-money option.

4.1. Base case

To help understand the relationship between the value of the option and the housing market's response to negative demand shocks, we examine, through examples, the relationship between the owner's equity positions and the value of the option inherent in home ownership. Using the above assumptions we estimate the value of the derivative representing the homeowner's interest in the property using the bias-corrected and lower bounds estimates of the volatility of the real estate returns described above. We utilize the LSMC option valuation methodology developed by Longstaff and Schwartz (2001) and account for the monthly interest payments and property taxes, which in this case are the only costs of maintaining the option. Appendix B provides a detailed description of our implementation of the option pricing method and examines the expected holding period.

Table 7 lists the resulting values of the option, net of the next monthly payments required to maintain the ownership interest and net of the current equity in the home (i.e., the time value of the option).[20] The option value includes the after tax interest payment, amortization amount, and property taxes in future periods, if it is not optimal to exercise the option by paying off the loan or by loan default.[21] If the option value is greater than the payments required to maintain the home for an additional month, it will be optimal for the motivated seller to reject an offer.

The amortization payment is computed for a fully amortizing mortgage with 23 years to maturity (e.g., a 30-year loan that has been outstanding for seven years). As evident from

Table 7. Time value of option representing the interest of the homeowner in a home where the bid price is $400,000 with various equity levels, net of monthly payments and equity in the home.

	Zero Equity Home
Assumptions	
Net bid price for home*	$400,000
Outstanding balance	$400,000
Interest (8% APR)	$2,667/month
After tax interest cost (30% income tax)	$1,867/month
Amortization amount (based on 23 years to maturity)	$507/month
Property tax (1% of purchase price)	$417/month
Total carrying cost	$2,791/month
Time value of option	
Lower bound using confidence intervals net service flow = 0	$3,387**
Bias-corrected estimate net service flow = 0	$5,362**
Lower bound using confidence intervals net service flow = 2% of value	$2,912**
Bias-corrected estimate net service flow = 2% of value	$4,607**

* With 6 percent transaction cost this would correspond to a transaction price of $425,530.
** Bold if the option value exceeds the payments necessary to maintain the option.

Figure 2, owners that are likely to have little or negative equity purchased their properties between 1988 and 1993. Thus, assuming 23 years to maturity generates an upper bound on the amortization amount.[22] To be consistent with the theme of the paper of developing a lower bound of the option value, we consider the entire amortization as a pure expense. This is also very conservative, since in our simulation there is at least 50 percent probability that the property will be sold (the option exercised) during the 5-year period being considered. When the property is sold, the owner receives back the amortization amount. This approach clearly underestimates the value of the option and overestimates the carrying costs.

Two sets of estimates are provided. The first assumes the typical owner receives no net service flows. The second set is very conservative as it assumes net service flows from home ownership of 2 percent per year (i.e., an amount that provides the owner a 10 percent rate of return on the original equity investment).

For a home with zero equity the option is ''at-the-money.'' Our most conservative estimate of volatility (the lower bound estimate) and our most conservative estimate of the net value of housing services (2 percent), yield an estimate of $2,912 for the time value of the homeowner's interest. This is greater than the one-month carrying costs of $2,791.[23] Consequently, it would not be optimal for a motivated seller to accept an offer that netted him $400,000 (e.g, $425,530 before 6 percent brokerage commissions); he should wait to observe what happens to the bid price for his house.[24] Using the best estimate of volatility, the bias corrected estimate, and conservative estimate of the net value of housing results in an estimated option value of $4,607. In this case, the seller's net reservation price, assuming he derives no valuable housing services from owning the home, would be

$401,818 (i.e., the mortgage loan balance plus $4,607–$2,791)). Even with a very conservative estimate of volatility and market value of net service flow, it is not optimal for an owner whose interest is equivalent to an at-the-money option to accept an offer that will net him $400,000.

4.2. Comparative statics

In the base case we assumed that the maximum net bid price for the house was $400,000 (i.e., an at the money option). Figure 4 pictures the relationship between the maximum net bid price (assuming a non-amortizing loan of $400,000) and the option value of home ownership. Region I corresponds to net bid prices less than $391,500 (i.e., a sales price of $416,489 before 6 percent brokerage commissions). In this region it would be optimal for an owner who receives no valuable housing services to ''walk'' from the house and default on the loan. For owners in Region II, a net bid price between $391,500 and $416,000, the option value is greater than carrying cost and it would be optimal for an owner who receives no valuable housing services not to transact and wait to see what happens to housing values. For bid prices in Region III, a net bid price greater than $416,000 the option is in-the-money, carrying costs are greater than the time value of the option, and it is optimal for the owner to accept the offer. For offers in all regions the desirability of waiting would be enhanced if the house provided valuable services to the owner. This would be pictured as a shifting up of the option value curve, which would raise the seller's reservation price and increase the range of bid prices where it would be optimal for the owner to wait. While the analysis presented in Figure 4 is for a specific example, the

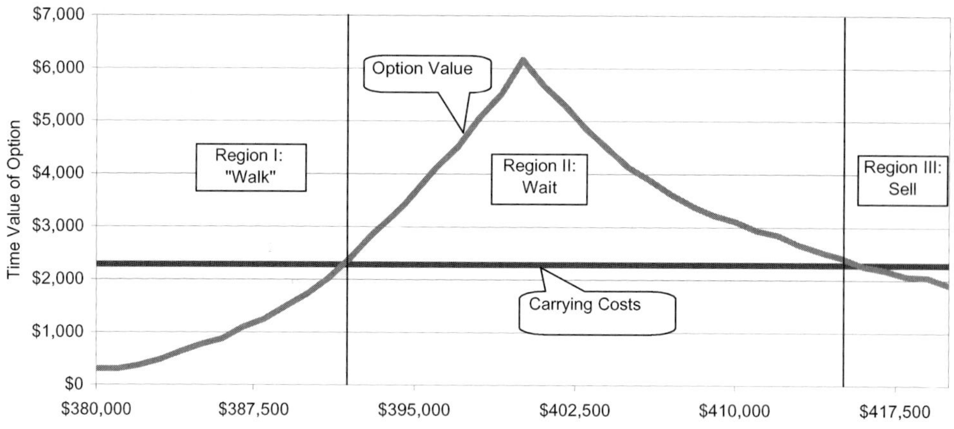

Figure 4. Bid price and the option value of home ownership (loan = $400,000).

conclusions are general: even though there may be no disagreement between sellers and potential buyers the option value of homeownership can preclude otherwise mutually advantageous transactions. Note, that if the net maximum bid price for the seller's home was $400,000 next month the optimal decision would be the same: do not accept the offer, make the mortgage loan payments and observe what happens to the bid price during the upcoming month. In this way, the option value of the home can result in long periods during which the volume of transactions and the liquidity of housing decline. In our example, the process stops when the house is sold or the owner defaults on the mortgage.

The impact of a minimum down-payment requirement can be seen when we consider the position of a person making an offer corresponding to a net sales price of $400,000. In the absence of transaction costs and with a minimum down payment of 20 percent, the buyer would be purchasing an option with an exercise price $320,000 for a price of $80,000 (the time value of the option is close to zero). With six percent transaction costs, for the seller to net $400,000 (a purchase price of $425,530) the buyer would be purchasing an option with an exercise price of $340,424 for a price of $85,106. Again, the time value of the option being purchased is very small, whereas the value of the option being sold is not. This example illustrates the economically important differences between the option that is being purchased and sold following a large negative demand.

Following a negative demand shock, similar to that which occurred in Los Angeles during the early 1990s, many homeowners will have "negative equity" and their ownership interest will correspond to an out-of-the money call option. For example, at the 1995 market trough, the owner's interest in a typical home purchased between April 1987 and October 1993 with 20 percent down payment would correspond to an out-of-the money option. In this situation, the time value of the option will make it optimal for many homeowners to make their monthly payments and observe what happens to the bid price for the house.

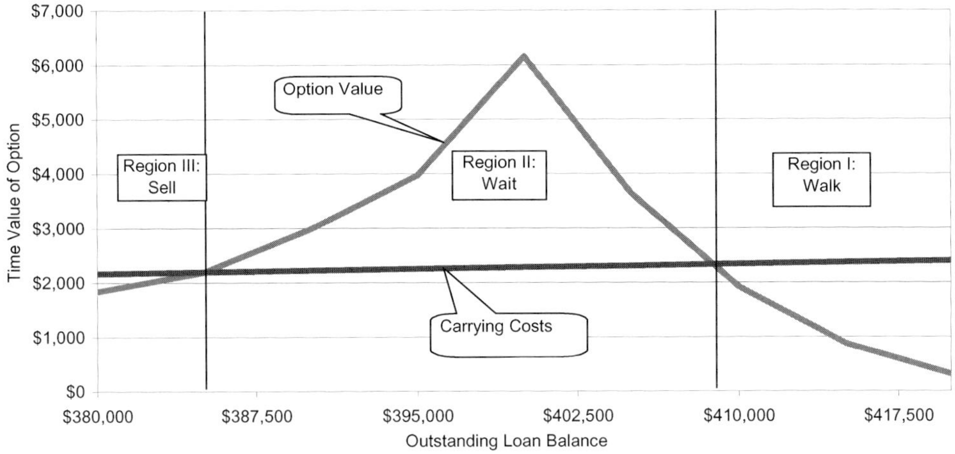

Figure 5. Option value and leverage (assuming maximum net bid price = $400,000).

At a point in time, comparable homes should receive comparable bids (offers) prices. The exercise price of the option that represents the owners' interest will differ because of differences in loan balance (e.g., from when the home was initially purchased). Figure 5 presents our best estimate of the relationship between the time value of the option and the outstanding loan balance, when the current maximum net bid price for the property is \$400,000.[25] The figure also pictures the relationship between loan balance and caring costs. For owners whose equity position is in Region III, a mortgage loan balance less than \$385,000, the option is in-the-money and carrying cost are greater than the time value of the option and the option is exercised. In this region it would be optimal for an owner who receives no valuable housing services to accept an offer of \$400,000. For owners whose equity position is in Region I, mortgage loan balances in excess of \$408,000, the option is out-of-the money and carrying costs are greater than the option value. It would be optimal for the owners in this region who receive no valuable housing services to ''walk'' and default on the loan. For owners in Region II, the option value is greater than carrying cost and it would be optimal for an owner who receives no valuable housing services not to transact and wait to see what happens to housing values.

5. Conclusion

This paper presented estimates of the option-like value of an owner's interest in a home, for a specific real estate market, for a particular period of time. Our estimates imply that, at least for the West Side of Los Angeles County, when an owner has little or negative home equity, the value of waiting to sell is likely to exceed the net carrying cost. Consequently, the option value of a potential seller's interest would eliminate the possibility of an otherwise mutually advantageous transaction. While our results are not directly applicable to commercial real estate markets, they strongly suggest that the combination of non-recourse loans and minimum down payment requirements are likely to contribute to the decline in asset liquidity that follows negative demand shocks for commercial real estate markets as well.

When a real estate market is subject to a positive demand shock the sellers would have ''excess equity'' (i.e., more than the minimum down-payment requirement). In this case, the seller and potential buyer could own options with the same exercise price. Consequently, the option value of the owner's interest would not be expected to preclude otherwise mutually advantageous transactions. Our results suggest that the option value of the owner's interest can, at least in part, explain the asymmetric response of real estate markets to positive and negative demand shocks.

Appendix A: Bias-corrected estimate

As discussed in the body of the paper, the ''naïve'' estimate of volatility contains an upward bias because the estimated returns used to calculate it are subject to sampling error. In particular, the estimated return $\hat{\beta}_t$ can be represented as mean (expected) return plus excess return for period t, plus sampling error:

$$\hat{\beta}_t = r + \delta_t + \eta_t, \tag{A1}$$

where $\hat{\beta}_t$ is the estimated return at time t, r is the expected return, δ_t is realized excess return at time t (thus $r + \delta_t$ is the true return for period t) and η_t is the sampling error contained in $\hat{\beta}_t$.

We are interested in the standard deviation of the monthly excess returns:

$$\text{std}(\delta_t)^2 = \frac{1}{T-1}\sum(\delta_t)^2. \tag{A2}$$

Since we do not observe the excess monthly returns, we approximate their standard deviation with the standard deviation of the estimated returns $\hat{\beta}_t$:

$$\text{std}(\hat{\beta}_t)^2 = \frac{1}{T-1}\sum(\hat{\beta}_t - \hat{\beta})^2. \tag{A3}$$

The standard deviation of the estimated rates of return (multiplied by $(T-1)$) is:

$$\begin{aligned}
(T-1)\ \text{std}(\hat{\beta}_t)^2 &= \sum\left(\hat{\beta}_t - \hat{\beta}\right)^2 = \frac{1}{T}\sum\left(r + \delta_t + \varepsilon_t - \frac{1}{T}\left(\sum r + \delta_t + \eta_t\right)\right)^2 \\
&= \sum(\delta_t + \eta_t - \delta - \eta)^2 \\
&= \sum\left[(\delta_t + \eta_t)^2 - 2(\delta_t + \eta_t)(\delta + \eta) + (\delta + \eta)^2\right] \\
&= \sum\left[\delta_t^2 + \eta_t^2 + 2\delta_t\eta_t\right] - 2T(\delta + \eta)^2 + T(\delta + \eta)^2 \\
&= \sum\left[\delta_t^2 + \eta_t^2 + 2\delta_t\eta_t\right] - T(\delta + \eta)^2 \\
&= \sum\left[\delta_t^2 + \eta_t^2 + 2\delta_t\eta_t\right] - T(\delta^2 + \eta^2 + 2\delta\eta) \\
&= \sum\left[\delta_t^2 + \eta_t^2 + 2\delta_t\eta_t\right] - \frac{1}{T}\left[\left(\sum \delta_t\right)^2 + \left(\sum \eta_t\right)^2 + 2\left(\sum \delta_t\right)\left(\sum \eta_t\right)\right].
\end{aligned} \tag{A4}$$

Taking the expectation and assuming independence between the monthly excess return and the errors (both η and δ) gives us:

$$
\begin{aligned}
(T-1)E\left\{\mathrm{std}(\hat{\beta}_t)^2\right\} &= E\left\{\sum[\delta_t^2+\eta_t^2] - \frac{1}{T}\left[\left(\sum\delta_t\right)^2 + \left(\sum\eta_t\right)^2\right]\right\} \\
&= E\left\{\sum[\delta_t^2+\eta_t^2] - \frac{1}{T}\left[\left(\sum\delta_t\right)^2 + \left(\sum\eta_t\right)^2\right]\right\} \\
&= E\left\{\sum[\delta_t^2+\eta_t^2] - \frac{1}{T}\left[\sum\delta_t^2 + \sum\eta_t^2\right]\right\} \\
&\quad \text{(cross terms have zero expectation)} \\
&= (T-1)\ \mathrm{std}(\delta)^2 + \frac{(T-1)}{T}\sum\ \mathrm{std}(\eta_t)^2 \qquad \text{(A5)}
\end{aligned}
$$

The above argument suggests the following bias-corrected estimate of the volatility

$$
\mathrm{std}(\delta_t)^2 = \mathrm{std}(\beta_t)^2 - \frac{1}{T}\sum\ \mathrm{std}(\eta_t)^2. \qquad \text{(A6)}
$$

Notice that the above argument assumes that the returns δ_t and the errors η_t are serially independent and independent among each other. Violation of this assumption will result in smaller bias-correction, which in turn will result in larger estimate of the volatility of monthly returns. Since our hypothesis is that the option value resulting from this volatility exceeds the carrying costs, a smaller bias reduction will make the results even stronger.

Appendix B: Option valuation methodology

In this paper we employ the LSMC simulation option valuation approach developed by Longstaff and Schwartz (2001). The key to this method is the use of least squares to estimate the expected payoff from continuation of the option conditional on the current home value. This allows comparisons between the payoff from immediate exercise and the expected payoff from continuation at each step. Once the optimal exercise strategy is estimated, computing the value of the option today becomes a simple present value calculation.

Home value paths in the future

The first step in the option valuation procedure is to estimate a large number of future paths for home values. Those paths are later used to estimate the conditional expected payoff from continuation of the option and they are thus essential to the procedure. To estimate these paths, according to the risk-neutral valuation, we use the risk-free rate of return, and two alternative estimates of the volatility: the bias-corrected estimate and the lower volatility bound. We further assume monthly appreciation in home values is normally distributed.

The implicit framework used in this valuation is that the home prices V are log-normally distributed and follow the typical generalized Wiener process:

$$\frac{\mathrm{d}V}{V} = (r - s)\mathrm{d}t + \sigma\ \mathrm{d}z, \tag{A7}$$

where r is the rate of return, s is the net service flow from owning the home, σ is the volatility of home prices, and $\mathrm{d}z$ is the standard Wiener process. Under the risk-neutral valuation, the above model of home prices is replaced by:

$$\frac{\mathrm{d}V}{V} = (r_f - s)\mathrm{d}t + \sigma\ \mathrm{d}z, \tag{A8}$$

where r_f is the risk-free rate of return.

In terms of generating the price paths in the future, this framework translates into the following. On an annual basis, we use the risk-free rate of return of 5 percent minus a 2 percent net value of housing services (i.e., 10 percent on the 20 percent equity investment) as the expected rate of appreciation to generate to generate the price path. In addition, we generate price paths assuming no net housing services. The appropriate standard deviation is the standard deviation of the home prices, which is approximated by the bias-corrected estimate and by the lower bound discussed above.

Estimating the value of the option representing the homeowner's interest in the home

The most important step in the option valuation procedure is estimating the expected payoff from continuation, conditional on the option not being exercised earlier. Then, assuming risk neutrality, the decision to exercise becomes a simple comparison between the immediate payoff and the expected payoff from continuation. More specifically, we employ the following steps:

(1) Compute the value of an unexercised option at the last period T for each of the estimated housing paths in the future. This is simply the equity in the home if the value of the home exceeds the outstanding loan balance, or zero otherwise.
(2) Compute the value of immediate exercise of an unexercised option in period $T - 1$. This is the equity in the home if the value of the home exceeds the outstanding loan balance in period $T - 1$, or zero otherwise.
(3) Compute the expected payoff of continuation. Below we discuss this step in greater detail.

(4) Compare the payoff from immediate exercise to the expected payoff from continuation minus the carrying costs of the option. This cost is assumed to be the monthly payment on the mortgage. If the immediate exercise is beneficial, the homeowner sells the home and foregoes expected payoffs in the future. If continuation is optimal, the homeowner makes the monthly payment and waits. If the homeowner has negative equity but the expected payoff from continuation does not justify the monthly payment, the homeowner defaults and gets zero cash flow at the time of default and in the future.

(5) Repeat steps 2 to 4 for periods $T-2$ to 1. This gives the cash flows for each period for each home value path. These cash flows will be negative and equal to the monthly payment for each period before option exercise, equal to the equity in the home or zero, whichever is greater, at time of exercise, and zero afterwards.

(6) Take the present value of all cash flows and average them across home value paths. This gives the estimate of the option value today.

The only non-trivial part of the above algorithm is the computation of the expected payoff from continuation (step 3 above). Since this payoff is essential to the optimal exercise strategy, it will have a substantial effect on the estimated option value. Since the housing returns are assumed to be independent, the expected payoff from continuation depends only on the current level of home values V_t. Let Y_t denote the corresponding discounted cash flows received at time $t+1$ to T if the option is not exercised at time t. Then, to estimate the expected cash flow from continuing the option conditional on the home value at time t, we regress using OLS Y_t on a constant, V_t, V_t^2 and V_t^3. This specification is one of the simplest possible. Longstaff and Schwartz (2001) discuss more general specifications. Using the above regression, we estimate the expected payoff from continuation for each home value at time t. Then, as described above, we compare this expected payoff to the value of the immediate option exercise.

For theoretical foundation and a more detailed description of this method see Longstaff and Schwartz (2001).

Acknowledgments

Special thanks for their comments and suggestions to Gareth James, Robert Gay and the participants of the Finance Seminars at UCLA, the University of Southern California and the Real Estate Seminar at the University of California, Berkeley. Financial support from the Social Science Research Council of Canada is gratefully acknowledged.

Notes

1. Cornell, Longstaff and Schwartz (1996) noted that the ''mortgage lock-in'' due to the value of the option to default may result in declines in volume following a negative demand shock.

2. The owner's interest in a home is analogous to stock in a levered firm. Merton (1974) first recognized that stock in a levered firm is equivalent to call option on the firm's assets. Geske (1977, 1979) extended Merton's model by analyzing stock as a compound option.
3. The value of the option can explain why it may not be optimal for an owner with negative equity to walk away from a home (default on the mortgage loan).
4. A seller with excess equity can always "borrow out" of the home and a potential purchaser can always put up extra equity at the time of purchase.
5. Increases in bid price would be due to evolution of home values not due to search.
6. The option of refinancing at a lower interest rate is ignored through out this paper. For a motivated seller the value of this option is likely to be very small.
7. For commercial real estate s is net cash flow from operations or the property. For homes s would be non-negative, but for commercial real estate negative cash flow is possible.
8. We are assuming a five-year, interest only balloon payment loan. Analysis of the optimal exercise of the option results in the conclusion that extending the life of the option, say to 30 years, will have little effect on the estimates of value. In our example, optimal exercise of the option through sale of the property or default on the mortgage always occurs before five years.
9. Conceptually the statistic should be the prospective standard deviation of the rate of appreciation of the home in question.
10. This model has all of the strengths and weakness of any hedonic home value model. The most important potential weakness is the assumption that the marginal (percentage) value placed upon a characteristic is constant over time. Alternatively, the repeat sales methodology could have been used to estimate rates of appreciation. It was not employed because there are too few repeat sales for this area.
11. The β_t are estimated as follows. If a transaction occurred during January 1985 (i.e., $t=1$), all time indicator variables are assigned a value of zero. If a transaction occurred during the second month, the first time indicator variable is assigned a value of one and all other time indicator variables are set to zero. If a transaction occurred during the third month, the first two indicators are set to one and all others are set to zero.
12. The transaction data were screened for outliers and influential observations.
13. The homogeneity of the area is important because the relevant risk should be that of an individual house, not a portfolio of houses such as those that comprise a large region.
14. The monthly appreciation rates obtained by estimating Model (1) exhibit some negative serial correlation (Durban–Watson statistic of 2.99). One could correct for this by estimating an auto-regressive model. We have performed the estimation utilizing AR(1) to AR(5) process and have found this to have small impact on the estimated standard deviation.
15. There is a clear cycle in home values as evident by Figure 2. We tried to allow for changing expected returns over time based on a number of economic variables such as unemployment, short and long interest rates, and dividend yield on stocks. Such attempts resulted in negligible decrease in the estimated standard deviation.
16. Conceptually, for commercial real estate this magnitude, the after tax cash flow from operation, would be much easier to estimate.
17. Loan amortization increases carrying costs and reduces the exercise price of the option (i.e., loan balance) over time. The shorter the time to maturity the larger the fraction of the payment is to principal. As will be seen below, amortization has no qualitative effect on our conclusions.
18. This is a very conservative assumption. In fact the marginal state and federal tax rate for individuals who own the homes being considered is likely to exceed 40 percent.
19. We are examining the decision of the seller to accept his best offer or to delay. Consequently, the relevant price for him is the maximum bid price, net of transaction cost. The bid price would be determined by the value of housing services and the value of the option to the potential buyer.
20. The total value would be the sum of the time and intrinsic values of the option.
21. Future mortgage loan payments are included as part of the cost of maintaining the ownership because they are an actual cash outflow for the current owner. In general, the market value of an asset is independent of how it

is financed. The perspective we are taking is the value to the owner and from his point of view differences in loan balances and interest payments are different assets.

22. Some homeowners may have refinanced to take advantage of lower interest rates or to remove equity from previously purchased homes. In these cases the remaining time to maturity of the loan would be more than 23 years.
23. The comparable amounts for a non-amortizing loan are an option value of $2953 and carrying costs of $2284.
24. Our analysis assumes that there are no costs of default. In this case a homeowner would default on his mortgage loan when the balance is approximately 2.5 percent greater than the net bid price.
25. For computation simplicity we assume a non-amortizing loan.

References

Black, F., and M. Scholes. (1973). ''The Pricing of Options and Corporate Liabilities,'' *Journal of Political Economy* 81, 637–659.

Brennan, M., and E. Schwartz. (1985). ''Evaluating Natural Resource Investments,'' *Journal of Business* 58, 135–157.

Cauley, S. D. (1994). ''Contingent Price Contracts and the Efficiency of Housing Markets,'' *Journal of the American Real Estate and Urban Economics Association*, Winter.

Cornell, B., F. Longstaff, and E. Schwartz. (1996). ''Throwing Good Money after Bad? Cash Infusions and Distressed Real Estate,'' *Real Estate Economics* 24(1), 23–41.

Copeland, T., R. Koller, and J. Murrin. (1991). *Valuation: Measuring and Managing the Value of Companies*. New York: John Wiley & Sons.

Dixit, A., and R. Pidyck. (1994). *Investment Under Uncertainty*. Princeton, New Jersey: Princeton University Press.

Efron, B., and R. Tibshirani. (1998). *An Introduction to the Bootstrap*. Boca Raton, Florida: Chapman & Hall/CRC.

Gabriel, S., J. Mattey, and W. Wascher. (1999). ''House Price Differentials and Dynamics: Evidence from the Los Angeles and San Francisco Metropolitan Areas,'' *Federal Reserve Bank of San Francisco Economic Review* 0(1), 3–22.

Geske, R. (1977). ''The Valuation of Corporate Libilities as Compound Options,'' *Journal of Financial and Quantitative Analysis*, 541–552.

Geske, R. (1979). ''The Valuation of Compound Options,'' *Journal of Financial Economics* 5, 63–81.

Hull, J. (1997). *Options, Futures, and other Derivatives*. Upper Saddle River, NJ: Prentice Hall.

Kallberg, J., C. Liu, and D. Greig. (1996). ''The Role of Real Estate in the Portfolio Allocation Process,'' *Real Estate Economics*, Fall.

Kau, J., and T. Kim. 1994. ''Waiting to Default: The Value of Delay,'' *Journal of the American Real Estate and Urban Economics Association* 22(3), 539–551.

Kester, C. (1984). ''Today's Options for Tomorrow's Growth,'' *Harvard Business Review* March/April, 153–160.

Liang, Y., F. Myer, and J. Webb. (1996). ''The Bootstrap Efficient Frontier for Mixed-Asset Portfolios,'' *Real Estate Economics*, Summer.

Longstaff, F., and E. Schwartz. (2001). ''Valuing American Options by Simulation: A Simple Least-Squares Approach,'' *Review of Financial Studies* 14(1), 32–39.

Mason, S., and R. Merton. (1985). ''The Role of Contingent Claims Analysis in Corporate Finance.'' In E. Altman and M. Subrahmanyam (eds), *Recent Advances in Corporate Finance*, Homewood, IL: Richard D. Irwin.

Meyer, R., and K. Wieand. (1996). ''Risk and Return to Housing, Tenure Choice and the Value of Housing in an Asset Pricing Context,'' *Real Estate Economics*, Spring.

McDonald, R., and D. Siegel. (1985). ''Investment and the valuation of Firms When There is an Option to Shut Down,'' *International Economic Review* 26 (June), 331–349.

Stein, J. (1995). ''Prices and Trading Volume in the Housing Market: A Model with Down-Payment Effects.'' *The Quarterly Journal of Economics* 110 (May): 379–406.

Tourino, O. (1979). *The Valuation of Reserves of Natural Resources: An Option Pricing Approach.* Unpublished Doctoral Dissertation, University of California, Berkeley.

Trigeorgis, L., and S. Manson. (1987). ''Valuing Flexibility as a Complex Option,'' *Journal of Finance* 45 (June), 594–565.

Williams, J. (1997). ''Redevelopment of Real Assets,'' *Real Estate Economics* 25, 387–407.

Winger, A. (1996). ''A Layman's Approach to Risk Analysis,'' *Real Estate Review* 25, 79–83.

Ziobrowski, B., and A. Ziobrowski. (1997). ''Higher Real Estate Risk and Mixed-Asset Portfolio Performance,'' *Journal of Real Estate Portfolio Management* 3, 107–115.

Ziobrowski, A., P. Cheng, and B. Ziobrowski. (1997). ''Using a Bootstrap to measure Optimum Mixed-Asset Portfolio Composition: A Comment,'' *Real Estate Economics*, 4.

Journal of Real Estate Finance and Economics, 24:1/2, 167–200, 2002

Hedging Housing Risk*

PETER ENGLUND
Stockholm School of Economics
Email: Peter.Englund@hhs.se

MIN HWANG
University of California, Berkeley
Email: min@econ.berkeley.edu

JOHN M. QUIGLEY
University of California, Berkeley
Email: quigley@econ.berkeley.edu

Abstract

An unusually rich source of data on housing prices in Stockholm is used to analyze the investment implications of housing choices. This empirical analysis derives market-wide price and return series for housing investment during a 13-year period, and it also provides estimates of the individual-specific, idiosyncratic, variation in housing returns. Because the idiosyncratic component follows an autocorrelated process, the analysis of portfolio choice is dependent upon the holding period. We analyze the composition of household investment portfolios containing housing, common stocks, stocks in real estate holding companies, bonds, and *t*-bills. For short holding periods, the efficient portfolio contains essentially no housing. For longer periods, low-risk portfolios contain 15 to 50 percent housing. These results suggest that there are large potential gains from policies or institutions that would permit households to hedge their lumpy investments in housing. We estimate the potential value of hedges in reducing risk to households, yet yielding the same investment returns. The value is surprisingly large, especially to poorer homeowners.

Key Words: portfolio risk, house price index, hedging

1. Introduction

Housing is a major component of household consumption expenditure. The average household in Western Europe and North America spends 25 to 35 percent of its income on housing, and young homeowners often spend even larger proportions. For a variety of reasons, most housing is owner-occupied. Differences in tax treatment and credit availability contribute to the substantial differences in the fraction of owner-occupied housing across countries. However, apart from these institutional factors, there are other reasons why most households choose to own their home, at least over a part of their life-

*A previous version of this paper was presented at the Maastricht-Cambridge Real Estate Finance and Investment Symposium, Maastricht, Netherlands, June 2000.

Table 1. Life-cycle housing investment. Mean house value as a percentage of mean net wealth by age category.

Age of Household Head	United States 1989	Sweden 1991
18–30 (25–34)	351.1	258.0
31–40 (35–44)	236.6	161.7
41–50 (45–54)	158.8	121.1
51–60 (55–64)	96.9	94.6
61–70 (65–74)	75.7	78.7
71 + (75+)	64.8	80.6

Note. Age intervals in parenthesis refer to Sweden.
Sources. Flavin and Yamashita (1998) Table 2 and Edin et al. (1995), Table 8b.

cycles. Homeownership gives the occupants full freedom to tailor the house to their specific tastes and needs. Homeowners also stand to benefit from the consequences of sound decisions about maintenance and renovation. These offer considerable financial advantages (see Sweeney, 1974, for a discussion of the maintenance cost advantages of homeownership.) The advantages of homeownership have to be weighed against the transaction costs of changing homes; these costs are typically larger for homeowners. Less frequent movers will be more likely to prefer homeownership, whereas households with shorter expected durations may be better-off renting.

Choosing to own a home is not only a consumption decision. It also entails a portfolio choice. In fact, most homeowners have strongly unbalanced portfolios. This is illustrated in Table 1 based on micro data, the PSID for the United States and the HINK[1] database for Sweden. Despite different institutional environments, the life-cycle pattern is relatively similar in these two countries. In both countries, the average household invests well above 100 percent of net wealth in its home up until 50 years of age. The age profile appears to be somewhat steeper for the U.S., where households below 30 years of age invest more than three times their net wealth in owner-occupied housing.

This wealth composition does not seem to be the outcome of an unrestricted portfolio choice. Rather, it suggests that current institutional arrangements do not allow an optimal sharing of the risks associated with homeownership. There is some econometric evidence to suggest that the high risks of homeownership have real consequences. For example, studies by Rosen et al. (1984) and Turner (2000) both conclude that house-price volatility discourages homeownership. Turner also finds that high-income households, presumably those with smaller investment shares in housing, are less sensitive to price volatility.

Recently, different proposals have been put forth to improve the possibilities to pool and share these risks. Case, Shiller and Weiss (1993) have proposed a market in futures contracts tied to regional house-price indexes, allowing households to hedge by taking short positions in these derivatives contracts. Caplin *et al.* (1997) have suggested setting up housing partnerships that would allow households to share the risk of owning the dwellings in which they live with other investors. So far, neither of these proposals for hedging and risk-sharing has met with much success in practice. This is undoubtedly partly due to legal and practical problems. Setting up housing partnerships would require new legislation, and the attractiveness of a derivatives market in price-index futures depends on the quality and integrity of the indexes. These new markets would take time to develop, and despite their immediate appeal, it is not clear to what extent households are adversely affected by their unbalanced investment portfolios.

This paper provides a detailed assessment of the potential gains for homeowners from improved hedging opportunities. Specifically, we investigate the benefits in mean-variance space which arise from introducing opportunities to take positions in a price index for owner-occupied homes. The next section of the paper briefly reviews available evidence on housing returns in a portfolio context. Section 3 presents the data that our analysis draws on and the methods we use for estimating house-price indexes and the returns to investing in an owner-occupied home. In order to generate long-term returns, we estimate a VAR model. This model and the properties of returns at different horizons are discussed in Section 4. Further details are reported in Appendix B. In Section 5 we use the variance-covariance structure of returns to derive mean-variance efficient portfolios under a series of conditions. We deal with three issues: the optimal allocation of investment to housing in efficient portfolios unrestricted by consumption motives; the inherent risk in housing chosen only for consumption motives; and the potential for risk-reduction which could be afforded by instruments to hedge housing investments. Households that hold a large fraction of their portfolios in their own homes—typically younger and poorer households—pay a high cost for this choice in terms of extra risk. Introducing a market in the housing index leads to a considerable reduction of this risk.

2. Evidence on housing returns and optimal portfolio choice

Empirical studies of the quantitative importance of the portfolio-imbalance problem are scarce. Exceptions are papers by Goetzmann (1993), Flavin and Yamashita (1998), Eichholtz et al. (2000), and Gatzlaff (2000).[2] Despite using different methods to measure the returns to housing, all three studies find low correlations between the returns to housing and other assets—Goetzmann uses repeat-sales price indexes for four U.S. cities estimated by Case and Shiller (1990); Gatzlaff uses indexes for 20 MSAs in Florida estimated by similar techniques; Flavin and Yamashita use panel information on the owners' own assessments of house values. The low correlation between housing and other assets suggests that housing should contribute to diversifying the portfolio and lowering the risk. Although the exact specification varies among these three studies, each indicates a portfolio share for housing around fifty percent for the minimum-variance portfolio.[3] At the riskier end of the efficient frontier, results differ more across studies, not surprisingly since this portion of the frontier is much more sensitive to estimation errors (see, for example, Jorion, 1985).

For a standard portfolio choice problem, the holding period of the investment is not a major concern. Because most asset returns are reasonably well described by random-walk processes, their variances and covariances over n periods are approximately equal to n

times their one-period counterparts. The solution to a portfolio-choice problem based on quarterly returns is, thus, almost identical to the solution based on multi-period returns. Despite the recent findings of high-frequency positive autocorrelation and long-term mean reversion in stock prices, the random-walk assumption remains a reasonable approximation for most asset returns. Housing is a major exception for two reasons. First, index returns exhibit positive autocorrelation for many markets; see Case and Shiller (1989) for U.S. cities and Englund and Ioannides (1996) for international comparative data. Second, houses are heterogeneous, as are the conditions of sale. Thus, there is a strong idiosyncratic component to the return from investing in an individual house. The importance of the idiosyncratic component can be expected to diminish over time in relation to the price-index uncertainty. For this reason, and since transaction costs are important, the assumed holding period (the investment horizon) may be quite important in analyzing a portfolio-choice problem in which housing is one of the assets. Goetzmann considers the impact of the holding period. He finds that the two aspects tend to have offsetting effects on the riskiness of housing. The annualized standard deviation of the index-based return tends to increase with the holding period, but the impact of the idiosyncratic component decreases. On balance, according to Goetzmann's study, the holding period does not appear to be a major concern.

The study by Eichholtz et al. (2000) focuses on the potential of bonds and common stocks as hedges against the risks of homeownership. Interestingly, they find that the demand for stocks and bonds in an optimal portfolio is not significantly affected by homeownership, implying that neither asset provides a good hedge for housing. This suggests that one has to look towards instruments more directly geared at housing returns in order to find good hedges.

3. Data and methods

Research on this issue has been hampered by the lack of reliable time-series data on housing prices and housing returns. In this paper, we draw upon a body of data consisting of observations on all sales of one-family houses in Sweden from January 1, 1981 through August 31, 1993. These data that have been used to estimate rather precise quarterly house-price indexes for eight major Swedish regions; see Englund et al. (1998) and Quigley and Redfearn (1999). This data series is much shorter than comparable price series that could be used to estimate stock returns. To focus on longer-term returns, this poses special problems. We address those by estimating a vector autoregression system, and we use the estimated VAR model to generate long term expected housing returns and autocovariances. The data set on housing includes every arm's length sale of owner-occupied housing in Sweden. Contract data reporting the transaction price for each sale have been merged with tax-assessment records containing detailed information about the characteristics of each house. Repeat sales are identified, as is the location of each unit down to the smallest geographical unit, the parish (akin to a census tract). The data set is exceptional in its detailed description of each dwelling at the date of sale and its identification of the panel nature of sales of the same property.

Assume that the sale price of a housing unit is the product of an index representing the level of services emitted by the unit and an index of price per quality unit. To represent this, suppose

$$V_{it} = P_t + Q_{it} + \omega_{it}, \tag{1}$$

where V_{it} is the logarithm of the observed selling price of house i at time t, Q_{it} is the log of the quality of house i sold at time t, P_t is the log of the constant quality housing-price index at time t, and ω_{it} is a random error reflecting idiosyncratic aspects of a particular transaction, e.g., a ''distressed'' sale. According to (1), each house emits a quality of service Q_{it} that is priced at P_t at a particular point in time. Q_{it} is unobserved, but

$$Q_{it} = \beta X_{it} + \xi_i + \eta_{it}. \tag{2}$$

According to (2), housing quality is a function of a vector of observable characteristics of dwellings at time t, X_{it}, a dwelling-unit-specific factor, ξ_i, and a random error η_{it}. The vector X_{it} may include the vintage (production year) of the dwelling as well as the accumulated physical depreciation of that dwelling at year t. The term ξ_i represents the unmeasured characteristics of house i. Combining (1) and (2) yields

$$V_{it} = \beta X_{it} + P_t + \xi_i + \varepsilon_{it}, \tag{3}$$

where ε_{it} is a composite error term,

$$\varepsilon_{it} = \eta_{it} + \omega_{it}. \tag{4}$$

We assume that this composite term, i.e., the idiosyncratic error net of the individual-specific error, is autocorrelated:

$$\varepsilon_{it} = \rho^{t-\tau}\varepsilon_{i,t-\tau} + \nu_{it}, \tag{5}$$

where

$$\begin{aligned} E(\xi_i) = 0 \quad E(\xi_i^2) &= \sigma_\xi^2; \\ E(\nu_{it}) = 0 \quad E(\nu_{it}^2) &= \sigma_\nu^2. \end{aligned} \tag{6}$$

The panel nature of the data identifies the key parameters: the price index P_t, the autoregressive term ρ, and the error variances. The methods of estimating these parameters are discussed in Englund et al. (1998). Table A1 reports the coefficient estimates of the price series and standard errors for eight regions in Sweden. The price indices are very precisely estimated. The indexes are estimated monthly and aggregated to quarter-year intervals in our analysis.

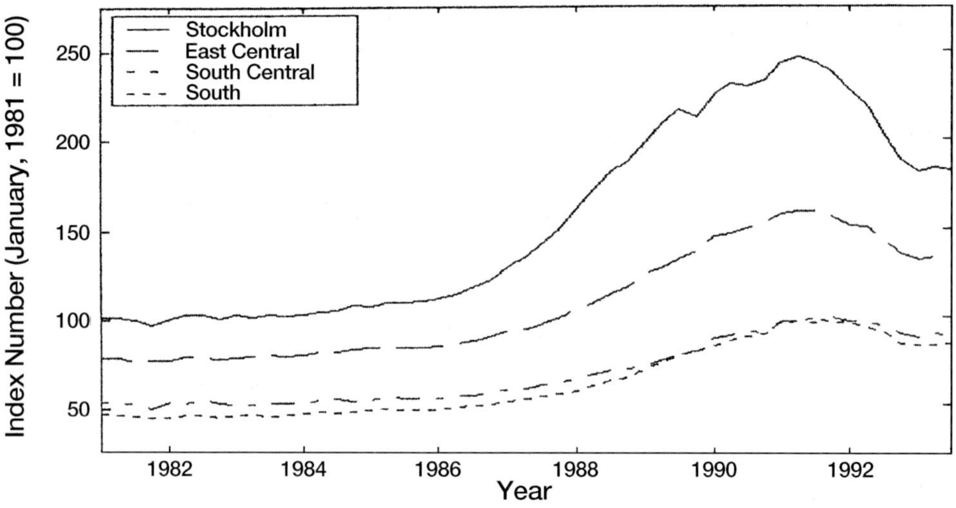

Figure 1A. House price indices for Sweden.

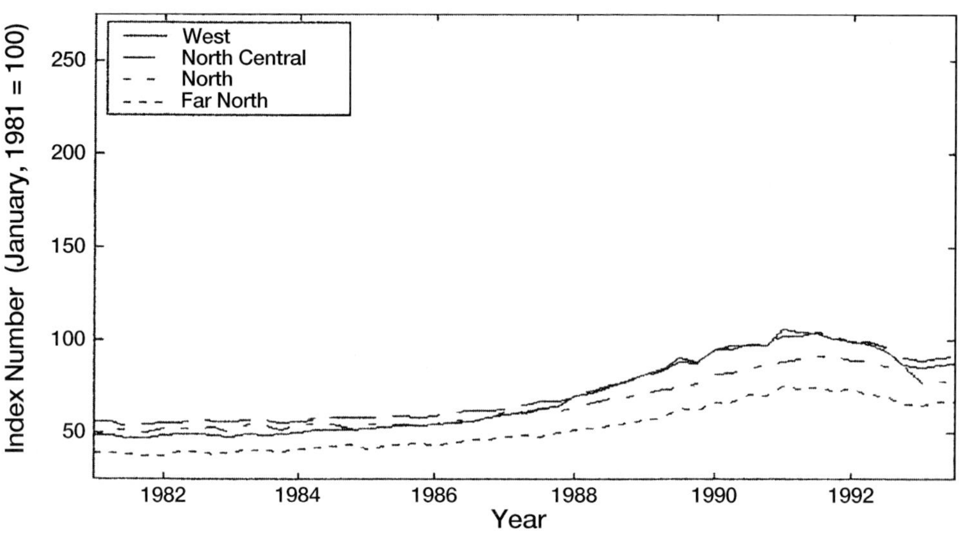

Figure 1B. House price indices for Sweden.

The estimated price indexes for all the eight regions identified in Table A.1 are depicted in Figures 1A and 1B. As the diagrams indicate, the course of housing returns across the different regions of Sweden during this period has been fairly well synchronized. Prices were stagnant nominally until 1985, when they started to increase. House prices reached a peak in 1991 followed by a sharp drop, as a major financial crisis hit Sweden during the early 1990s. Stockholm has the highest and most volatile housing prices.

The return from investing in an owner-occupied home consists of three components: the rate of change of the housing-price index, P, the rental value of the service flow generated by the housing unit (net of operating costs and depreciation), and the rate of change of the idiosyncratic component of the house price. We impute a rental value using the index of rents for residential apartments in each region, i.e., we assume the apartment index to be valid for one-family houses as well.[4] We set the rent in the first quarter of 1981 at 1 percent of house value. This follows the widely-used one-in-one-hundred rule.[5] This gives us two return series. The housing index return, r^H, is given by

$$r_t^H = P_t - P_{t-1} + 0.01. \tag{7}$$

And the return on an individual housing unit, r^h, by

$$r_t^h = r_t^H + \varepsilon_{it} - \varepsilon_{it-1}. \tag{8}$$

Housing returns are highly correlated across all eight regions, indicating that there are only small diversification benefits from holding a multi-regional housing portfolio within the country. This contrasts with the United States where the benefits from regional diversification are considerable; see Goetzmann (1993). For this reason, we limit ourselves to including the Stockholm housing market in the portfolio analysis. Figure 2A depicts the temporal pattern of the real quarterly return on Stockholm housing defined according to (7) as the weighted change in the monthly price index (see Table A1) aggregated to quarters plus the quarterly rental service stream minus the change in CPI.

Following Goetzmann (1993) we include general stocks (the AFGX index, produced by a leading business periodical), five-year bonds and three-month treasury bills among the investment alternatives. In order to highlight the opportunities for hedging using currently traded instruments, we also include an index for real-estate corporations traded on the Stockholm stock exchange. This index covers a group of companies whose main source of income comes from real-estate holdings (office and residential). To varying degrees, they also have other lines of business, primarily in construction. In the absence of REITs, this is the most natural vehicle for investing in real estate for a Swedish investor. Figures 2A and 2B report the real returns on these assets which could be used to form an investment portfolio.

The data cover a dramatic period in Swedish economic history.[6] The 1980s was a decade of major asset revaluations, as seen by the high returns to stocks throughout the decade, and to homes, during the second half of the decade. During the 1980s, the Stockholm stock exchange outperformed all major stock markets in industrialized countries. The development of asset prices can be explained by the deregulation of credit markets around 1985 and by an expansionary fiscal policy. Returns to fixed-income instruments were also extraordinary. Since the parity of the krona was maintained at a fixed level after a devaluation in 1982 despite the fact that inflation was higher in Sweden than abroad, the currency had to be defended by high interest rates. The early 1990s saw an end to the asset-price boom with a sharp drop in prices, particularly for real estate, in 1991 and 1992. This

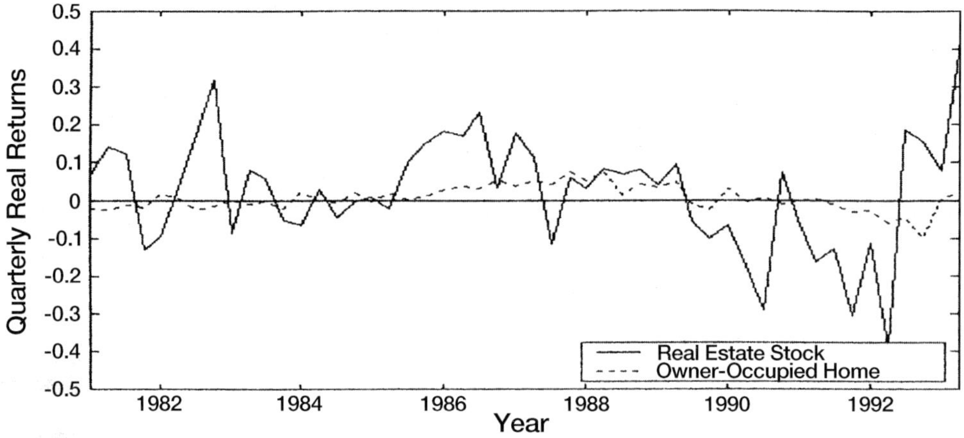

Figure 2A. Stockholm owner-occupied homes and real estate stock index.

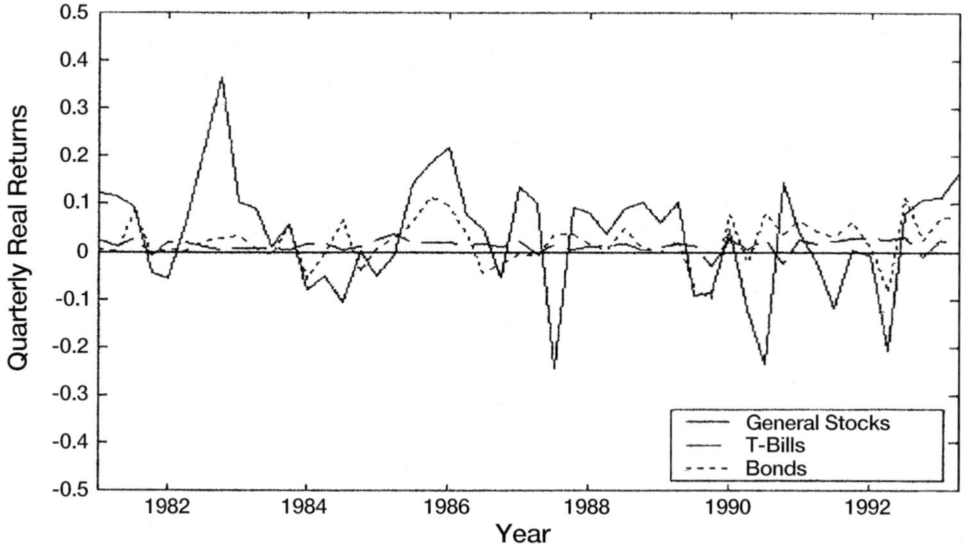

Figure 2B. General stock index, *t*-bills and bonds.

was associated with a banking crisis, with total credit losses between 1990 and 1993 on the order of 12 percent of one year's GDP. A general economic crisis persisted and GDP fell for three consecutive years. In the fall of 1992, the Swedish krona was allowed to float, resulting in a depreciation by twenty percent by the end of the year. In 1994 the Swedish economy started to recover. The recovery period is not part of our data, however.

4. Investment returns

Since most households take a long-term perspective on their home investment, it is important to analyze the returns to housing over different investment horizons. But with only 13 years of data, we cannot observe long-horizon variances and covariances directly. To circumvent this problem, we assume that returns are generated from a fourth order vector autoregression system on a quarterly basis in the five asset returns. Once the parameters for the VAR system are estimated, it is fairly straightforward to compute moments over long horizons; see Appendix B for details. The estimated model is presented in Table B1. The model explains much of the variation in housing returns (R^2adj = 0.72) but, as expected, it works less well for financial assets. Tests for Granger-causality fail to reject the null hypothesis of no causality. Exceptions are the returns to bonds and houses; both are predicted by stock returns, the general index as well as the real-estate stock index. Interestingly, high returns to real-estate stocks predict high housing returns, while high general stock returns predict low housing returns. Closely related findings, that the returns to securitized real estate help predict the returns to direct investment in individual properties, have been reported for commercial real estate. See Barkham and Geltner (1995).

The first two moments of investment returns at different horizons, based on the estimated VAR parameters, are presented in Tables 2 and 3. As noted in Table 2, expected real returns are generally quite high, ranging from 1.3 percent per quarter for *t*-bills and homes to 3.7 percent for the general stock index, reflecting the strong performance of Swedish asset prices discussed above. The lower panel of Table 2 displays variances at different horizons. To maintain comparability, the table presents long-horizon variances on a per quarter basis, i.e., the variance of n-quarter returns divided by n. In terms of variance, housing returns are considerably riskier than nominal assets, but are less risky than stocks. Real estate stocks have two to four times the variance of stocks in general. In comparing the different horizons, we note that the

Table 2. Means and variances of real quarterly asset returns.

	R.E. Stocks	Gen. Stocks	*t*-bills	Bonds	H. Index	Houses
			Expected returns			
	0.0251	0.0365	0.0129	0.0186	0.0127	0.0127
			Variances			
Time Horizon						
1 quarter	0.0436	0.0194	0.00021	0.0029	0.0022	0.0126
10 quarters	0.1467	0.0409	0.00031	0.0033	0.0116	0.0193
20 quarters	0.0523	0.0183	0.00018	0.0014	0.0064	0.0122
40 quarters	0.0397	0.0167	0.00014	0.0011	0.0051	0.0087

Notes. Returns are generated from the VAR model of Table B1. For comparability, variances are expressed in quarterly terms by dividing by the number of quarters.

Table 3. Correlation coefficients among asset returns at different time horizons.

Time Horizon	R.E. Stocks	Gen. Stocks	*t*-bills	Bonds	H. Index	Houses
R.E.Stocks						
1 quarter	1	0.8161	− 0.1420	0.1612	0.3473	0.1458
10 quarters		0.8961	0.1559	0.0826	0.5171	0.4006
20 quarters		0.7710	0.0813	0.0230	0.5270	0.3822
40 quarters		0.7533	0.0281	0.0104	0.4961	0.3798
Gen Stocks						
1 quarter		1	− 0.0696	0.3579	0.1609	0.0676
10 quarters			0.2263	0.2818	0.2231	0.1729
20 quarters			0.0402	0.2520	0.0503	0.0365
40 quarters			− 0.0531	0.2334	− 0.0292	− 0.0223
t-bills						
1 quarter			1	0.4100	− 0.0694	− 0.0292
10 quarters				0.8097	− 0.5137	− 0.3980
20 quarters				0.6949	− 0.3528	− 0.2558
40 quarters				0.6720	− 0.3009	− 0.2303
Bonds						
1 quarter				1	− 01316	− 0.0552
10 quarters					− 0.6167	− 0.4778
20 quarters					− 0.4923	− 0.3571
40 quarters					− 0.4711	− 0.3606
Housing index						
1 quarter					1	0.4199
10 quarters						0.7748
20 quarters						0.7252
40 quarters						0.7654

10-quarter horizon displays higher variances for all assets than any other horizons. Generally variances are lower at the 40-quarter than at the one-quarter horizon; the housing index is the only exception.

For housing, we distinguish between index returns and the returns to an individual house, as defined in (7) and (8). We note that the difference is sizeable for short holding periods. At the one-period horizon, the variance of the housing-index return equals that of bonds, whereas the variance of the return to an individual home is six times as large. At longer horizons, it is less than twice as large. Yet, even at the 40-quarter horizon, the individual home is a relatively risky investment, with a variance half that of common stocks and eight times that of bonds.

Table 3 reports simple correlation coefficients between the investment vehicles for the different time horizons. The returns to housing are positively correlated with real-estate stocks and negatively correlated with *t*-bills and bonds. All correlations with housing are stronger at longer horizons. The correlation with the general stock index is close to zero. Our results may be compared with those of Goetzmann (1993) and Gatzlaff (2000), both of which apply to one-year horizons. Each of these studies finds a negative correlation between housing and bond returns (− 0.54 and − 0.23), a small correlation with *t*-bills (− 0.22 and + 0.19), and a small negative correlation with the S&P 500 stock index. Only Gatzlaff considers securitized real estate, surprisingly finding a negative correlation (− 0.13). Our results confirm the general conclusion from these studies that the correlations between housing and other key assets are sufficiently low as to make housing a potentially attractive addition to a portfolio, at least at lower risk levels. Whether this warrants the observed portfolio shares of 100 percent or more is an issue discussed in the next section.

5. Optimal portfolios

We now use the structure of this information to construct mean-variance efficient portfolios. We focus on three sets of issues: the optimal allocation of investment to housing in efficient portfolios unrestricted by consumption motives; the inherent risk in housing chosen only for consumption motives; and the potential for risk reduction which could be afforded by instruments to hedge housing investments.

5.1. Unrestricted portfolios

We start by considering a benchmark where the amount of housing is chosen freely by mean-variance optimization. We analyze two cases; both include the four financial assets, with housing represented either by a single house or by the housing index (Tables 4 and 5, and Figure 3). Portfolio shares, except for a single house, are only restricted to be between plus and minus 500 percent. The share of a single house is restricted to be non-negative, reflecting the fact that it is difficult in practice to short-sell individual houses. The benchmark cases are not intended to capture real life investment opportunities, but rather to bring out the implications of the return patterns in the data for portfolio choice. We illustrate the solutions to this problem for two horizons, one-quarter and 40-quarters.[7] From Table 4 we see that the optimal portfolio share in an individual house is close to zero in the minimum-variance portfolio at both horizons. Moving out along the frontier, it increases at first, for the one-quarter horizon only modestly to at most 15 percent, but for the longer horizon more sharply to more than 100 percent. With further increased risk, the optimal portfolio share in an individual house decreases to become zero at high risk levels. The minimum variance portfolio invests more than 100 percent in *t*-bills and borrows in bonds, but at higher risk levels this is reversed, with borrowing in bills and investment in bonds and shares. Real estate stocks are generally unattractive except far out on the efficient frontier.

The results of the same exercise assuming that the investor can invest in the housing index, but not in an individual house,[8] are displayed in Table 5. This case can be thought of as applying to a renter household if an index market were available. Since the housing index offers a lower variance but the same expected return as a single house, it comes as no surprise that the housing index portfolio shares in Table 5 are consistently larger than the

Table 4. Optimal unrestricted portfolios. Four financial instruments and a house.

Standard Deviation	Expected Returns	R.E. Stocks	Gen. Stocks	*t*-bill	Bonds	Houses
			40-quarter horizon			
0.0089	0.0131	−0.0500	0.0821	1.1226	−0.2127	0.0580
0.0636	0.0304	−0.2696	0.5591	−1.0208	1.3529	0.3784
0.1263	0.0477	−0.4892	1.0361	−3.1642	2.9185	0.6988
0.1895	0.0650	−0.7454	1.6095	−5.0000	4.1588	0.9771
0.2640	0.0823	−1.2203	2.7586	−5.0000	3.4581	1.0036
0.3477	0.0997	−1.6952	3.9078	−5.0000	2.7574	1.0300
0.4352	0.1170	−2.1035	5.0000	−5.0000	2.1456	0.9579
0.6161	0.1343	−0.3167	5.0000	−5.0000	1.3167	0.0000
1.0428	0.1516	2.3417	5.0000	−5.0000	−1.3417	0.0000
1.5396	0.1689	5.0000	5.0000	−5.0000	−4.0000	0.0000
			One-quarter horizon			
0.0136	0.0131	0.0065	0.0177	1.0298	−0.0676	0.0136
0.0802	0.0304	−0.4017	0.9185	0.3201	0.1230	0.0401
0.1586	0.0477	−0.8098	1.8193	−0.3895	0.3135	0.0666
0.2375	0.0650	−1.2179	2.7201	−1.0992	0.5040	0.0930
0.3164	0.0823	−1.6261	3.6209	−1.8089	0.6945	0.1195
0.3953	0.0997	−2.0342	4.5217	−2.5185	0.8850	0.1460
0.4778	0.1170	−2.1526	5.0000	−4.2136	2.2120	0.1542
0.6787	0.1343	−0.3167	5.0000	−5.0000	1.3167	0.0000
1.1250	0.1516	2.3417	5.0000	−5.0000	−1.3417	0.0000
1.6360	0.1689	5.0000	5.0000	−5.0000	−4.0000	0.0000

corresponding housing shares in Table 4, except when non-negativity restrictions on a single house becomes binding. In fact, the housing-index shares are quite large. For the 40- and one-quarter horizons, the portfolio shares start at 9 and 15 percent for the minimum variance portfolios and peak at close to 100 and 200 percent respectively. This suggests that access to a housing index should prove attractive for a renter household. Other features of the efficient frontiers are much the same as in Table 4. Figure 3 compares the efficient investment frontiers when households can invest in financial instruments and a house with the frontier when they can invest in financial instruments and a housing index. The gains from an index at higher levels of risk are apparent.

We have also computed optimal portfolio shares imposing non-negativity restrictions on stocks but not on bonds and *t*-bills. This reflects the fact that short-selling is difficult in practice, while short positions in nominal instruments may be interpreted as borrowing. The general pattern of optimal portfolio holdings (see Table 6) along the efficient frontier is roughly the same under these assumptions. With increasing risk, the housing fraction goes from close to zero over positive values (peaking at around 40 percent) to zero at the high-risk end of the frontier.

Table 5. Optimal unrestricted portfolios. Four financial instruments and the housing index.

Standard Deviation	Expected Returns	R.E. Stocks	Gen. Stocks	*t*-bill	Bonds	H. Index
			40-quarter horizon			
0.0011	0.0138	– 0.0812	0.1126	0.9602	– 0.1376	0.1460
0.0107	0.0343	– 0.4574	0.7320	– 1.9567	1.7621	0.9200
0.0213	0.0549	– 0.8336	1.3514	– 4.8737	3.6618	1.6941
0.0345	0.0754	– 1.3996	2.6934	– 5.0000	2.9248	1.7814
0.0504	0.0959	– 1.9742	4.0681	– 5.0000	2.0684	1.8377
0.0676	0.1164	– 2.0731	5.0000	– 5.0000	1.9932	1.0798
0.0919	0.1370	– 1.1705	5.0000	– 5.0000	3.5621	– 1.3916
0.1204	0.1575	– 0.2056	5.0000	– 5.0000	5.0000	– 3.7944
0.1592	0.1780	1.8488	5.0000	– 5.0000	4.1512	– 5.0000
0.2335	0.1986	5.0000	5.0000	– 5.0000	1.0000	– 5.0000
			One-quarter horizon			
0.0132	0.0131	– 0.0038	0.0231	0.9483	– 0.0532	0.0855
0.0946	0.0337	– 0.5094	1.0996	– 0.0768	0.2049	0.2817
0.1878	0.0543	– 1.0151	2.1761	– 1.1020	0.4630	0.4779
0.2813	0.0749	– 1.5207	3.2526	– 2.1271	0.7211	0.6742
0.3749	0.0955	– 2.0263	4.3291	– 3.1523	0.9792	0.8704
0.4717	0.1161	– 2.2425	5.0000	– 5.0000	2.2985	0.9440
0.6093	0.1368	– 1.5997	5.0000	– 5.0000	4.4252	– 1.8255
0.8017	0.1574	– 0.2176	5.0000	– 5.0000	5.0000	– 3.7824
1.1034	0.1780	1.8373	5.0000	– 5.0000	4.1627	– 5.0000
1.6355	0.1986	5.0000	5.0000	– 5.0000	1.0000	– 5.0000

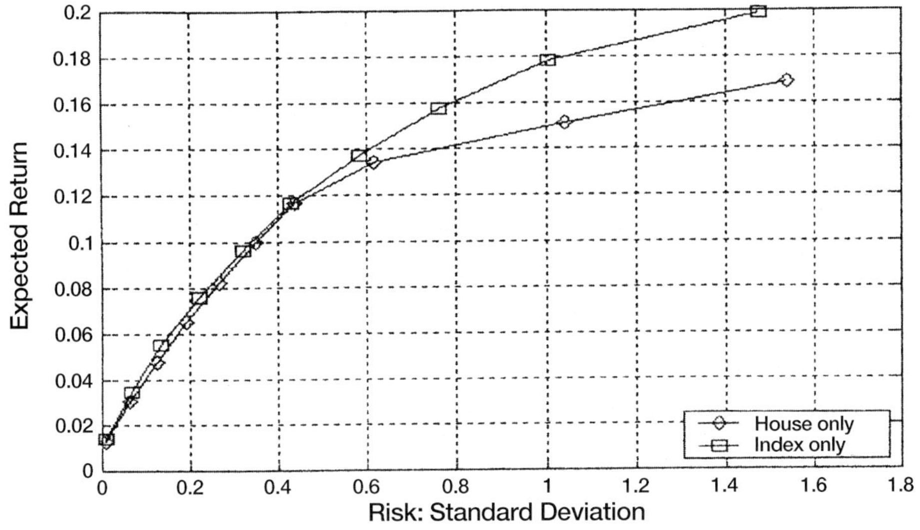

Figure 3. Investment in house only or in index only: 40 quarters.

Table 6. Optimal portfolios. Four financial instruments and a house. No short selling of stocks.

Standard Deviation	Expected Returns	R.E. Stocks	Gen. Stocks	*t*-bill	Bonds	Houses
			40-quarter horizon			
0.0104	0.0125	0.0000	0.0227	1.1237	−0.1708	0.0244
0.0689	0.0299	0.0000	0.2741	−1.3666	1.8669	0.2255
0.1366	0.0473	0.0000	0.5256	−3.8568	3.9045	0.4267
0.2101	0.0647	0.0000	1.0918	−5.0000	4.6139	0.2943
0.3049	0.0820	0.0000	1.9652	−5.0000	4.0348	0.0000
0.4127	0.0994	0.0000	2.9362	−5.0000	3.0638	0.0000
0.5268	0.1168	0.0000	3.9071	−5.0000	2.0929	0.0000
0.6438	0.1342	0.0000	4.8780	−5.0000	1.1220	0.0000
1.0412	0.1516	2.3324	5.0000	−5.0000	−1.3324	0.0000
1.5396	0.1689	5.0000	5.0000	−5.0000	−4.0000	0.0000
			One-quarter horizon			
0.0136	0.0131	0.0065	0.0177	1.0298	−0.0676	0.0136
0.0992	0.0304	0.0000	0.6017	−0.1783	0.5766	0.0000
0.1976	0.0477	0.0000	1.1796	−1.4124	1.2328	0.0000
0.2963	0.0650	0.0000	1.7576	−2.6465	1.8890	0.0000
0.3951	0.0823	0.0000	2.3355	−3.8807	2.5451	0.0000
0.4940	0.0997	0.0000	2.9497	−5.0000	3.0503	0.0000
0.5989	0.1170	0.0000	3.9172	−5.0000	2.0828	0.0000
0.7107	0.1343	0.0000	4.8848	−5.0000	1.1152	0.0000
1.1250	0.1516	2.3417	5.0000	−5.0000	−1.3417	0.0000
1.6360	0.1689	5.0000	5.0000	−5.0000	−4.0000	0.0000

5.2. Housing consumption choice and risk

Households do not make their housing choices purely from an investment perspective. Under current institutional arrangements, it is not feasible to disentangle the consumption and investment aspects of housing choices. Taking the consumption choice as exogenous, we now analyze at the optimal portfolio composition conditional on given fractions of wealth invested in housing.[9] We do this for four different cases: ''rich'' homeowners, for whom we assume the housing share is 100 percent of net wealth; ''average'' homeowners (housing share = 200 percent); ''poor'' homeowners (housing share = 400 percent); and renters (housing share = 0). These portfolio shares span the average shares reported in Table 1 for households of different ages (see also Flavin and Yamashita, 1998). How large is the loss, in mean-variance terms, attributable to these restrictions relative to a fully efficient portfolio? The answer to this question is reported in Figures 4A and 4B which depict mean-variance efficient frontiers for holding periods of 40 quarters and one quarter calculated under the assumption that short selling of stocks is not possible but negative positions in bonds and *t*-bills are.

Renters experience almost no losses relative to the unrestricted portfolio; efficient

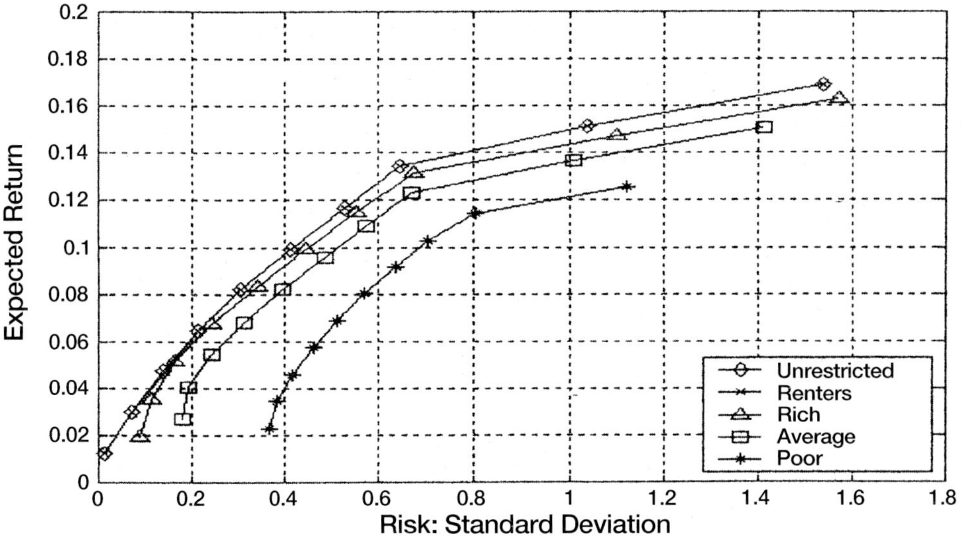

Figure 4A. Optimal portfolios for different classes of homeowners: 40 quarters.

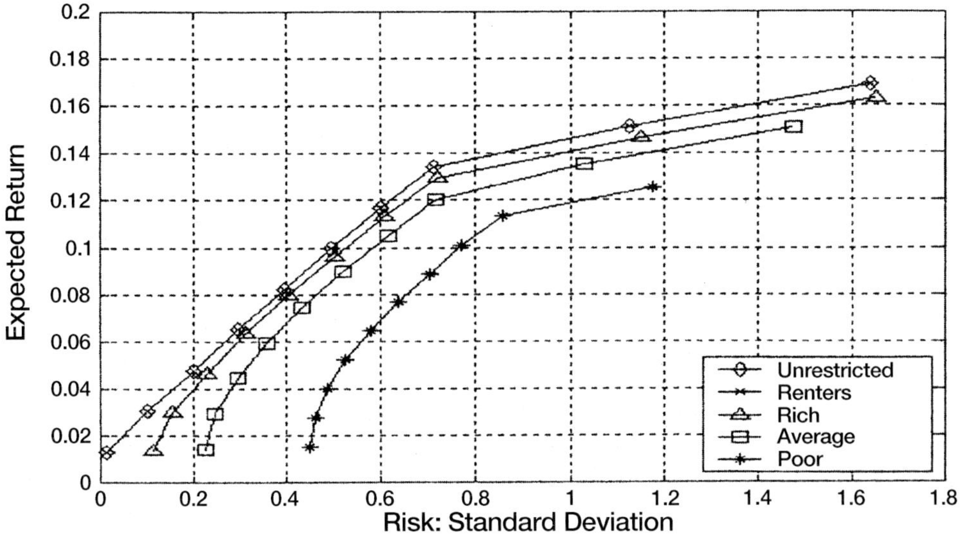

Figure 4B. Optimal portfolios for different classes of homeowners: 1 quarter.

frontiers of both classes are almost identical for all different horizons. For the three homeowner categories, return losses get larger with increasing portfolio shares in housing. This is evident from the differences in minimum variance attainable. At the 40-quarter horizon the minimum standard deviation is less than 1.1 percent for the renter portfolio compared to 8.8, 17.8 and 36.7 percent for the three homeowner portfolios. At the one-quarter horizon, the corresponding minimum variances are even farther apart: 1.4, 11.2, 22.5, and 45.1 percent respectively. A part of these differences is compensated for by higher expected returns. Comparing at the same standard deviation (47 percent) at one-quarter horizon, the loss in expected return relative to the unrestricted portfolio is modest, less than 0.3 percent for a rich owner, but very large (6.3 percent) for a poor owner.

Table 7 represents the corresponding portfolio compositions for renters and poor homeowners. The renter invests more than 100 percent in *t*-bills, financed by borrowing in bonds, at the minimum-variance end of the frontier. However, with increasing risk tolerance, the renter reverses positions between *t*-bills and bonds; she borrows in *t*-bills and invests in bonds and stocks. The share of stocks is larger in riskier portfolios while the share of bonds is larger in less-risky portfolios. Only far out on the frontier do we see any investment in real estate stocks. These general patterns hold at all horizons. For the poor homeowner, in contrast, the minimum variance portfolio is a corner solution with maximum short-term borrowing financing the house and an investment in bonds. As in case of the renter, with increasing risk the poor homeowner gradually raises the share of stocks by borrowing in bonds.

5.3. Hedging housing risk

Now consider the opportunities for hedging. Among currently available instruments, the most obvious hedging opportunity would be short sales of securitized real estate: shorting real-estate stocks. In this section, we first explore the gains that the real estate stocks afford. We then consider the extra benefits from allowing positions in the housing index. We illustrate the hedging gains for the four household types in Figures 5A–D for a 40-quarter horizon. Each panel graphs three efficient frontiers, one allowing neither hedging opportunity, one allowing short sales in real estate and other stocks and one allowing both short sales in stocks and positions in the housing index. The corresponding portfolios for the poor homeowner are given in Table 8.

Figure 5 shows the gains that real estate stocks and the housing index can respectively bring to homeowners. Starting from portfolios that allow neither short-selling of real-estate stocks nor trading in the housing index, we see that the two frontiers diverge for less-risky portfolios, but converge for riskier portfolios. Comparing the two efficient frontiers with short positions allowed for real-estate stocks, but with and without access to the housing index, we note that the frontiers start very close at the minimum variance portfolios, but diverge substantially for riskier portfolios. The housing index brings extra benefits to homeowners even after real estate stocks are used as a hedge. Importantly, while real estate stocks tend to benefit more risk averse homeowners, the housing index can bring substantial gains to less risk averse homeowners in terms of reducing risk for their riskier portfolios.

The portfolio compositions in Table 8 shows that when an index is available, real-estate stocks, index and *t*-bills are used to finance long positions in general stocks and bonds, except for high-risk portfolios. At high risks, even bonds are held in short positions,

Table 7. Optimal portfolios. No short selling. No index.

Standard Deviation	Expected Returns	R.E. Stocks	Gen. Stocks	*t*-bill	Bonds	Houses
(A) Renters (housing = 0)						
40-quarter horizon						
0.0106	0.0124	0.0000	0.0251	1.1825	− 0.2076	0.0000
0.0714	0.0298	0.0000	0.3166	− 0.9726	1.6560	0.0000
0.1417	0.0472	0.0000	0.6081	− 3.1277	3.5196	0.0000
0.2126	0.0646	0.0000	0.9916	− 4.9916	5.0000	0.0000
0.3044	0.0820	0.0000	1.9607	− 5.0000	4.0393	0.0000
0.4123	0.0993	0.0000	2.9326	− 5.0000	3.0674	0.0000
0.5265	0.1167	0.0000	3.9044	− 5.0000	2.0956	0.0000
0.6436	0.1341	0.0000	4.8762	− 5.0000	1.1238	0.0000
1.0407	0.1515	2.3299	5.0000	− 5.0000	− 1.3299	0.0000
1.5396	0.1689	5.0000	5.0000	− 5.0000	− 4.0000	0.0000
One-quarter horizon						
0.0137	0.0130	0.0084	0.0166	1.0453	− 0.0703	0.0000
0.0991	0.0304	0.0000	0.6013	− 0.1775	0.5762	0.0000
0.1975	0.0477	0.0000	1.1793	− 1.4117	1.2324	0.0000
0.2963	0.0650	0.0000	1.7573	− 2.6459	1.8886	0.0000
0.3951	0.0823	0.0000	2.3353	− 3.8802	2.5449	0.0000
0.4940	0.0996	0.0000	2.9494	− 5.0000	3.0506	0.0000
0.5989	0.1170	0.0000	3.9170	− 5.0000	2.0830	0.0000
0.7107	0.1343	0.0000	4.8846	− 5.0000	1.1154	0.0000
1.1249	0.1516	2.3415	5.0000	− 5.0000	− 1.3415	0.0000
1.6360	0.1689	5.0000	5.0000	− 5.0000	− 4.0000	0.0000
(B) Poor homeowners (housing = 4)						
40-quarter horizon						
0.3673	0.0231	0.0000	0.0000	− 5.0000	2.0000	4.0000
0.3842	0.0345	0.0000	0.6364	− 5.0000	1.3636	4.0000
0.4161	0.0459	0.0000	1.2729	− 5.0000	0.7271	4.0000
0.4598	0.0573	0.0000	1.9093	− 5.0000	0.0907	4.0000
0.5124	0.0687	0.0000	2.5457	− 5.0000	− 0.5457	4.0000
0.5714	0.0801	0.0000	3.1822	− 5.0000	− 1.1822	4.0000
0.6350	0.0915	0.0000	3.8186	− 5.0000	− 1.8186	4.0000
0.7020	0.1029	0.0000	4.4550	− 5.0000	− 2.4550	4.0000
0.8044	0.1143	0.2514	5.0000	− 5.0000	− 3.2514	4.0000
1.1216	0.1257	2.0000	5.0000	− 5.0000	− 5.0000	4.0000
One-quarter horizon						
0.4507	0.0152	0.0000	0.0000	− 3.5978	0.5978	4.0000
0.4610	0.0275	0.0000	0.2430	− 5.0000	1.7570	4.0000
0.4862	0.0398	0.0000	0.9286	− 5.0000	1.0714	4.0000
0.5254	0.0520	0.0000	1.6142	− 5.0000	0.3858	4.0000
0.5760	0.0643	0.0000	2.2998	− 5.0000	− 0.2998	4.0000
0.6352	0.0766	0.0000	2.9855	− 5.0000	− 0.9855	4.0000
0.7007	0.0889	0.0000	3.6711	− 5.0000	− 1.6711	4.0000
0.7711	0.1011	0.0000	4.3567	− 5.0000	− 2.3567	4.0000
0.8581	0.1134	0.1162	5.0000	− 5.0000	− 3.1162	4.0000
1.1777	0.1257	2.0000	5.0000	− 5.0000	− 5.0000	4.0000

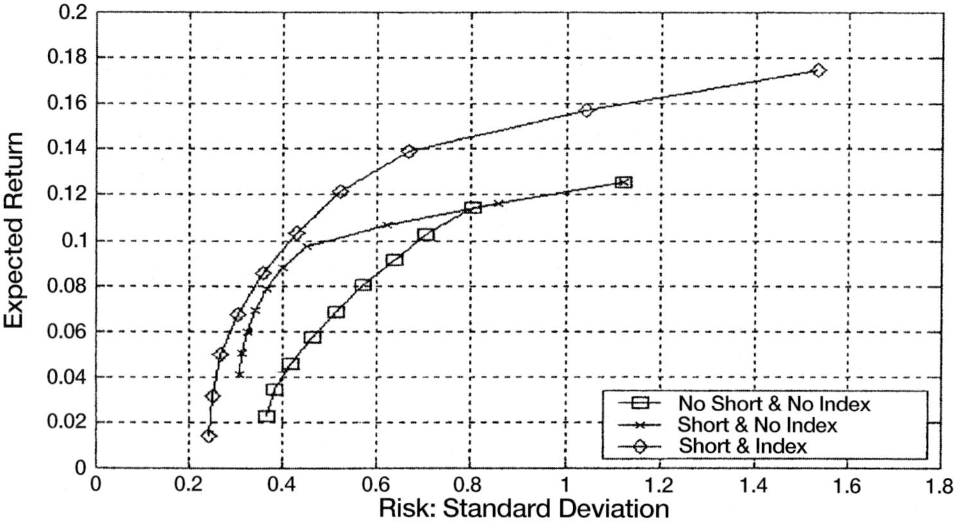

Figure 5A. Efficient frontiers for poor homeowner with 40-quarter horizon.

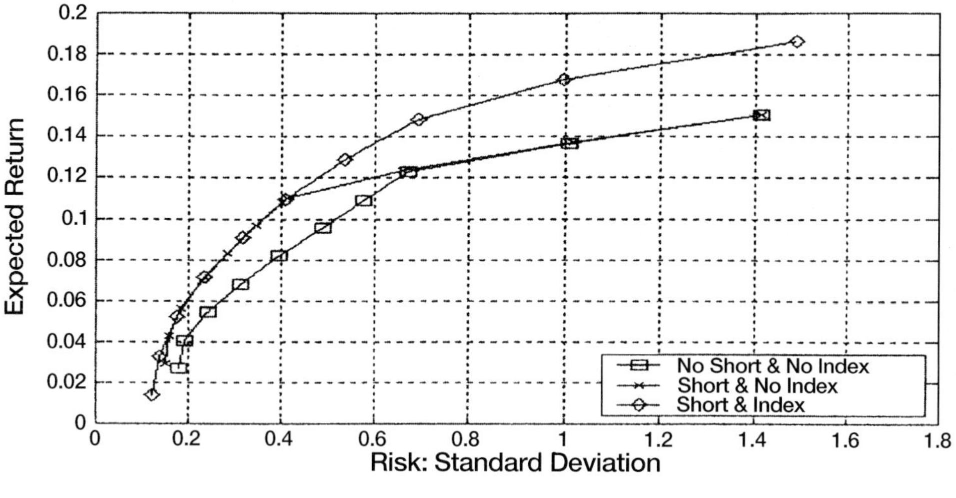

Figure 5B. Efficient frontiers for average homeowner with 40-quarter horizon.

leaving only general stocks in long positions. The role of real-estate stocks as a hedge is explained by the high variance and low expected return of real-estate stocks (relative to other stocks) and by the relatively strong positive correlation between real-estate stocks and houses. The correlation coefficient is around 0.4 at longer horizons. When housing investment is suboptimally large from a portfolio perspective, as it is in these homeowner portfolios, investment shares in real estate stocks become generally smaller (and short positions are larger). The figures illustrate the resulting gains from short positions in real-

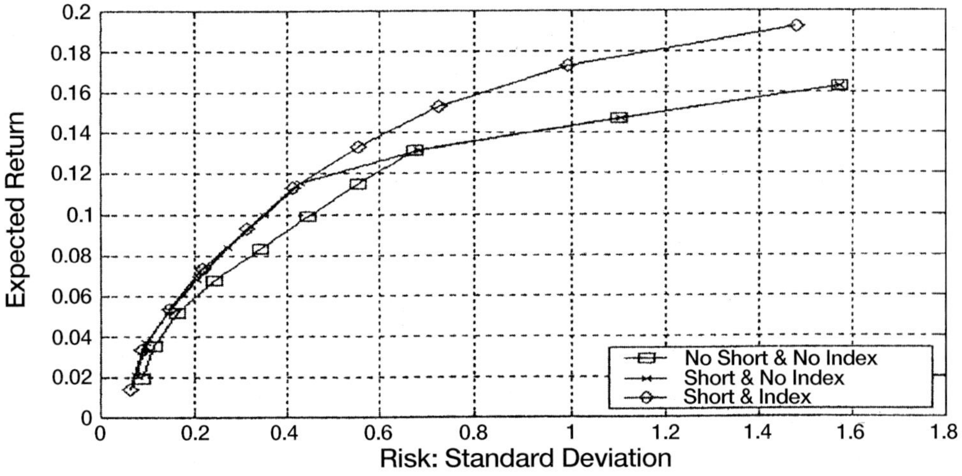

Figure 5C. Efficient frontiers for rich homeowner with 40-quarter horizon.

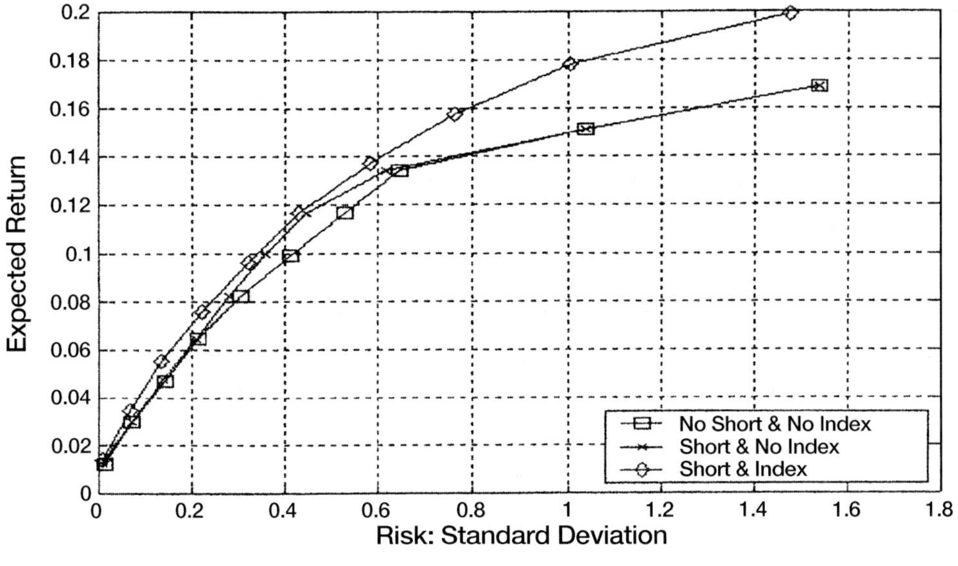

Figure 5D. Efficient frontiers for renter with 40-quarter horizon.

estate stocks in mean-variance terms. For poor homeowners, the gains are quite large indeed. At the 40-quarter horizon, the standard deviation of the minimum variance portfolio is reduced from 36.7 to 30.6 percent, while the expected return is increased from 2.3 to 4.1 percent. At the one-quarter horizon, gains are much smaller. The variance of the minimum variance portfolio for a poor homeowner is reduced from 45.1 without short selling of stocks to 44.3 percent with short selling while the increase in expected return is merely 0.2 percent, from 1.5 to 1.7.

Table 8. Optimal portfolios for poor homeowners (Housing = 4) with short selling and the housing index.

Standard Deviation	Expected Returns	R.E. Stocks	Gen. Stocks	*t*-bill	Bonds	Index	Houses
(A) 40-quarter horizon							
Short selling no index							
0.3069	0.0412	−1.5267	1.5637	−5.0000	1.9630	0.0000	4.0000
0.3111	0.0506	−1.7774	2.1794	−5.0000	1.5980	0.0000	4.0000
0.3231	0.0600	−2.0281	2.7951	−5.0000	1.2330	0.0000	4.0000
0.3423	0.0693	−2.2787	3.4107	−5.0000	0.8680	0.0000	4.0000
0.3674	0.0787	−2.5294	4.0264	−5.0000	0.5030	0.0000	4.0000
0.3973	0.0881	−2.7801	4.6421	−5.0000	0.1381	0.0000	4.0000
0.4475	0.0975	−2.3227	5.0000	−5.0000	−0.6773	0.0000	4.0000
0.6196	0.1069	−0.8818	5.0000	−5.0000	−2.1182	0.0000	4.0000
0.8582	0.1163	0.5591	5.0000	−5.0000	−3.5591	0.0000	4.0000
1.1216	0.1257	2.0000	5.0000	−5.0000	−5.0000	0.0000	4.0000
Short selling and index							
0.2408	0.0138	−0.0812	0.1126	0.9602	−0.1376	−3.8540	4.0000
0.2478	0.0317	−0.4091	0.6525	−1.5824	1.5183	−3.1793	4.0000
0.2677	0.0496	−0.7370	1.1924	−4.1251	3.1742	−2.5046	4.0000
0.3022	0.0675	−1.1784	2.1642	−5.0000	3.2544	−2.2402	4.0000
0.3588	0.0854	−1.6793	3.3624	−5.0000	2.5080	−2.1912	4.0000
0.4298	0.1033	−2.1802	4.5607	−5.0000	1.7616	−2.1421	4.0000
0.5184	0.1212	−1.8654	5.0000	−5.0000	2.3541	−3.4887	4.0000
0.6636	0.1391	−0.4937	5.0000	−5.0000	2.4937	−5.0000	4.0000
1.0447	0.1570	2.2532	5.0000	−5.0000	−0.2532	−5.0000	4.0000
1.5350	0.1749	5.0000	5.0000	−5.0000	−3.0000	−5.0000	4.0000
(B) One quarter horizon							
Short selling no index							
0.4425	0.0167	−0.5631	0.3201	−3.4883	0.7313	0.0000	4.0000
0.4459	0.0288	−0.8463	0.9496	−3.9643	0.8610	0.0000	4.0000
0.4561	0.0409	−1.1295	1.5791	−4.4403	0.9907	0.0000	4.0000
0.4725	0.0530	−1.4127	2.2085	−4.9163	1.1204	0.0000	4.0000
0.4951	0.0651	−1.7700	2.9888	−5.0000	0.7812	0.0000	4.0000
0.5239	0.0772	−2.1431	3.8013	−5.0000	0.3418	0.0000	4.0000
0.5579	0.0893	−2.5162	4.6137	−5.0000	−0.0975	0.0000	4.0000
0.6287	0.1014	−1.7183	5.0000	−5.0000	−1.2817	0.0000	4.0000
0.8619	0.1136	0.1408	5.0000	−5.0000	−3.1408	0.0000	4.0000
1.1777	0.1257	2.0000	5.0000	−5.0000	−5.0000	0.0000	4.0000
Short selling and index							
0.4071	0.0131	−0.0038	0.0231	0.9483	−0.0532	−3.9145	4.0000
0.4152	0.0311	−0.4448	0.9620	0.0543	0.1719	−3.7434	4.0000
0.4387	0.0491	−0.8858	1.9008	−0.8398	0.3970	−3.5722	4.0000
0.4752	0.0670	−1.3267	2.8397	−1.7339	0.6221	−3.4011	4.0000
0.5220	0.0850	−1.7677	3.7785	−2.6280	0.8472	−3.2300	4.0000
0.5767	0.1030	−2.2087	4.7174	−3.5221	1.0722	−3.0589	4.0000
0.6440	0.1209	−2.0929	5.0000	−5.0000	2.7937	−3.7008	4.0000
0.7874	0.1389	−0.5166	5.0000	−5.0000	2.5166	−5.0000	4.0000
1.1803	0.1569	2.2417	5.0000	−5.0000	−0.2417	−5.0000	4.0000
1.6788	0.1749	5.0000	5.0000	−5.0000	−3.0000	−5.0000	4.0000

The usefulness of real-estate stocks as a hedge is limited by the relatively low correlation with housing returns. The housing-price index, in contrast, has a stronger correlation with returns from a single house, ranging from 0.42 at the shortest horizon to 0.77 at longer horizons. Allowing positions in the index has a dramatic impact on the composition of the minimum variance portfolios for the poor homeowners. When a position in the housing index is allowed, the results in Table 8 indicate that there is a large negative position (390 percent) in that index, a positive position in *t*-bills and positions close to zero in other instruments. To minimize risk, housing should be financed, almost exclusively, by going short in the housing index. Compared to the case when a housing index is not available, there is some reduction in the minimum variance portfolio, at the one-quarter horizon, from 44.3 percent to 40.7 percent (and at the 40-quarter horizon from 30.7 to 24.1 percent). This safety comes at the expense of a sharp drop in expected returns, however. To account for this, we may compare the expected returns at the minimum variances achievable without the housing index with those with the housing index available. The return increases from 4.1 to 6.9 percent, at the 40-quarter horizon, and from 1.7 percent to 5.1 percent, at the one-quarter horizon.

These results indicate clearly that there is substantial scope for welfare improvement by allowing trade in more direct hedging instruments such as home-price index futures. We have also seen that the index appears in positive amounts in the efficient portfolios for renters. Renters as well as institutional investors would seem to be the natural market counterparts of owners. With both a supply side and a demand side, the basic requirements for a market are fulfilled.

6. Conclusion

We have used an unusually rich source of data on housing prices in Stockholm to analyze the investment implications of housing choices. Our empirical analysis derives market-wide price and return series for housing investment during a 13-year period, and it also provides estimates of the individual specific, idiosyncratic, variation in housing returns. Because index changes and the idiosyncratic component follow autocorrelated processes, the analysis of portfolio choice is dependent upon the holding period specified.

We analyze the composition of household investment portfolios containing housing, common stocks, stocks in real-estate holding companies, bonds, and *t*-bills. For short holding periods, the efficient portfolio contains essentially no housing. For longer periods, low-risk portfolios contain 15–50 percent housing. These results suggest that there are large potential gains from policies or institutions that would permit households to hedge their lumpy investments in housing. We estimate the potential value of hedges in reducing risk for the same investment returns. The value is surprisingly large, especially for poorer homeowners.

This is the first systematic evidence on the topic. Given the ways in which data on house sales are collected centrally in Sweden, it would seem that one could develop a transparent and reliable price index that should be useful for trading in these derivatives. This market would permit households to hedge their most important investment and to diversify their current risks in owner-occupied housing. Currently, these risks are quite large, especially for young households. Our analysis suggests that financial instruments could reduce these risks quite considerably.

Appendix A

Table A.1. Monthly estimates of regional price changes for Sweden, 1981–1993 January, 1981 = 1.000 (entries are the logarithms of estimated price increase during each month) *t*-ratios in parentheses.

	Region							
Year/ Month	Stockholm	East Central	South Central	South	West	North Central	North	Far North
1981:	0.047	− 0.023	0.026	− 0.043	0.004	− 0.009	− 0.060	− 0.064
Feb	(2.34)	(1.29)	(0.81)	(1.80)	(0.20)	(0.34)	(1.10)	(1.25)
	− 0.058	0.032	− 0.027	0.033	− 0.044	0.024	− 0.038	0.047
	(2.54)	(1.61)	(0.77)	(1.28)	(2.02)	(0.82)	(0.61)	(0.77)
	0.038	− 0.002	− 0.010	− 0.020	0.020	− 0.031	0.134	− 0.034
	(1.66)	(0.10)	(0.31)	(0.80)	(0.91)	(1.13)	(2.31)	(0.52)
	− 0.005	− 0.005	0.006	− 0.020	0.015	0.012	− 0.039	0.019
	(0.22)	(0.26)	(0.18)	(0.79)	(0.69)	(0.44)	(0.72)	(0.31)
	− 0.029	− 0.017	0.009	0.007	− 0.010	0.036	0.015	− 0.004
	(1.45)	(1.00)	(0.32)	(0.32)	(0.52)	(1.47)	(0.33)	(0.09)
	0.009	− 0.021	0.043	− 0.021	− 0.007	− 0.043	0.017	0.007
	(0.42)	(1.23)	(1.59)	(0.99)	(0.36)	(1.82)	(0.40)	(0.15)
	0.005	0.020	− 0.048	0.034	− 0.012	− 0.051	− 0.002	− 0.031
	(0.21)	(1.00)	(1.63)	(1.45)	(0.57)	(1.99)	(0.04)	(0.61)
	− 0.017	− 0.014	− 0.053	− 0.037	− 0.008	0.001	− 0.047	− 0.017
	(0.80)	(0.77)	(1.90)	(1.61)	(0.40)	(0.04)	(1.01)	(0.36)
	− 0.013	0.042	0.075	0.007	0.002	0.052	0.006	0.028
	(0.67)	(2.54)	(2.69)	(0.31)	(0.10)	(2.19)	(0.13)	(0.59)
	0.006	− 0.030	− 0.068	− 0.041	0.002	− 0.024	− 0.053	− 0.027
	(0.31)	(1.83)	(2.44)	(1.83)	(0.10)	(0.99)	(1.18)	(0.55)
	− 0.031	− 0.042	− 0.090	0.076	− 0.024	− 0.006	0.103	− 0.004
	(1.30)	(2.14)	(2.80)	(2.81)	(1.08)	(0.20)	(2.04)	(0.07)
1982:	0.057	0.048	0.193	− 0.036	0.066	0.045	0.007	0.063
Jan	(2.12)	(2.13)	(5.35)	(1.17)	(2.69)	(1.33)	(0.12)	(0.98)
	− 0.026	− 0.016	− 0.067	− 0.009	− 0.042	0.002	0.012	− 0.025
	(0.99)	(0.73)	(1.95)	(0.31)	(1.77)	(0.06)	(0.21)	(0.38)
	0.029	0.013	0.001	− 0.007	0.047	− 0.025	− 0.052	− 0.080
	(1.25)	(0.66)	(0.03)	(0.27)	(2.19)	(0.89)	(1.00)	(1.44)
	− 0.001	0.004	− 0.022	0.046	− 0.011	− 0.022	0.038	0.087
	(0.05)	(0.23)	(0.76)	(2.00)	(0.57)	(0.89)	(0.77)	(1.70)
	0.029	0.011	0.072	0.005	− 0.001	0.042	− 0.006	0.053
	(1.56)	(0.67)	(2.65)	(0.23)	(0.06)	(1.79)	(0.14)	(1.10)
	− 0.020	0.023	− 0.042	0.001	0.008	0.029	− 0.029	− 0.045
	(1.15)	(1.54)	(1.79)	(0.05)	(0.47)	(1.36)	(0.76)	(1.05)
	0.005	− 0.017	0.061	0.008	− 0.001	− 0.003	0.023	0.015
	(0.27)	(1.13)	(2.73)	(0.42)	(0.06)	(0.14)	(0.62)	(0.37)

Table A.1. (continued)

	Region							
Year/ Month	Stockholm	East Central	South Central	South	West	North Central	North	Far North
	0.010	– 0.011	– 0.016	– 0.003	0.003	0.017	0.020	0.025
	(0.47)	(0.63)	(0.59)	(0.14)	(0.16)	(0.74)	(0.45)	(0.58)
	– 0.018	– 0.021	– 0.024	– 0.023	– 0.001	– 0.039	– 0.025	– 0.026
	(0.90)	(1.23)	(0.87)	(1.03)	(0.05)	(1.75)	(0.59)	(0.60)
	0.012	0.035	– 0.014	0.005	0.005	0.015	0.024	– 0.072
	(0.61)	(2.00)	(0.50)	(0.22)	(0.26)	(0.65)	(0.57)	(1.51)
	– 0.039	– 0.016	0.020	– 0.045	– 0.036	– 0.025	– 0.036	0.077
	(2.00)	(0.94)	(0.74)	(1.87)	(1.90)	(1.08)	(0.83)	(1.61)
	0.005	– 0.020	– 0.056	0.007	0.019	– 0.005	0.056	– 0.030
	(0.22)	(1.07)	(1.89)	(0.25)	(0.89)	(0.19)	(1.09)	(0.59)
1983:	0.029	0.042	0.034	0.068	– 0.025	– 0.008	– 0.101	0.054
Jan	(1.16)	(2.06)	(1.00)	(2.27)	(1.07)	(0.26)	(1.64)	(0.90)
	– 0.012	– 0.024	– 0.021	– 0.056	0.018	0.028	0.071	– 0.013
	(0.51)	(1.21)	(0.65)	(2.03)	(0.81)	(0.91)	(1.18)	(0.20)
	0.019	0.001	0.002	0.054	– 0.013	0.004	– 0.063	– 0.045
	(0.90)	(0.05)	(0.06)	(2.05)	(0.61)	(0.13)	(1.10)	(0.69)
	– 0.052	0.015	– 0.008	– 0.026	0.019	– 0.023	0.065	0.022
	(2.64)	(0.85)	(0.26)	(1.04)	(0.96)	(0.85)	(1.19)	(0.37)
	0.054	– 0.011	0.018	0.006	0.007	0.012	0.029	0.024
	(3.04)	(0.69)	(0.70)	(0.27)	(0.39)	(0.51)	(0.59)	(0.49)
	– 0.006	0.016	0.024	0.017	0.002	0.034	0.026	0.020
	(0.38)	(1.08)	(0.99)	(0.86)	(0.12)	(1.59)	(0.63)	(0.51)
	– 0.010	0.020	– 0.032	– 0.048	– 0.011	– 0.020	– 0.059	– 0.017
	(0.58)	(1.31)	(1.29)	(2.43)	(0.64)	(0.90)	(1.55)	(0.43)
	– 0.001	– 0.015	0.022	0.024	– 0.010	– 0.004	0.011	– 0.049
	(0.05)	(0.87)	(0.81)	(1.13)	(0.51)	(0.16)	(0.25)	(1.09)
	0.020	– 0.021	– 0.008	– 0.011	0.037	0.003	0.049	0.074
	(1.12)	(1.28)	(0.30)	(0.52)	(1.93)	(0.13)	(1.19)	(1.71)
	– 0.031	0.012	0.026	0.026	– 0.005	– 0.039	– 0.033	– 0.058
	(1.82)	(0.75)	(1.00)	(1.24)	(0.26)	(1.79)	(0.78)	(1.29)
	0.017	– 0.002	– 0.024	– 0.027	– 0.007	0.025	– 0.059	0.009
	(1.08)	(0.13)	(0.97)	(1.34)	(0.38)	(1.16)	(1.37)	(0.19)
	– 0.001	– 0.009	– 0.010	0.012	– 0.016	– 0.011	0.001	0.047
	(0.05)	(0.51)	(0.33)	(0.49)	(0.79)	(0.44)	(0.02)	(0.90)
1984:	– 0.007	0.013	– 0.004	0.011	0.039	0.012	0.090	– 0.050
Jan	(0.32)	(0.67)	(0.12)	(0.40)	(1.74)	(0.41)	(1.62)	(0.87)
	0.019	– 0.008	0.016	0.020	– 0.028	0.008	– 0.050	0.012
	(0.90)	(0.41)	(0.49)	(0.79)	(1.31)	(0.26)	(0.89)	(0.21)
	– 0.004	0.018	0.008	– 0.026	0.022	– 0.005	0.051	0.094
	(0.20)	(0.96)	(0.25)	(1.08)	(1.09)	(0.18)	(0.91)	(1.63)
	– 0.007	– 0.008	0.026	0.001	0.027	0.015	– 0.039	– 0.088
	(0.36)	(0.45)	(0.90)	(0.05)	(1.42)	(0.60)	(0.77)	(1.67)
	0.021	0.019	– 0.031	0.033	– 0.009	– 0.009	– 0.014	0.026
	(1.19)	(1.18)	(1.18)	(1.62)	(0.52)	(0.39)	(0.33)	(0.54)

Table A.1. (continued)

	Region							
Year/ Month	Stockholm	East Central	South Central	South	West	North Central	North	Far North
	– 0.005	0.012	0.034	0.007	0.005	0.016	0.069	0.070
	(0.32)	(0.84)	(1.41)	(0.38)	(0.31)	(0.77)	(1.87)	(1.73)
	– 0.004	– 0.013	0.043	– 0.039	0.002	0.024	– 0.035	– 0.045
	(0.25)	(0.89)	(1.81)	(2.09)	(0.12)	(1.18)	(0.95)	(1.20)
	0.016	0.011	– 0.038	0.029	– 0.002	0.014	0.023	– 0.000
	(0.87)	(0.66)	(1.50)	(1.42)	(0.11)	(0.64)	(0.54)	(0.00)
	0.001	– 0.006	– 0.033	– 0.010	– 0.012	– 0.056	– 0.054	– 0.018
	(0.06)	(0.36)	(1.27)	(0.47)	(0.68)	(2.50)	(1.30)	(0.42)
	0.003	0.004	0.016	– 0.002	0.003	0.023	– 0.008	– 0.029
	(0.17)	(0.25)	(0.61)	(0.09)	(0.17)	(1.03)	(0.20)	(0.68)
	– 0.002	0.017	– 0.015	0.029	0.008	– 0.007	0.022	0.036
	(0.12)	(1.14)	(0.58)	(1.42)	(0.47)	(0.32)	(0.54)	(0.82)
	0.053	– 0.008	0.006	– 0.020	0.037	0.057	– 0.042	0.033
	(2.57)	(0.46)	(0.20)	(0.85)	(1.83)	(2.30)	(0.91)	(0.67)
1985:	– 0.042	– 0.001	0.020	0.021	– 0.027	– 0.032	0.069	– 0.070
Jan	(1.90)	(0.05)	(0.64)	(0.82)	(1.25)	(1.12)	(1.26)	(1.24)
	0.021	– 0.007	– 0.030	0.008	0.020	– 0.020	– 0.014	– 0.005
	(1.02)	(0.39)	(0.98)	(0.33)	(1.02)	(0.72)	(0.26)	(0.09)
	– 0.033	0.037	0.050	– 0.015	0.003	0.027	– 0.007	– 0.039
	(1.73)	(2.08)	(1.66)	(0.62)	(0.16)	(1.03)	(0.14)	(0.71)
	0.015	– 0.020	– 0.009	0.022	– 0.004	– 0.027	– 0.028	0.061
	(0.85)	(1.20)	(0.34)	(0.97)	(0.23)	(1.14)	(0.57)	(1.07)
	0.015	0.006	0.009	– 0.004	0.001	0.030	0.060	– 0.009
	(0.92)	(0.41)	(0.37)	(0.20)	(0.06)	(1.40)	(1.39)	(0.17)
	0.018	0.018	0.021	0.006	0.018	0.012	– 0.006	0.039
	(1.13)	(1.26)	(0.87)	(0.31)	(1.11)	(0.57)	(0.16)	(0.90)
	– 0.022	0.005	– 0.013	– 0.012	0.018	– 0.000	– 0.027	0.024
	(1.33)	(0.33)	(0.53)	(0.61)	(1.11)	(0.00)	(0.68)	(0.57)
	0.021	– 0.031	– 0.036	– 0.006	– 0.030	– 0.006	– 0.033	– 0.067
	(1.16)	(1.80)	(1.36)	(0.27)	(1.65)	(0.25)	(0.76)	(1.47)
	– 0.023	– 0.011	0.020	– 0.001	0.003	– 0.027	0.074	0.041
	(1.32)	(0.66)	(0.80)	(0.05)	(0.17)	(1.17)	(1.73)	(0.97)
	0.020	0.011	– 0.004	0.014	– 0.006	– 0.001	– 0.027	0.015
	(1.25)	(0.69)	(0.16)	(0.67)	(0.36)	(0.05)	(0.67)	(0.34)
	– 0.003	0.004	– 0.016	– 0.005	0.016	– 0.006	– 0.030	0.036
	(0.19)	(0.26)	(0.62)	(0.24)	(0.97)	(0.28)	(0.74)	(0.81)
	– 0.005	– 0.006	0.014	– 0.015	– 0.010	0.009	– 0.003	– 0.084
	(0.24)	(0.34)	(0.49)	(0.61)	(0.51)	(0.37)	(0.06)	(1.79)
1986:	– 0.008	0.029	0.010	– 0.006	0.007	0.026	0.024	0.025
Jan	(0.35)	(1.51)	(0.33)	(0.22)	(0.33)	(0.95)	(0.43)	(0.48)
	0.042	– 0.033	– 0.002	0.031	0.010	– 0.004	0.010	0.026
	(2.00)	(1.79)	(0.07)	(1.24)	(0.50)	(0.15)	(0.19)	(0.48)
	– 0.001	0.007	– 0.029	– 0.011	0.014	– 0.015	– 0.021	– 0.060
	(0.05)	(0.37)	(1.03)	(0.46)	(0.71)	(0.58)	(0.41)	(1.18)

Table A.1. (*continued*)

	Region							
Year/ Month	Stockholm	East Central	South Central	South	West	North Central	North	Far North
	– 0.012	0.008	0.034	0.030	– 0.014	0.037	0.025	0.042
	(0.62)	(0.47)	(1.38)	(1.40)	(0.81)	(1.61)	(0.55)	(0.92)
	0.017	0.029	0.022	– 0.002	0.035	0.004	0.008	0.049
	(1.02)	(2.11)	(0.96)	(0.11)	(2.28)	(0.20)	(0.22)	(1.20)
	0.024	0.002	0.001	– 0.003	– 0.003	0.009	0.059	– 0.043
	(1.65)	(0.16)	(0.05)	(0.18)	(0.20)	(0.48)	(1.92)	(1.24)
	0.002	0.009	0.008	0.022	0.008	0.009	– 0.033	0.049
	(0.13)	(0.69)	(0.38)	(1.32)	(0.53)	(0.50)	(1.02)	(1.42)
	0.006	0.001	– 0.031	– 0.020	– 0.010	– 0.008	– 0.018	0.020
	(0.34)	(0.07)	(1.32)	(1.05)	(0.60)	(0.41)	(0.50)	(0.52)
	0.017	– 0.017	0.012	0.000	0.007	0.009	0.000	– 0.048
	(0.98)	(1.19)	(0.51)	(0.00)	(0.43)	(0.47)	(0.00)	(1.24)
	0.004	0.028	0.028	0.027	0.033	– 0.011	– 0.005	0.052
	(0.23)	(1.91)	(1.25)	(1.41)	(2.03)	(0.57)	(0.13)	(1.35)
	0.018	– 0.002	0.021	– 0.015	0.001	0.020	0.092	– 0.007
	(1.03)	(0.14)	(0.93)	(0.78)	(0.06)	(1.02)	(2.40)	(0.17)
	0.011	0.037	– 0.027	0.009	0.009	– 0.007	– 0.049	– 0.033
	(0.54)	(2.18)	(1.02)	(0.40)	(0.48)	(0.31)	(1.01)	(0.71)
1987:	0.075	0.012	0.019	0.067	0.024	– 0.006	0.043	0.099
Jan	(3.23)	(0.63)	(0.64)	(2.63)	(1.11)	(0.23)	(0.76)	(1.81)
	– 0.053	– 0.019	0.012	– 0.039	– 0.015	0.021	0.016	– 0.100
	(2.35)	(1.04)	(0.40)	(1.58)	(0.70)	(0.81)	(0.30)	(1.74)
	0.025	0.033	0.000	– 0.010	0.005	0.002	– 0.011	0.055
	(1.15)	(1.93)	(0.00)	(0.43)	(0.25)	(0.08)	(0.22)	(1.03)
	0.034	– 0.027	– 0.006	0.034	0.015	– 0.015	– 0.040	– 0.040
	(1.65)	(1.70)	(0.24)	(1.62)	(0.84)	(0.66)	(0.89)	(0.88)
	– 0.013	0.020	0.027	0.004	0.030	0.057	0.052	0.094
	(0.67)	(1.35)	(1.20)	(0.21)	(1.84)	(2.82)	(1.33)	(2.31)
	0.048	0.024	– 0.004	0.012	– 0.009	– 0.015	– 0.010	– 0.045
	(2.70)	(1.81)	(0.19)	(0.70)	(0.59)	(0.84)	(0.31)	(1.34)
	0.028	– 0.002	0.044	0.011	0.025	0.025	0.023	– 0.032
	(1.54)	(0.15)	(2.14)	(0.63)	(1.59)	(1.38)	(0.69)	(0.92)
	– 0.009	0.023	– 0.010	– 0.011	0.017	0.008	– 0.005	0.041
	(0.44)	(1.52)	(0.44)	(0.56)	(0.98)	(0.41)	(0.13)	(1.06)
	0.015	– 0.018	– 0.021	0.024	– 0.025	– 0.014	0.024	– 0.020
	(0.76)	(1.22)	(0.92)	(1.22)	(1.47)	(0.73)	(0.63)	(0.54)
	0.019	0.027	0.041	– 0.003	0.027	0.006	– 0.024	0.020
	(1.01)	(1.82)	(1.84)	(0.16)	(1.61)	(0.31)	(0.65)	(0.52)
	0.038	– 0.000	– 0.015	0.014	0.010	– 0.009	0.003	0.072
	(2.02)	(0.00)	(0.68)	(0.76)	(0.60)	(0.48)	(0.08)	(1.81)
	0.027	0.041	0.005	0.024	– 0.026	0.043	0.003	– 0.087
	(1.24)	(2.49)	(0.19)	(1.12)	(1.32)	(1.86)	(0.07)	(1.93)
1988:	0.046	0.029	0.045	0.025	0.130	0.005	0.067	0.098
Jan	(1.79)	(1.51)	(1.54)	(1.03)	(5.68)	(0.19)	(1.34)	(1.88)

Table A.1. (continued)

Year/ Month	Region: Stockholm	East Central	South Central	South	West	North Central	North	Far North
	– 0.027	– 0.027	– 0.021	– 0.068	– 0.085	– 0.012	– 0.100	– 0.056
	(1.14)	(1.45)	(0.79)	(3.05)	(3.93)	(0.48)	(2.14)	(1.13)
	0.026	0.024	0.007	0.089	0.060	0.040	0.059	0.025
	(1.18)	(1.36)	(0.27)	(4.15)	(2.93)	(1.69)	(1.29)	(0.51)
	0.031	0.001	0.005	– 0.008	– 0.019	– 0.000	0.017	– 0.002
	(1.54)	(0.06)	(0.21)	(0.40)	(1.00)	(0.00)	(0.40)	(0.04)
	0.022	0.019	0.048	0.020	0.044	0.005	0.011	0.028
	(1.17)	(1.34)	(2.11)	(1.05)	(2.48)	(0.24)	(0.29)	(0.74)
	0.040	0.025	0.006	0.032	0.022	0.054	0.030	0.010
	(2.26)	(1.89)	(0.28)	(1.80)	(1.32)	(3.06)	(0.93)	(0.32)
	0.022	0.040	0.007	0.019	0.019	– 0.030	0.045	– 0.004
	(1.24)	(2.92)	(0.34)	(1.05)	(1.10)	(1.70)	(1.39)	(0.12)
	0.000	– 0.030	– 0.006	– 0.019	– 0.011	0.037	– 0.062	0.043
	(0.00)	(1.93)	(0.27)	(0.98)	(0.58)	(1.98)	(1.70)	(1.11)
	– 0.002	0.023	0.022	0.030	0.009	0.015	0.003	– 0.035
	(0.11)	(1.56)	(1.02)	(1.56)	(0.48)	(0.81)	(0.08)	(0.93)
	0.028	0.009	– 0.017	– 0.001	0.009	– 0.003	– 0.012	0.049
	(1.49)	(0.61)	(0.76)	(0.05)	(0.47)	(0.16)	(0.32)	(1.31)
	– 0.011	– 0.009	0.008	– 0.005	0.037	0.029	0.066	0.031
	(0.59)	(0.61)	(0.34)	(0.26)	(1.93)	(1.51)	(1.73)	(0.80)
	0.026	0.055	0.028	0.044	0.005	– 0.018	– 0.007	– 0.106
	(1.34)	(3.43)	(1.11)	(2.06)	(0.25)	(0.83)	(0.17)	(2.59)
1989:	0.026	0.033	0.025	0.048	0.027	0.052	– 0.003	0.075
Jan	(1.18)	(1.87)	(0.96)	(2.08)	(1.26)	(2.12)	(0.06)	(1.57)
	0.022	0.005	– 0.018	– 0.012	– 0.016	– 0.029	0.044	– 0.001
	(1.01)	(0.29)	(0.69)	(0.54)	(0.81)	(1.20)	(0.84)	(0.02)
	0.012	– 0.028	– 0.029	0.015	0.043	– 0.003	– 0.031	0.026
	(0.58)	(1.69)	(1.13)	(0.70)	(2.32)	(0.13)	(0.60)	(0.55)
	0.032	0.034	0.078	0.019	0.001	0.022	0.015	– 0.014
	(1.62)	(2.14)	(3.10)	(0.93)	(0.06)	(1.02)	(0.34)	(0.31)
	0.000	0.005	– 0.010	0.027	0.009	0.029	0.007	0.037
	(0.00)	(0.33)	(0.42)	(1.41)	(0.53)	(1.46)	(0.18)	(0.94)
	0.023	0.038	0.014	0.016	0.037	0.029	0.064	0.012
	(1.32)	(2.73)	(0.65)	(0.93)	(2.33)	(1.59)	(1.90)	(0.36)
	0.034	0.001	0.042	0.058	0.033	0.037	– 0.049	0.048
	(1.92)	(0.07)	(1.90)	(3.19)	(1.93)	(2.02)	(1.41)	(1.39)
	– 0.012	0.007	– 0.007	– 0.066	– 0.030	– 0.022	0.025	– 0.013
	(0.61)	(0.44)	(0.28)	(3.21)	(1.62)	(1.04)	(0.63)	(0.34)
	– 0.027	– 0.008	– 0.029	0.057	0.065	0.015	– 0.028	0.063
	(1.38)	(0.51)	(1.10)	(2.66)	(3.49)	(0.68)	(0.68)	(1.61)
	0.012	0.017	0.027	0.014	– 0.067	– 0.025	0.058	– 0.025
	(0.62)	(1.02)	(0.98)	(0.62)	(3.43)	(1.06)	(1.32)	(0.58)
	– 0.013	0.021	0.032	– 0.004	0.032	0.008	– 0.030	– 0.060
	(0.67)	(1.25)	(1.24)	(0.18)	(1.66)	(0.34)	(0.65)	(1.37)

Table A.1. (*continued*)

	Region							
Year/ Month	Stockholm	East Central	South Central	South	West	North Central	North	Far North
	−0.008	0.012	−0.025	−0.004	−0.021	0.024	0.002	−0.000
	(0.38)	(0.66)	(0.93)	(0.17)	(1.02)	(0.97)	(0.04)	(0.00)
1990:	0.094	0.072	0.127	0.036	0.137	0.076	0.120	0.132
Jan	(3.64)	(3.09)	(3.65)	(1.28)	(5.28)	(2.49)	(2.15)	(2.27)
	−0.021	−0.055	−0.060	0.009	−0.085	−0.044	−0.080	−0.043
	(0.89)	(2.60)	(1.89)	(0.37)	(3.68)	(1.51)	(1.53)	(0.77)
	−0.029	0.041	0.038	−0.016	−0.017	0.038	0.024	−0.035
	(1.39)	(2.31)	(1.47)	(0.73)	(0.88)	(1.53)	(0.49)	(0.74)
	0.061	0.003	−0.005	0.024	0.025	−0.001	0.006	0.066
	(2.78)	(0.16)	(0.19)	(1.07)	(1.25)	(0.04)	(0.12)	(1.44)
	−0.019	−0.008	0.021	−0.013	0.017	−0.004	0.023	−0.010
	(0.88)	(0.45)	(0.83)	(0.61)	(0.91)	(0.17)	(0.52)	(0.24)
	0.007	0.017	0.006	0.076	0.001	0.045	0.017	−0.039
	(0.36)	(1.07)	(0.26)	(3.92)	(0.06)	(2.15)	(0.45)	(1.05)
	−0.032	0.015	0.005	−0.036	0.036	−0.016	0.022	0.088
	(1.64)	(0.93)	(0.22)	(1.87)	(2.08)	(0.80)	(0.61)	(2.47)
	0.059	−0.010	0.011	0.032	−0.001	−0.023	−0.009	0.010
	(2.76)	(0.56)	(0.45)	(1.55)	(0.05)	(1.09)	(0.23)	(0.25)
	−0.034	−0.004	0.012	−0.005	−0.018	0.017	−0.018	−0.003
	(1.63)	(0.22)	(0.50)	(0.23)	(0.95)	(0.79)	(0.47)	(0.08)
	0.025	0.023	−0.044	−0.024	0.000	−0.020	0.006	0.007
	(1.19)	(1.30)	(1.79)	(1.09)	(0.00)	(0.89)	(0.15)	(0.18)
	−0.008	−0.021	0.014	0.029	−0.010	0.012	0.006	−0.056
	(0.38)	(1.19)	(0.59)	(1.38)	(0.53)	(0.54)	(0.15)	(1.44)
	−0.002	0.076	0.008	0.030	0.030	0.056	0.045	0.045
	(0.09)	(4.23)	(0.31)	(1.35)	(1.52)	(2.45)	(1.05)	(1.17)
1991:	0.081	0.016	0.098	0.085	0.123	0.029	0.012	0.096
Jan	(4.06)	(0.91)	(3.65)	(3.79)	(6.12)	(1.21)	(0.26)	(2.23)
	−0.044	−0.064	−0.042	−0.085	−0.096	−0.036	0.015	−0.097
	(2.71)	(3.95)	(1.59)	(4.15)	(5.42)	(1.52)	(0.33)	(2.17)
	−0.023	0.033	−0.011	0.037	0.016	−0.009	−0.072	0.072
	(1.32)	(1.93)	(0.40)	(1.70)	(0.84)	(0.37)	(1.61)	(1.56)
	0.049	−0.012	−0.012	0.008	0.007	−0.002	0.040	−0.020
	(3.07)	(0.76)	(0.45)	(0.38)	(0.37)	(0.09)	(0.93)	(0.46)
	−0.012	0.045	0.043	−0.009	0.002	0.028	0.007	−0.009
	(0.81)	(2.90)	(1.69)	(0.47)	(0.12)	(1.38)	(0.18)	(0.24)
	0.001	−0.029	−0.004	0.027	0.010	−0.007	0.030	−0.013
	(0.07)	(1.85)	(0.17)	(1.45)	(0.62)	(0.35)	(0.80)	(0.36)
	0.015	0.011	0.007	0.005	−0.019	0.022	0.011	0.053
	(0.92)	(0.68)	(0.30)	(0.25)	(1.10)	(1.05)	(0.28)	(1.37)
	−0.036	−0.019	−0.014	0.013	0.017	−0.010	−0.013	−0.016
	(1.91)	(1.01)	(0.51)	(0.61)	(0.91)	(0.44)	(0.31)	(0.37)
	0.009	0.013	−0.033	−0.008	−0.024	0.005	−0.019	−0.056
	(0.48)	(0.68)	(1.20)	(0.37)	(1.31)	(0.22)	(0.47)	(1.29)

Table A.1. (*continued*)

Year/ Month	Region Stockholm	East Central	South Central	South	West	North Central	North	Far North
	−0.028	−0.026	0.074	−0.019	0.024	0.006	0.082	0.047
	(1.52)	(1.43)	(2.77)	(0.88)	(1.26)	(0.25)	(1.97)	(1.06)
	0.011	0.028	−0.034	0.026	−0.032	−0.009	−0.148	−0.029
	(0.58)	(1.53)	(1.22)	(1.19)	(1.62)	(0.36)	(3.29)	(0.65)
	0.010	−0.042	0.007	−0.095	−0.061	−0.029	0.096	−0.030
	(0.40)	(1.85)	(0.22)	(3.57)	(2.66)	(0.95)	(1.81)	(0.56)
1992:	−0.070	0.004	−0.032	0.096	0.056	0.006	0.043	0.076
Jan	(2.49)	(0.16)	(0.93)	(3.13)	(2.22)	(0.17)	(0.72)	(1.21)
	0.026	−0.030	0.053	−0.053	−0.022	−0.029	−0.142	−0.065
	(0.98)	(1.20)	(1.50)	(1.79)	(0.91)	(0.84)	(2.29)	(1.06)
	−0.003	0.011	−0.051	−0.004	−0.012	−0.038	0.033	0.032
	(0.12)	(0.44)	(1.47)	(0.14)	(0.49)	(1.15)	(0.54)	(0.55)
	−0.027	−0.006	−0.001	0.000	0.010	0.064	0.045	−0.073
	(1.19)	(0.26)	(0.03)	(0.00)	(0.43)	(2.03)	(0.79)	(1.30)
	−0.021	0.008	0.022	−0.001	−0.031	−0.045	−0.025	0.028
	(0.94)	(0.36)	(0.68)	(0.04)	(1.44)	(1.51)	(0.49)	(0.54)
	−0.021	0.000	−0.005	−0.026	0.016	0.023	0.014	0.025
	(0.93)	(0.00)	(0.17)	(1.07)	(0.77)	(0.81)	(0.29)	(0.54)
	−0.24	−0.026	−0.003	0.017	−0.024	0.008	−0.048	−0.018
	(1.05)	(1.14)	(0.10)	(0.68)	(1.08)	(0.29)	(0.99)	(0.36)
	−0.021	−0.038	−0.068	−0.045	−0.020	−0.059	0.026	−0.039
	(0.85)	(1.48)	(2.12)	(1.64)	(0.81)	(1.94)	(0.51)	(0.69)
	−0.038	−0.007	0.086	0.012	0.010	0.002	−0.019	0.020
	(1.43)	(0.28)	(2.58)	(0.42)	(0.41)	(0.06)	(0.35)	(0.34)
	−0.011	−0.023	−0.048	−0.046	−0.084	−0.030	0.038	−0.052
	(0.38)	(0.85)	(1.34)	(1.52)	(3.11)	(0.85)	(0.65)	(0.79)
	−0.032	−0.040	−0.039	−0.014	−0.002	0.027	−0.148	0.002
	(1.13)	(1.43)	(1.08)	(0.45)	(0.07)	(0.72)	(2.35)	(0.03)
	−0.045	0.020	−0.068	−0.055	0.014	−0.088	0.182	−0.043
	(1.45)	(0.60)	(1.70)	(1.43)	(0.46)	(2.07)	(2.36)	(0.58)
1993:	0.054	−0.038	0.059	0.019	−0.037	0.062	−0.164	−0.003
Jan	(1.62)	(1.05)	(1.37)	(0.44)	(1.11)	(1.26)	(2.08)	(0.03)
	−0.075	0.033	−0.030	0.035	−0.001	−0.010	−0.100	0.080
	(2.45)	(0.98)	(0.71)	(0.91)	(0.03)	(0.22)	(1.34)	(0.92)
	−0.002	−0.037	−0.011	−0.026	0.032	−0.061	0.151	−0.084
	(0.07)	(1.17)	(0.27)	(0.77)	(1.08)	(1.53)	(2.22)	(1.01)
	0.059	0.038	0.028	−0.001	−0.025	0.046	−0.081	0.040
	(2.40)	(1.30)	(0.76)	(0.03)	(0.95)	(1.24)	(1.35)	(0.55)
	−0.053	−0.035	0.010	0.027	0.056	0.044	0.038	0.052
	(2.22)	(1.30)	(0.28)	(0.94)	(2.32)	(1.25)	(0.72)	(0.88)
	0.046	0.040	0.028	−0.055	−0.052	−0.054	0.013	−0.054
	(2.00)	(1.54)	(0.82)	(2.07)	(2.31)	(1.56)	(0.26)	(0.99)
	−0.024	−0.005	−0.025	−0.024	0.048	0.049	−0.002	0.037
	(0.95)	(0.17)	(0.54)	(0.78)	(1.93)	(1.28)	(0.03)	(0.59)

Table A.1. (*continued*)

	Region							
Year/ Month	Stockholm	East Central	South Central	South	West	North Central	North	Far North
1993:	−0.004	−0.014	−0.043	−0.024	0.050	0.051	−0.019	−0.306
Aug	(0.06)	(0.21)	(0.38)	(0.28)	(0.69)	(0.51)	(0.11)	(1.33)

Note. Equation also includes a large number of variables reflecting the quality and amenity of individual dwellings. See Englund et al., 1998, Table IV.

Appendix B

In this appendix, we indicate how the variance-covariance matrix of asset returns is estimated for different time periods using the 164 months of home sales data available. It is convenient tc consider the case of investment in the four financial instruments and the housing index first and then to consider investment in the index and in an individual house.

Let $\mathbf{r}_t$ be a vector of the logarithms of (gross) returns on assets, $\mathbf{r}_t = [r_t^R, r_t^E, r_t^N, r_t^L, r_t^H]$ where r_t^R is the return on real-estate stocks, r_t^E the return on general stocks, r_t^N the return on long term bonds, r_t^L the return on short-term bonds and r_t^H is the return on housing indices. Then the variance-convariance matrix of n-period returns is

$$E\left[\left(\sum_{t=1}^{n}(\mathbf{r}_t - \mu)\right)\left(\sum_{t=1}^{n}(\mathbf{r}_t - \mu)\right)'\right] = \sum_{i=1}^{n}\sum_{j=1}^{n} E[(\mathbf{r}_t - \mu)(\mathbf{r}_j' - \mu')] = \sum_{p=0}^{n-1}\sum_{q=0}^{n-1}\Gamma_{p-q} \tag{B.1}$$

where $\Gamma_k = E[(r_t - \mu)(r_{t-k}' - \mu')]$.

To compute Γ_k, we assume that log returns follow a VAR(4) process, i.e.,

$$\mathbf{r}_t - \boldsymbol{\mu} = \Phi_1(\mathbf{r}_{t-1} - \boldsymbol{\mu}) + \Phi_2(\mathbf{r}_{t-1} - \boldsymbol{\mu}) + \Phi_3(\mathbf{r}_{t-1} - \boldsymbol{\mu}) + \Phi_4(\mathbf{r}_{t-1} - \boldsymbol{\mu}) + \varepsilon_t. \tag{B.2}$$

Following Hamilton (1994), this VAR relation can be transformed into

$$\xi_t = \mathbf{F}\xi_{t-1} + \mathbf{v}_t \tag{B.3}$$

where

$$\xi_t = \begin{bmatrix} \mathbf{r}_t - \boldsymbol{\mu} \\ \mathbf{r}_{t-1} - \boldsymbol{\mu} \\ \mathbf{r}_{t-2} - \boldsymbol{\mu} \\ \mathbf{r}_{t-3} - \boldsymbol{\mu} \end{bmatrix}, \quad \mathbf{F} = \begin{bmatrix} \Phi_1 & \Phi_2 & \Phi_3 & \Phi_4 \\ \mathbf{I}_n & \mathbf{0} & \mathbf{0} & \mathbf{0} \\ \mathbf{0} & \mathbf{I}_n & \mathbf{0} & \mathbf{0} \\ \mathbf{0} & \mathbf{0} & \mathbf{I}_n & \mathbf{0} \end{bmatrix}, \quad \mathbf{v}_t = \begin{bmatrix} \boldsymbol{\varepsilon}_t \\ \mathbf{0} \\ \mathbf{0} \\ \mathbf{0} \end{bmatrix},$$

$$\mathbf{Q} = E(\mathbf{v}_t\mathbf{v}_t') = \begin{bmatrix} \Omega & \mathbf{0} & \mathbf{0} & \mathbf{0} \\ \mathbf{0} & \mathbf{0} & \mathbf{0} & \mathbf{0} \\ \mathbf{0} & \mathbf{0} & \mathbf{0} & \mathbf{0} \\ \mathbf{0} & \mathbf{0} & \mathbf{0} & \mathbf{0} \end{bmatrix} \quad \text{and} \quad E(\boldsymbol{\varepsilon}_t\boldsymbol{\varepsilon}_t') = \boldsymbol{\Omega}.$$

To extract $\boldsymbol{\Gamma}_k$, first note that

$$\boldsymbol{\Sigma} = E(\xi_t\xi_t') = \begin{bmatrix} \boldsymbol{\Gamma}_0 & \boldsymbol{\Gamma}_1 & \boldsymbol{\Gamma}_2 & \boldsymbol{\Gamma}_3 \\ \boldsymbol{\Gamma}_1' & \boldsymbol{\Gamma}_0 & \boldsymbol{\Gamma}_1 & \boldsymbol{\Gamma}_2 \\ \boldsymbol{\Gamma}_2' & \boldsymbol{\Gamma}_1' & \boldsymbol{\Gamma}_0 & \boldsymbol{\Gamma}_1 \\ \boldsymbol{\Gamma}_3' & \boldsymbol{\Gamma}_2' & \boldsymbol{\Gamma}_1' & \boldsymbol{\Gamma}_0 \end{bmatrix}. \tag{B.4}$$

Note also that

$$\boldsymbol{\Sigma} = E(\xi_t\xi_t') = E[(\mathbf{F}\xi_{t-1} + \mathbf{v}_t)(\mathbf{F}\xi_{t-1} + \mathbf{v}_t)'] = \mathbf{F}\boldsymbol{\Sigma}\mathbf{F}' + \mathbf{Q}. \tag{B.5}$$

Therefore,

$$\text{vec}(\Sigma) = [\mathbf{I} - (\mathbf{F} \otimes \mathbf{F})]^{-1}\mathbf{vec}(\mathbf{Q}). \tag{B.6}$$

From this, we recover $\boldsymbol{\Gamma}_0$ to $\boldsymbol{\Gamma}_3$. The remaining elements of $\boldsymbol{\Gamma}_k$ may be recovered by recursion,

$$\boldsymbol{\Gamma}_k = \Phi\boldsymbol{\Gamma}_{k-1} + \Phi\boldsymbol{\Gamma}_{k-2} + \Phi\boldsymbol{\Gamma}_{k-3} + \Phi\boldsymbol{\Gamma}_{k-4}. \tag{B.7}$$

Now, consider adding an individual house, whose return follows an AR(1) process, to the above system. Note that

$$r_t^H - \mu^H = \sum_j \sum_{i=1}^{4} \beta_i^{H,j}(r_{t-i}^j - \mu^j) + \varepsilon_t^H \tag{B.8}$$

where r_t^H is the return on the housing index.

Let r_t^h be the log return on an individual house. Since

$$r_t^h - \mu^h = r_t^H - \mu^H + \nu_t - \nu_{t-1}, \tag{B.9}$$

where,

$$\nu_t = \rho\nu_{t-1} + \eta_t, \tag{B.10}$$

then the return on individual house can be written as

$$\begin{aligned} r_t^h - \mu^h &= \sum_j \sum_{i=1}^4 \beta_i^{H,j}(r_{t-i}^j - \mu^j) + \nu_t - \nu_{t-1} + \varepsilon_t^H \\ &= \sum_j \sum_{i=1}^4 \beta_i^{H,j}(r_{t-i}^j - \mu^j) + (\rho - 1)\nu_{t-1} + \eta_t + \varepsilon_t^H. \end{aligned} \tag{B.11}$$

Note that (B.11) is in VAR form with ν_{t-1} as a new variable. That is, we can simply augment (B.1) with (B.9) and (B.11), such that

$$\begin{bmatrix} r_t^R - \mu^R \\ r_t^E - \mu^E \\ r_t^N - \mu^N \\ r_t^L - \mu^L \\ r_t^H - \mu^H \\ r_t^h - \mu^H \\ \nu_t \end{bmatrix} = \begin{bmatrix} \beta_1^{R,R} & \beta_1^{R,E} & \beta_1^{R,N} & \beta_1^{R,L} & \beta_1^{R,H} & 0 & 0 \\ \beta_1^{E,R} & \beta_1^{E,E} & \beta_1^{E,N} & \beta_1^{E,L} & \beta_1^{E,H} & 0 & 0 \\ \beta_1^{N,R} & \beta_1^{N,E} & \beta_1^{N,N} & \beta_1^{N,L} & \beta_1^{N,H} & 0 & 0 \\ \beta_1^{L,R} & \beta_1^{L,E} & \beta_1^{L,N} & \beta_1^{L,L} & \beta_1^{L,H} & 0 & 0 \\ \beta_1^{H,R} & \beta_1^{H,E} & \beta_1^{H,N} & \beta_1^{H,L} & \beta_1^{H,H} & 0 & 0 \\ \beta_1^{H,R} & \beta_1^{H,E} & \beta_1^{H,N} & \beta_1^{H,L} & \beta_1^{H,H} & 0 & \rho - 1 \\ 0 & 0 & 0 & 0 & 0 & 0 & \rho \end{bmatrix} \begin{bmatrix} r_{t-1}^R - \mu^R \\ r_{t-1}^E - \mu^E \\ r_{t-1}^N - \mu^N \\ r_{t-1}^L - \mu^L \\ r_{t-1}^H - \mu^H \\ r_{t-1}^h - \mu^H \\ \nu_{t-1} \end{bmatrix}, \tag{B.12}$$

$$\tilde{\mathbf{r}}_t - \mu = \tilde{\Phi}_1(\tilde{\mathbf{r}}_{t-1} - \tilde{\mu}),$$

$$+ \sum_{i=2}^4 \begin{bmatrix} \beta_i^{R,R} & \beta_i^{R,E} & \beta_i^{R,N} & \beta_i^{R,L} & \beta_i^{R,H} & 0 & 0 \\ \beta_i^{E,R} & \beta_i^{E,E} & \beta_i^{E,N} & \beta_i^{E,L} & \beta_i^{E,H} & 0 & 0 \\ \beta_i^{N,R} & \beta_i^{N,E} & \beta_i^{N,N} & \beta_i^{N,L} & \beta_i^{N,H} & 0 & 0 \\ \beta_i^{L,R} & \beta_i^{L,E} & \beta_i^{L,N} & \beta_i^{L,L} & \beta_i^{L,H} & 0 & 0 \\ \beta_i^{H,R} & \beta_i^{H,E} & \beta_i^{H,N} & \beta_i^{H,L} & \beta_i^{H,H} & 0 & 0 \\ \beta_i^{H,R} & \beta_i^{H,E} & \beta_i^{H,N} & \beta_i^{H,L} & \beta_i^{H,H} & 0 & 0 \\ 0 & 0 & 0 & 0 & 0 & 0 & 0 \end{bmatrix} \begin{bmatrix} r_{t-i}^R - \mu^R \\ r_{t-i}^E - \mu^E \\ r_{t-i}^N - \mu^N \\ r_{t-i}^L - \mu^L \\ r_{t-i}^H - \mu^H \\ r_{t-i}^H - \mu^H \\ \nu_{t-i} \end{bmatrix} + \begin{bmatrix} \varepsilon_t^R \\ \varepsilon_t^E \\ \varepsilon_t^N \\ \varepsilon_t^L \\ \varepsilon_t^H \\ \eta_t + \varepsilon_t^H \\ \eta_t \end{bmatrix},$$

$$+ \sum_{i=2}^4 \tilde{\Phi}_i(\tilde{\mathbf{r}}_{t-i} - \tilde{\boldsymbol{\mu}}) + \tilde{\varepsilon}_t,$$

where

$$
E\left(\tilde{\varepsilon}_t \tilde{\varepsilon}_t^{'}\right) = \tilde{\boldsymbol{\Omega}} = \begin{bmatrix} \sigma_R^2 & \sigma_{R,E} & \sigma_{R,N} & \sigma_{R,L} & \sigma_{R,H} & \sigma_{R,H} & 0 \\ \sigma_{R,E} & \sigma_E^2 & \sigma_{E,N} & \sigma_{E,L} & \sigma_{E,H} & \sigma_{E,H} & 0 \\ \sigma_{R,N} & \sigma_{E,N} & \sigma_N^2 & \sigma_{N,L} & \sigma_{N,H} & \sigma_{N,H} & 0 \\ \sigma_{R,L} & \sigma_{E,L} & \sigma_{N,L} & \sigma_L^2 & \sigma_{L,H} & \sigma_{L,H} & 0 \\ \sigma_{R,H} & \sigma_{E,H} & \sigma_{N,H} & \sigma_{L,H} & \sigma_H^2 & \sigma_H^2 & 0 \\ \sigma_{R,H} & \sigma_{E,H} & \sigma_{N,H} & \sigma_{L,H} & \sigma_H^2 & \sigma_H^2 + \sigma_\eta^2 & \sigma_\eta^2 \\ 0 & 0 & 0 & 0 & 0 & \sigma_\eta^2 & \sigma_\eta^2 \end{bmatrix}.
$$

Thus, to compute the variance-covariance matrix of n period returns, we only need compute

$$
\mathrm{vec}\left(\tilde{\boldsymbol{\Sigma}}\right) = \left[\mathbf{I} - \left(\tilde{\mathbf{F}} \bigotimes \tilde{\mathbf{F}}\right)\right]^{-1} \mathrm{vec}(\tilde{\mathbf{Q}}), \tag{B.13}
$$

and we can extract $\{\tilde{\boldsymbol{\Gamma}}_0, \tilde{\boldsymbol{\Gamma}}_1, \tilde{\boldsymbol{\Gamma}}_3, \ldots, \tilde{\boldsymbol{\Gamma}}_r\}$ from $\tilde{\boldsymbol{\Sigma}}$ as in the previous example.

Table B.1. VAR model with five assets. Quarterly data: 1982 I through 1993 II.

	R.E. Stocks		Gen Stocks		*t*-bill		Bond		House	
R.E. Stocks, *t*-1	– 0.0267	(0.0862)	– 0.0463	(0.1689)	– 0.0327	(1.2673)	0.0403	(0.4458)	0.0146	(0.3634)
R.E. Stocks, *t*-2	0.5703	(1.9616)	0.3356	(1.3057)	0.0046	(0.1894)	0.0657	(0.7743)	0.1391	(3.7004)
R.E. Stocks, *t*-3	– 0.3907	(1.0727)	– 0.2790	(0.8665)	0.0387	(1.2738)	– 0.2069	(1.9456)	0.1242	(2.6382)
R.E. Stocks, *t*-4	– 0.6479	(1.4259)	– 0.0088	(0.0220)	0.0761	(2.0105)	0.3178	(2.3954)	0.0799	(1.3603)
Gen Stocks, *t*-1	0.4664	(1.2062)	0.4874	(1.4261)	0.0091	(0.2828)	0.0085	(0.0753)	– 0.0518	(1.0363)
Gen Stocks, *t*-2	– 0.5491	(1.5524)	– 0.4666	(1.4924)	– 0.0027	(0.0931)	– 0.1163	(1.1264)	– 0.1168	(2.5545)
Gen Stocks, *t*-3	0.6769	(1.6935)	0.4907	(1.3886)	– 0.0776	(2.3312)	0.1605	(1.3748)	– 0.1113	(2.1540)
Gen Stocks, *t*-4	0.2166	(0.4874)	– 0.2736	(0.6964)	– 0.0812	(2.1924)	– 0.4212	(3.2463)	– 0.0823	(1.4327)
t-bill, *t*-1	0.3049	(0.1272)	– 0.3843	(0.1813)	– 0.3595	(1.7999)	– 1.2086	(1.7266)	– 0.7212	(2.3266)
t-bill, *t*-2	1.1395	(0.4652)	0.4621	(0.2134)	0.2426	(1.1885)	1.3475	(1.8841)	– 0.4096	(1.2934)
t-bill, *t*-3	6.8644	(2.3700)	4.7512	(1.8557)	– 0.1337	(0.5538)	0.1577	(0.1865)	0.2099	(0.5605)
t-bill, *t*-4	2.1984	(0.8143)	– 2.1389	(0.8962)	– 0.0268	(0.1193)	– 0.6922	(0.8782)	0.1286	(0.3685)
Bond, *t*-1	– 0.7503	(1.1301)	0.0195	(0.0331)	0.0200	(0.3614)	0.2224	(1.1473)	0.1601	(1.8655)
Bond, *t*-2	– 0.7113	(1.1696)	– 0.2588	(0.4814)	0.0368	(0.7265)	– 0.1413	(0.7956)	0.1368	(1.7391)
Bond, *t*-3	– 0.2158	(0.3258)	– 0.1469	(0.2508)	0.1143	(2.0708)	0.2255	(1.1660)	0.1066	(1.2448)
Bond, *t*-4	– 0.5097	(0.7675)	0.2202	(0.3750)	0.1309	(2.3648)	– 0.1781	(0.9186)	– 0.0028	(0.0320)
House, *t*-1	2.7190	(1.4996)	0.4812	(0.3002)	0.0316	(0.2093)	0.3578	(0.6759)	– 0.0532	(0.2269)
House, *t*-2	2.7806	(1.6294)	1.0475	(0.6944)	– 0.1942	(1.3658)	– 0.5979	(1.2001)	0.3071	(1.3921)
House, *t*-3	– 1.5334	(0.9683)	– 0.5320	(0.3800)	– 0.1297	(0.9829)	– 0.6392	(1.3824)	– 0.0296	(0.1448)
House, *t*-4	– 2.6471	(1.7865)	– 1.0180	(0.7772)	0.0792	(0.6412)	0.2703	(0.6247)	0.1095	(0.5717)
Constant	– 0.1041	(1.6038)	– 0.0037	(0.0644)	0.0170	(3.1446)	0.0371	(1.9544)	0.0155	(1.8441)
R^2 adjusted	0.2099		– 0.0173		0.1991		0.3008		0.7192	
Q-statistics	1.6900		0.6286		1.2679		1.5033		1.1645	
$F_{\mathrm{realestate}}$	1.5514	(0.2181)	0.6224	(0.6508)	1.9151	(0.1392)	3.6806	(0.0173)	5.4469	(0.0027)
F_{stocks}	1.4109	(0.2593)	1.4352	(0.2517)	2.3909	(0.0778)	3.6590	(0.0177)	3.2926	(0.0268)

Table B.1. (*continued*)

	R.E. Stocks		Gen Stocks		*t*-bill		Bond		House	
$F_{t\text{-bills}}$	1.8780	(0.1457)	1.2327	(0.3224)	1.6750	(0.1872)	1.6508	(0.1929)	1.8899	(0.1436)
F_{bonds}	0.7199	(0.5864)	0.1114	(0.9774)	2.6823	(0.0548)	0.9308	(0.4621)	1.5894	(0.2081)
F_{houses}	1.2523	(0.3148)	0.2218	(0.9237)	1.4851	(0.2367)	1.5324	(0.2233)	2.0219	(0.1220)

Estimated variance–covariance matrix of residuals

	R.E. Stocks	Gen Stocks	*t*-bill	Bond	House
R.E. Stocks	0.0103826	0.0074665	−0.0001042	0.0009854	0.0003317
Gen Stocks	0.0074665	0.0081131	−0.0000167	0.0012473	0.0001372
t-bill	−0.0001042	−0.0000167	0.0000721	0.0000882	0.0000391
Bond	0.0009854	0.0012473	0.0000882	0.0008851	0.0001490
House	0.0003317	0.0001372	0.0000391	0.0001490	0.0001736

Notes. This table shows the slope coefficients of a VAR model along with adjusted R^2, Box–Pierce Q-statistics and Granger-causality test results, expressed as F-statistics. The values in the parenthesis with the estimated parameters are t-statistics and the values in the parenthesis with Granger-causality tests are p-values.

Acknowledgments

We are especially grateful for comments of Frans A. de Roon which led to a substantial improvement in the analysis. We also wish to thank Stefan Nydahl for research assistance.

Notes

1. This data set is based on tax returns for a random sample of 10,000 Swedish households. Asset valuations made for tax purposes are translated into approximate market values.
2. See also Devaney and Rayburn (1988).
3. Goetzmann derives the efficient frontier based on four assets all with non-negativity constraints. Flavin and Yamashita impose non-negativity constraints on all four assets but also include mortgage loans constrained only by house value. Gatzlaff includes commercial real estate and REITs among the assets, again with non-negativity constraints.
4. This is the only consistent rent series available, and it is based upon comprehensive data. However, use of this index is problematic since apartment rents are regulated, with the objective of following production costs. Our use of this index probably leads to an underestimate of the short-term variation in the value of rental services. However, the variation in rents should, in any case, be small relative to the variation in the value of the stock, so this is probably not very serious.
5. See Kain and Quigley, 1975, for an early statement.
6. See Englund (1999) for an account of the events leading up to the banking crisis.
7. Since the correlation structures are not very different between the 10, 20, and 40 quarter horizons, the optimal portfolios are also quite similar.
8. The case of an unrestricted portfolio with all six assets, i e including both housing index and an individual house, is uninteresting. The optimal investment in an individual house will always be zero unless the position in the index is restricted by a constraint (in our case $\pm$ 500 percent).

9. Of course the fact that a large housing consumption leads to an unbalanced investment portfolio implies an additional cost to housing consumption, which should be taken into account when choosing housing consumption. Brueckner (1997) analyzes the complete choice problem when portfolio and consumption aspects are treated simultaneously. See also Heaton and Lucas (2000).

References

Barkham, R., and D. Geltner. (1995). ''Price Discovery in American and British Property Markets,'' *Real Estate Economics* 23(1), 21–44.

Brueckner, J. (1997). ''Consumption and Investment Motives and the Portfolio Choices of Homeowners,'' *Journal of Real Estate Finance and Economics* 15, 159–180.

Caplin, A. et al. (1997). *Housing Partnerships*. Cambridge, MA: MIT Press.

Case, K. E., and R. J. Shiller. (1989). ''The Efficiency of the Market for Single-Family Homes,'' *American Economic Review* 79(1), 125–137.

Case, K. E., and R. J. Shiller. (1990). ''Forecasting Prices and Excess Returns in the Housing Market,'' *AREUEA Journal* 18(3), 253–273.

Case, K. E., R. J. Shiller, and A. N. Weiss. (1993). ''Index-Based Futures and Options Markets in Real Estate,'' *Journal of Portfolio Management* 19(2), 83–92.

Devaney, M., and W. Rayburn. (1988). ''When a House is More Than a Home: Performance of the Household Portfolio,'' *Journal of Real Estate Research*.

Edin, P. A., P. Englund, and E. Ekman. (1995). ''Avregleringen och hushållens skulder'' (Deregulation and Household Debt). In *Bankerna under krisen*, Bankkriskommittén, Stockholm.

Eichholtz, P. M. A., K. G. Koedijk, and F. A. de Roon. (2000). ''The Portfolio Implication of Home Ownership,'' Manuscript, Maastricht University.

Englund, P. (1999). ''The Swedish Banking Crisis: Roots and Consequences,'' *Oxford Review of Economic Policy* 15(3), 80–97.

Englund, P., J. M. Quigley, and C. L. Redfearn. (1998). ''Improved Price Indexes For Real Estate: Measuring the Course of Swedish Housing Prices,'' *Journal of Urban Economics* 44(2), 171–196.

Englund, P., and Y. M. Ioannides. (1996). ''House Price Dynamics. An International Empirical Perspective,'' *Journal of Housing Economics*, 6, 119–136.

Flavin, M., and T. Yamashita. (1998). ''Owner-Occupied Housing and the Composition of the Household Portfolio Owner the Life Cycle,'' Working Paper No. 6389, National Bureau of Economic Research, January.

Gatzlaff, D. H. (2000). ''The Effect of Single-Family Housing on Multi-Asset Portfolio Allocations,'' unpublished manuscript.

Goetzmann, W. N. (1993). ''The Single Family Home in the Investment Portfolio,'' *Journal of Real Estate Finance and Economics* 6(3), 201–222.

Hamilton, J. D. (1994). *Time Series Analysis*, Princeton, NJ: Princeton University Press.

Heaton, J., and D. Lucas. (2000). ''Portfolio Choice in the Presence of Background Risk,'' *Economic Journal* 110, 1–26.

Jorion, P. (1985). ''International Portfolio Diversification with Portfolio Risk,'' *Journal of Business* 58(3), 259–278.

Kain, J. F., and J. Quigley. (1975). *Housing Markets and Racial Discrimination* New York, NY: Columbia University Press.

Quigley, J. M., and C. L. Redfearn. (1999). ''Housing Market Efficiency and the Opportunities for Excess Returns,'' Paper prepared for the National Bureau of Economic Research Conference on Real Estate, Cambridge, MA, November.

Rosen, H. S., K. T. Rosen, and D. Holtz-Eakin. (1984). ''Housing Tenure, Uncertainty, and Taxation,'' *Review of Economics and Statistics*, 66, 405–416.

Sweeney, J. L. (1974). ''Housing Unit Maintenance and the Modes of Tenure,'' *Journal of Economic Theory* 8, 111–138.

Turner, T. M. (2000). ''Does Investment Risk Affect the Housing Decisions of Families?'' Manuscript, UC Davis.